A GUIDE TO
Fashion
Sewing

FOURTH EDITION

Connie Amaden-Crawford

Fairchild Publications, Inc.

New York

Executive Editor: Olga T. Kontzias

Art Director: Adam B. Bohannon

Production Manager: Ginger Hillman

Associate Production Editor: Beth Cohen

Copy Editor: Chernow Editorial Services, Inc.

Interior Design: Ellen Pettengell

Cover Design: Adam B. Bohannon

Second Printing,2006

Fourth Edition, Copyright © 2006
Fairchild Publications, Inc.

Third Edition, Copyright © 2000
Fairchild Publications, Inc.

Second Edition, Copyright © 1994
Fairchild Publications, Inc.

First Edition, Copyright © 1986
Fairchild Publications, Inc.

Library of Congress Catalog Card Number: 2006921194

ISBN: 1-56367-450-5

GST R 133004424

Printed in the United States of America

CH01, TP13

Brief Contents

Extended Contents

Preface

A Guide to Fashion Sewing, Fourth Edition, continues to illustrate the many special industry-used techniques that will save time and help both students and experienced sewers create more fashionable, professional looking garments. The information builds steadily from basic theory to more advanced sewing projects. This newest edition offers updated fashion illustrations, as well as current information on sewing machines and textiles. A new chapter on tailoring illustrates the sewing process used in the garment industry, a process some home clothiers call "bagging the lining." Chapters 6 through 22 open with a section entitled Key Terms and Concepts that serves as a thumbnail dictionary to each chapter's content.

Our goal in preparing this new edition was to create an easy-to-read text, with step-by-step instructions and illustrations to guide the beginner or experienced designer in the creation of basic, simple, and more complicated designs. This edition continues to provide a comprehensive sewing education, with professional and updated information for fashion educators that helps them transition from the traditional elements of sewing to current methods.

A Guide to Fashion Sewing, Fourth Edition, is written for educators, students, and professionals. The step-by-step illustrations and easy-to-read text provides a complete understanding of sewing techniques. The author teaches readers to sew without the aid of a direction sheet, a unique concept proven through the education of students. This book helps the designer create fashionable and professional garments. This book includes:

- Measurement Charts
- Identifying Fashion Fabrics
- Sewing Machines
- Sewing Methods
- Seams
- Darts and Tucks
- Interfacings
- Fourteen Pocket Applications
- Five Various Zipper Applications
- Sleeve, Cuff, and Sleeve Placket Treatments
- Attaching Various Collars with facings and without facings
- Neckline Plackets and Neckline Treatments
- Lining Applications Pants, Skirts, Vests, and Bustier
- Pants
- Waistbands and Waist Seams
- Hems
- Closures
- Tailored Jackets
- Tailored Shirts

This text promises to be an excellent teaching guide for courses in fashion design, clothing, and dressmaking. It book is a valuable tool for students in an introductory course in fashion design or for those who are taking only a single course in fashion. In fact, it will interest anyone who want to know more about fashion sewing.

Acknowledgments

I wish to thank my many friends and business associates who continue to ask questions, make suggestions, review chapters, and add clarity during the revision of this book. I am particularly indebted to:

Olga Kontzias, Fashion Editor for Fairchild, for keeping this book on track and continuing to organize me till I would understand the concept.

Mary Stephens, Chair of the Fashion Design Department at The Fashion Institute of Design & Merchandising, for her continued support in creating a finer text for students.

Also, my colleagues for reviewing the old and new text: Moira Doyle, Alice Kaku.

I am especially indebted to Jimmy Hebert for creating the new art for this edition.

A special thank you to Barbara Chernow and Olga Kontzias for their fine attention to this project's production in creating newer and cleaner art, book layout and editing expertise, and opinions on this fourth edition.

A very gracious thank you to Amy Elam, my most wonderful and deserving assistant, for her constant help in the design room and her computer skills that would allow me time to continue with this text.

And, finally, to my husband, Wayne, for his support and encouragement to complete the project and not worry about the housework or meals.

Connie Amaden-Crawford
Hansville, WA 2006
President, Fashion Patterns by Coni

A GUIDE TO

Fashion Sewing

CHAPTER 1
Identifying Fashion Fabrics

IDENTIFYING FASHION FABRICS

A wise sewer understands the importance of matching fabric to a particular style, the same way professional designers select fabric and create ready-to-wear clothing. Selecting the correct fabric quality and suitability is important because they determine the appearance, durability, maintenance, and comfort of the finished garment. You should select fabrics using the same criteria as a designer: color, texture, weight, and price. The fabric should be attractive when sewn into the desired garment. You should be aware of the fiber content, the weave, and the finish. In general, you should choose fabric that is easy to maintain and comfortable.

The information in this chapter is intended to serve as a guide to selecting the most appropriate fabric. Many texts are available to provide a more comprehensive and deeper understanding of textiles.

You can either select the pattern and then shop for a fabric suggested on the pattern envelope, or you can purchase the fabric and then look for a pattern suitable for the fabric. The latter method is used more often than one would think, even though it is not considered "by the book;" this select group of sewers can visualize the garments they want.

Fabrics are constantly becoming more versatile and more appealing to fit the mood of the current fashion trends. Many kinds of stretch knits are used for activewear. Sportswear garments are made of denim, single knits, and a variety of woven cottons and synthetics. Sheer, see-through fabrics are used to capture the body's sleek lines. Tulle, organza, sheer cottons, and knits are used for discreetly revealing effects. Special evening fabrics enhance the contemporary lifestyles of women.

When you select a fabric, carefully drape a yard or more over your arm, holding it next to your body. Check the fabric for any flaws in the weave or imperfections in the color shading. Usually the fabric store will add extra yardage at no extra cost if this occurs on a piece of fabric yardage.

Learn to compare the fabrics used in ready-to-wear clothes. Table 1.1 lists categories of clothes, the fabrics most often used for these categories, and care, and the sewing tips necessary for these fabrics. The information is arranged by difficulty, with the simplest type of design and the least difficult-to-handle fabric listed first, the more difficult listed next, and so forth.

The process of producing fabric is the same, regardless of the texture of the fabric or the type of fiber. Fibers are usually twisted together to form yarns. The yarns are then woven or knitted to form a fabric. Color is applied by either dyeing or printing. Finally, a finishing technique, usually chemical, is applied to improve the performance and provide fabric characteristics that are desirable to the customer and suitable for the end use.

The feel of a fabric is referred to as the *hand*. The *appearance* is the flexibility of the fabric. *Texture* refers to the weight, body, or drape of fabric, and is created by using different types and combinations of fibers and yarns and methods of construction, colorings, and finishes.

TABLE 1.1 GUIDE TO SELECTING FABRICS

Garment Category	Typical Fabrics	Care & Pressing Tips	Sewing Tips
Sportswear, warm weather clothes, casual day dresses, skirts, and pants, men's dress shirts, and playclothes.	**Medium-weight woven or knit 100% cotton** Corduroy, denim, poplin, seersucker, broadcloth, pique, flannel, challis, and oxford cloth.	Machine wash. Shrinks unless preshrunk or treated. Very durable. Allows for good air circulation. Press while damp with hot iron.	
	Medium-weight woven or knit cotton/ polyester. Medium-weight wool or wool flannel, and cotton knits.	Machine wash. Does not shrink. May use bleach. Press with hot steam iron. Woolens should be dry cleaned.	**Helpful Sewing Tip:** *Usually a very good fabric for beginning sewers.*
	Medium-weight linen or rayon challis.	Wrinkles; has a tendency to shrink when machine washed. Dry-clean. Stretches when wet if not preshrunk.	**Thread & Needle:** *Use cotton-wrapped polyester, or mercerized cotton. Use size 11 needle.*
	Open-weave cottons. Monks cloth, homespun, and gauze.	Machine wash. Shrinks unless preshrunk.	
Active Sportswear, swimwear, costumes, and specialty clothes such as lycra pants or skirts.	**Stretch knits.** Spandex and lycra.	Machine wash. Dry at low temperature. Do not bleach. Press with cool iron.	**Helpful Sewing Tip: Thread & Needle:** *Use cotton-wrapped polyester, or mercerized cotton. Use size 11 needle. FOR KNITS: Use a ball-point needle and use cotton-wrapped polyester thread. (Refer to KNITS chapter for a specific knit chart.)*
	Woven cotton/polyester.	Machine wash. Does not shrink. Dries quickly. Little or no ironing.	

TABLE 1.1 GUIDE TO SELECTING FABRICS (CONTINUED)

Garment Category	Typical Fabrics	Care & Pressing Tips	Sewing Tips
Tailored jackets, medium-weight to heavier-weight coats, suits, and sport coats.	**Heavyweight hair blends.** Wool, cashmere, camel, alpaca, wool tweed, cheviot.	Dry-clean only unless otherwise instructed.	**Helpful Sewing Tip: Thread & Needle:** *Use cotton-wrapped polyester, or heavy duty (any fiber). Use size 14 or 16 needle.*
	Heavy woven cottons. Denim and duck.	Machine wash. Shrinks unless preshrunk or treated.	
	Heavyweight or medium-weight leather and fake fur.	Specially dry-clean. Needs special seam construction.	
	Nylon or quilted nylon with an inner layer of down or polyester fill.	Machine wash or dry-clean. Needs little or no ironing.	
Sleepwear, intimate apparel, blouses, or better dresses.	**Sheer cottons.** Batiste, dotted swiss, lawn, voile, and gauze.	Machine wash. Shrink unless preshrunk or treated. Wrinkles. Press with steam iron or when damp.	**Helpful Sewing Tip: Thread & Needle:** *Use extra fine silk or mercerized cotton. Use size 9 needle.*
	100% polyester or polyester blend. Georgette, chiffon, poly/silk, butter crepe, and poly/cotton.	Machine wash. Needs little or no ironing.	
	Light-weight fabrics. Silk fabrics such as peau de soie, chiffon, organza, raw silk, satin, shantung, rayon, and crepe de chine.	Dry-clean only unless otherwise instructed.	
Evening dresses and evening jackets.	**Light-weight fabrics.** Rayon organza, silk, peau de soie, raw silk, satin, taffeta, organdy, brocade, velvet, velveteen, and lightweight wool (challis, flannel, crepe, or jersey).	Dry-clean only unless otherwise instructed.	**Helpful Sewing Tip: Thread & Needle:** *Use cotton-wrapped silk or mercerized cotton (extra fine). Use size 9 needle.*
	Sheer fabrics. Chiffon or transparent cotton, and beaded fabrics.		

Fibers

The various fibers used and the methods with which these fibers are put together define the differences among fabrics. Fibers are either *natural* or *manufactured*. Natural fibers include cotton from the cotton plant, linen that is made from flax, wool from sheep, and silk from the silkworm. Manufactured fibers are not found in nature and are produced using combinations of chemicals. Manufactured fibers include acrylic, nylon, polyester, rayon, and spandex.

A major development of the 1990s was the production of microfibers. These are very thin manufactured fibers—thinner than a human hair or a strand of silk. Fabrics produced from microfibers are very soft and drapable. The result is that nylon or polyester fibers, for example, can be produced to look and feel like silk.

Fabrics can be made by using 100% of one fiber or by blending or combining different fibers. This is done when a fiber does not possess all the properties required to make the most desirable fabric. For example, one of cotton's unfavorable features is that it wrinkles easily. However, if polyester, which possesses excellent wrinkle resistance, and cotton are combined, the fabric will wrinkle less and still maintain the most favorable properties of cotton, such as its absorbency and softness.

Testing Fiber Content

Federal law requires that all uncut fabric be labeled and identified with the correct fiber content and care instruction. It is important to know the fiber content so that you can handle it correctly. For example, the fabric might need to be preshrunk before you can cut out a garment. Usually this is noted on the end of each bolt of fabric. If this information is not appropriately labeled, ask the salesperson. Sometimes fabric manufacturers send additional tags so that the store can distribute them to their customers.

However, sometimes the fiber content of fabric is not identified. A piece of fabric might be on a markdown table in a fabric shop, fabric may have been placed on a spare bolt from the store, or a piece of fabric may be incorrectly labeled. If the fiber content is unknown, you can perform a simple burn test, identify the ash and other burn characteristics, and use these to determine the fiber content.

Hold a small swatch of fabric with a pair of tweezers. Touch this fabric with a lighted match. When cotton, linen, or rayon is burned, the ash is feathery, and it floats away and disintegrates. Wool burns slowly and has a distinctive odor. The ash is easily crushed, feels crispy, and turns to soot. Burning silk is similar to wool, but the ash feels more delicate. Most synthetics react and burn in the same manner: They usually melt and drip when burned and are very hot. When the ash cools, it can be crushed easily with the fingers but cannot be brushed off.

FABRIC CONSTRUCTION

Although several construction methods can be used to create fabric, the two basic methods of producing fabrics—weaving and knitting—are the most pertinent for this text.

WOVEN FABRICS

Woven fabrics have two sets of yarns: warp and weft. The *warp* is the lengthwise yarns. The *weft* is the filling yarns or crosswise threads. The warp and weft yarns cross at right angles. Yarns can be interlaced to form plain weave, twill weave, or satin weave. Some common woven fabrics are calico, linen, denim, poplin, broadcloth, gingham, sharkskin, corduroy, chambray, and gabardine. A common characteristic of all woven fabrics is that they fray at the cut edge—the looser the weave, the more the cut edge frays. Loosely woven fabrics are usually less durable than tightly woven fabrics.

KNITTED FABRICS

The important characteristic of a knitted fabric is its capacity to stretch. The amount and direction (one-way or two-way) of stretch varies according to the knitting process used to create the fabric.

Knitted fabrics are formed by interlooping yarns. The most common knits are flat jersey knits, purl knits, and rib knits (often known as weft knits). Rib knits stretch more in the width than in the length direction. Double knits are also weft knits; they are firmer, heavier, less stretchy, and more resilient than single knits. Tricot and raschel knits are warp knits that have less stretch than weft knits and tend to be resistant to runs.

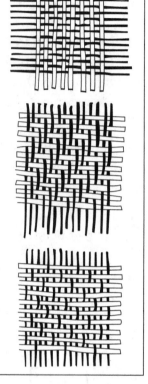

PLAIN WEAVE
Each yarn passes over and under each of the yarns going in the opposite direction.

TWILL WEAVE
Twill weave is recognized by the diagonal lines in the fabric. Yarns cross at least two yarns before going under one or more yarns.

SATIN WEAVE
Yarn goes over one and under several to create more luster on the correct side of the fabric.

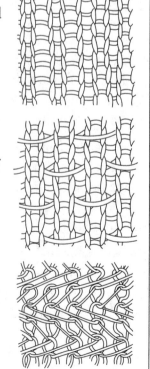

SINGLE KNIT
One set of needles is used to form loops across the fabric width.

DOUBLE KNIT
Two sets of needles are used, giving both sides of the fabric a similar appearance.

TRICOT KNIT
Several loops formed in a lengthwise direction.

TABLE 1.2 COMMON FASHION FABRICS

Fashion fabrics are available in a multitude of weaves, fiber contents, and weights.
The following chart is only a selection of fabrics commonly used in fashion sewing.

Fabric	Description	Weight	Common Uses	Fiber Content	Machine Needle
Boucle	A basket weave fabric woven with novelty looped yarns. Has an uneven texture and a thick, soft hand.	Medium to Heavy	Tailoring, Fitted garments	Various Fiber Blends: Wool, Silk, Cotton, Rayon, Acrylic	Universal Point Size: 11–14 (US) 75–90 (EU)
Brocade	A Jacquard weave fabric with a textured, raised pattern and crisp, firm hand	Medium-light to Heavy	Tailored garments, Evening wear, Home Decor	Various Fibers and Blends: Cotton, Silk, Rayon, Poly	Universal Point Size: 11–14 (US) 75–90 (EU)
Cotton Batiste	A fine, delicate, transparent plain weave fabric. Drapes and gathers in soft folds.	Light	Heirloom Sewing, Blouses, Lingerie	Cotton, Cotton/Poly Blend	Universal Point Size: 9 (US) 65 (EU)
Broadcloth	A tightly woven plain weave fabric with a slight sheen and a firm, soft hand	Light	Shirts, Blouses, Dresses	Cotton, Silk, Cotton/Poly Blends, Wool	Universal Point Size: 9–11 (US) 65–75 (EU)
Challis	A plain or twill weave fabric with a soft, supple hand	Light	Dresses, Skirts, Blouses	Cotton, Rayon, Rayon/Poly Blends, Wool	Universal Point Size: 9–11 (US) 65–75 (EU)
Chambray	A plain weave fabric with colored warp yarns and white filling yarns. Drapes in moderate flares with a dry, firm hand.	Medium-light	Shirts, Blouses, Dresses	Cotton, Cotton/Poly Blends	Universal Point Size: 9–11 (US) 65–75 (EU)
Chiffon	A plain weave sheer fabric with a soft, supple hand. Drapes in a soft, fluid flow	Light	Evening/Bridal wear, Home Decor	Silk, Polyester	Universal Point Size: 9 (US) 65 (EU)
Chintz	A glazed, usually printed, closely woven plain weave fabric with a crisp hand. Drapes in stiff folds, holds pleats well.	Medium	Dresses, Skirts, Children's wear	Cotton	Universal Point Size: 11 (US) 75 (EU)
Coating	A twill weave fabric with a lofty, thick, soft hand. Retains shape of garment.	Heavy	Outerwear, Tailored Coats and Jackets	Various Animal Hair Blends: Wool, Cashmere, Alpaca	Hair Blends: Size: 12–16 (US) 80–100 (EU)
Corduroy	A ribbed fabric with a filling pile face and plain weave back. Retains shape of garment.	Medium to Heavy	Jackets, Vests, Pants, Skirts,	Cotton, Cotton/Poly Blends	Universal Point Size: 11–14 (US) 75–90 (EU)
Crepe	A fabric woven with crimped yarns: wool crepe, Satin-back crepe, crepe georgette, crinkle crepe, crepe faille	Light to Medium	Evening/Bridal wear, Tailored garments, Dresses	Wool, Silk, Rayon, Poly, Various Blends	Universal Point Size: 9–11 (US) 65–75 (EU)
Damask	A woven fabric with a patterned Jacquard weave and smooth texture. Has a soft to firm hand depending on weight and finish.	Light to Medium-heavy	Tailored garments, Home Decor	Cotton, Silk, Various Fiber Blends	Universal Point Size: 9–14 (US) 65–90 (EU)
Denim	A closely woven warp-faced twill weave with heavier warp yarns. Has a firm hand and grainy texture.	Medium to Heavy	Jeans, Pants, Skirts, Jumpers, Jackets, Shirts, Children's wear	Cotton, Cotton/Poly or Cotton/Stretch Blends	Universal Point Size: 11–18 (US) 75–110 (EU)

TABLE 1.2 COMMON FASHION FABRICS (CONTINUED)

Fabric	Description	Weight	Common Uses	Fiber Content	Machine Needle
Faille	A plain weave fabric with heavier fill yarns that form crosswise ribs. Has a soft, textured hand and drapes into slightly crisp flares.	Light to Medium	Evening/Bridal wear, Dresses	Silk, Rayon, Nylon	Universal Point Size: 9–11 (US) 65–75 (EU)
Flannel	A supple, plain or twill weave fabric with a brushed, napped face and flat back	Light to Medium	Shirts, Tailored garments, Children's wear	Cotton, Wool	Universal Point Size: 11–14 (US) 75–90 (EU)
Fleece	A twill or knit weave fabric with a lofty, brushed, napped, and sheared surface.	Medium to Heavy	Outerwear, Sportswear, Children's wear	Wool, Acrylic, Polyester, nylon	Universal Point Size: 11–16 (US) 75–100 (EU)
Gabardine	A compact twill weave with a slight sheen and a raised diagonal rib on the face side. Has a firm, crisp or soft hand depending on the fiber content.	Medium to Heavy	Tailoring, Pants	Wool, Cotton, Poly Blends	Universal Point Size: 11–14 (US) 75–90 (EU)
Gauze	A loosely woven plain weave with a delicate, limp hand and porous texture.	Light to Medium	Casual wear, Skirts, Blouses, Lingerie	Cotton, Cotton/Poly Blends	Universal Point Size: 9–11 (US) 65–75 (EU)
Georgette	A plain weave fabric woven of textured yarns. Sheer to semi sheer, grainy appearance, drapes in soft, fluid folds	Light	Evening/Bridal wear, Dresses, Skirts	Silk, Polyester	Universal Point Size: 9 (US) 65 (EU)
Gingham	A closely and firmly woven plain weave fabric with a printed or woven checked appearance	Light to Medium	Blouses, Shirts, Dresses, Skirts, Home Decor	Poly/Cotton Blends	Universal Point Size: 9–11 (US) 65–75 (EU)
Hand-kerchief Linen	A plain weave fabric woven of fine yarns with slight irregular-ities. Drapes in crisp, stiff cones.	Light	Skirts, Dresses	Linen	Universal Point Size: 9–11 (US) 65–75 (EU)
Knit	An interlocking loop weave that creates stretch capabilities. Many knit variations are available: Interlock, Jersey, Tricot, Jacquard, Raschel, Sweater, Rib	Light to Medium	Sportswear, Athletic wear, Swimwear, Lingerie	Various Blends: Cotton, Poly, Rayon, Spandex, Nylon, Wool	Stretch / Ball Point Size: 9–11 (US) 65–75 (EU)
Muslin	A plain weave basic fabric of varying thread counts. Has a dry, soft to firm hand.	Light to Medium	Blouses, Heirloom garments, Lingerie, Quilting, Test garments	Cotton	Universal Point Size: 9–11 (US) 65–75 (EU)
Oxford Shirting	A finely woven basket weave fabric with a soft, firm hand and flat, soft luster	Light to Medium-light	Shirts, Blouses	Cotton	Universal Point Size: 9–11 (US) 65–75 (EU)
Pique	A pique weave produces a textured, raised pattern of various designs. Holds shape of garments well.	Medium-light to Medium-heavy	Fitted garments, Tailoring	Cotton, Cotton/Poly Blends	Universal Point Size: 12–14 (US) 80–90 (EU)
Plisse	A plain weave fabric put through a chemical process that produces a crinkling effect. Has a crisp, springy hand and an all over blistered texture.	Medium-light	Shirts, Blouses	Cotton, Polyester	Universal Point Size: 9–11 (US) 65–75 (EU)

TABLE 1.2 COMMON FASHION FABRICS (CONTINUED)

Fabric	Description	Weight	Common Uses	Fiber Content	Machine Needle
Poplin	A plain weave fabric with a rib effect in the crosswise direction. Has a firm to stiff hand and a papery, harsh texture.	Medium to Medium-heavy	Pants, Skirts, Shirts	Polyester, Poly/Cotton, Wool, Silk	Universal Point Size: 11–14 (US) 75–90 (EU)
Satin	A Satin weave produces a lustrous, smooth face fabric with a dull back. Common Satins include Brocade, Charmeuse, Crepe-back satin, Duchess, Jacquard Satin.	Light to Heavy	Evening/Bridal wear, Dresses, Skirts, Blouses, Tailored Jackets	Silk, Polyester, Acetate, Acetate/Rayon	Universal Point Size: 9–14 (US) 65–90 (EU)
Suiting	Suitings come in a variety of weaves and appearances. It is mainly characterized by its ability to retain its shape.	Medium to Medium-heavy	Tailored garments—Suits, Jackets, Skirts, Pants	Various Fibers and Blends: Silk, Linen, Wool, Rayon, Polyester	Universal Point Size: 11–14 (US) 75–90 (EU)
Seersucker	A crisp, textured plain weave fabric with alternating crinkled stripes permanently woven by weaving warp yarns slack and tight.	Medium-light to Medium-heavy	Shirts, Blouses, Dresses, Skirts, Children's wear	Cotton, Cotton/Poly Blends	Universal Point Size: 9–11 (US) 65–75 (EU)
Taffeta	A crisp fabric characterized by a fine crosswise rib. Available in a variety of types producing a soft to crisp hand and dull to lustrous finishes.	Light to Medium	Evening/Bridal wear, Dresses, Skirts	Silk, Acetate, Polyester	Universal Point Size: 9–11 (US) 65–75 (EU)
Tweed	Tweeds are a wide range of fabric types characterized by a mixed color appearance (woven of 2+ color yarns).	Medium-light to Heavy	Tailoring, Outerwear, Jackets, Coats	Various Fibers and Blends: Wool, Silk, Acrylic, Polyester	Universal Point Size: 12–16 (US) 80–100 (EU)
Twill	Twill is a close weave that creates a diagonal ridge side and a plain side. Common twills include Khaki Cloth, Drill, Herringbone, Denim, Tweed	Medium to Heavy	Pants, Rugged wear, Skirts, Tailoring	Various Blends: Cotton, Wool, Polyester, Silk	Universal Point Size: 12–16 (US) 80–100 (EU)
Velvet	A woven fabric with a cut warp pile face and a plain or knit base. There are many variations of velvet ranging from soft and spongy to firm and compact.	Medium-light to Heavy	Evening/Bridal wear, Dresses, Skirts, Home Decor	Various Blends: Rayon, Acetate, Nylon, Cotton	Universal Point Size: 11–14 (US) 75–90 (EU)
Velveteen	A filling pile fabric with a shorter, more closely set pile than velvet	Medium-heavy	Tailoring, Jackets, Children's wear, Home Decor	Cotton	Universal Point Size: 11–14 (US) 75–90 (EU)
Velour	A soft, spongy fabric with a cut pile face and a jersey knit back. Stretches in crosswise direction, pile is pressed flat in one direction.	Medium	Evening wear, Sportswear, Dresses, Skirts, T-tops	Cotton, Poly, Poly/Rayon Blends	Stretch / Ball Point Size: 11–14 (US) 75–90 (EU)
Voile	A loosely woven plain weave fabric with a delicate, semi-sheer appearance. Drapes in moderately soft flares.	Light	Dresses, Skirts, Blouses, Children's wear	Cotton/Poly Blends	Universal Point Size: 9–11 (US) 65–75 (EU)

PRE-SHRINKING FABRIC

When heat or steam is applied to fabric, the threads relax and shrink. Many fabrics shrink when laundered or dry-cleaned. The most common fabrics that shrink a good deal are untreated, 100%, cotton, linen, and wool. It is important to preshrink many fabrics so that the size of a garment will not be altered after washing or dry-cleaning.

To preshrink 100% cotton, place it in a washing machine on the spin cycle (the spin cycle adds a minimum of water without soaking the fabric). Then, place the fabric in an automatic dryer; the heat applied shrinks the damp fabric.

To preshrink 100% wool, take it to a dry-cleaners, and ask the cleaner to steam and press the fabric. The cleaning process is unnecessary because the heat from the steam process relaxes the threads and shrinks the fabric.

To preshrink 100% linen, you can use either the washer/dryer or dry-cleaning methods described above. Because untreated 100% linen wrinkles, the dry-cleaning method is simpler.

Silk, rayon, polyester, and other synthetic fabrics do not need to be preshrunk.

BLOCKING

A finished sewn garment must hang correctly. Therefore, it is important to check the fabric before cutting to determine whether the crossgrain threads are distorted. This is called blocking, which is the process of making sure the lengthwise and cross-grain threads are at right angles to each other.

To block fabric that is distorted, fold the fabric selvage to selvage, pin all the fabric edges together (excluding the folded side), tack the grainline to a board or table, and gently pull on the crossgrain threads until all the threads are at a 90-degree angle.

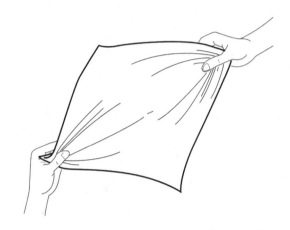

GRAINLINES

Lengthwise Grain (Straight of Grain). The lengthwise *grain* of the fabric is always parallel to the *selvage* of the fabric and is also sometimes referred to as the *warp*. The *selvage* is the firmly woven edge that runs lengthwise to the fabric on both sides. The strongest threads run in the lengthwise direction and have the best stretch.

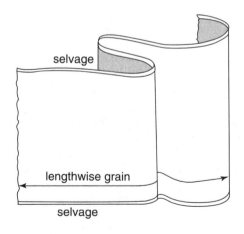

selvage

lengthwise grain

selvage

Crossgrain. The crosswise grain, or *crossgrain* is the weave that runs perpendicular to the lengthwise grain of the fabric from selvage to selvage. These crossgrain yarns are the *filling yarns*, or *weft*. The crossgrain has slightly more give than the straight of the grain in fabrics.

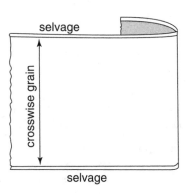

Bias. Bias fabric gives and stretches a great deal more than the grain or crossgrain of the fabric. Bias-cut garments are used when a design requires draping contours that fall gracefully over the body. To find the bias, fold the grain of the fabric to the crossgrain to create a perfect 45 degree foldline.

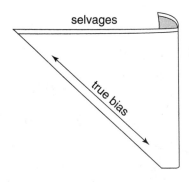

LINING FABRICS

The lining essentially is a duplicate of the garment, made in a suitable lining fabric and then sewn into the garment. Lining a garment adds more body and durability to the outer garment and also provides a more attractive inside finish. A lining fabric is usually a lighter weight than the garment fabric (see Table 1.3). It should be compatible to the fabric selected for the garment so it doesn't add too much body and distort the garment. For instance, a wool skirt would use a light-weight 100% acetate or a poly/cotton blend.

TABLE 1.3 GUIDELINES TO SELECTING LININGS

Lining Weight	Typical Fabrics	Qualities	Care Tips
Light-weight linings used for suit jackets, coats, tailored pants, and skirts.	100% cotton or polyester blend	Ravels and could pull apart at the seams.	Machine Wash. May need preshrinking. May need dry-cleaning.
	100% acetate	Smooth, slick finish. Ravels and could pull apart at the seams.	Dry-clean only.
	Polyester/rayon blend acetate	Smooth finish. Ravels and could pull apart at the seams.	Machine wash.
	Crepe (polyester)	Strong and durable.	Machine wash. Press at low temperature.
	Crepe-back satin (either rayon or acetate)	Smooth and flexible, with a bit more body than acetate.	Dry-clean.
Medium-weight linings used for lining bustier dresses or evening gowns.	Satin (polyester or acetate) or Taffeta (acetate or polyester)	Adds body and maintains shape.	Machine wash polyester. Dry-clean acetate.

Helpful Sewing Tip:
Thread & Needle: *Use cotton-wrapped polyester, or mercerized cotton. Use size 11 needle.*

INTERFACINGS

Interfacing, like fabric, is made of various fibers and constructions. You should select an interfacing that is compatible with the weight, hand, or stretch of the garment fabric. The interfacing should not change the weight of the fabric or drastically affect the appearance of the garment. Do not select interfacing by feel as all properties may change when an interfacing is attached or laundered. There are a number of interfacings characterized by weight, finish, fiber blends, and textures. Select interfacing based on the following criteria: fiber content, weave, finish (press-on or sew-in), color, and weight.

Use Table 1.4 as a guide for the most appropriate interfacing to complement the appearance durability, maintenance, and comfort of a garment.

Fiber Content

Interfacings are manufactured of natural fibers (such as cotton) or manufactured fibers (such as nylon, polyester, or rayon). They can also be manufactured of combined fibers using a percentage of a natural fiber and a percentage of a manufactured fiber. Using an interfacing with the correct fiber content allows the interfacing to work suitability with the fashion fabric in care, shrinkage, or washability. Conversely, using an interfacing with the wrong fiber content can damage the fashion fabric. For instance, 100% nylon interfacing shrinks with fabric such as lycra or stretch denim, and a nylon/polyester blend interface works with 100% rayon, 100% cotton, and 100% challis. Refer to Table 1.4 for guidance in choosing the correct interfacing.

Weave

Interfacings are made with five different weaving processes: (1) woven; (2) weft; (3) weft insertion; (4) tricot knit; (5) nonwoven.

All five processes are made sew-in or fusible (press-on). This may determine the appearance of the finished look and comfort of the garment. Please do not select interfacings by feel as all properties may change as soon as the interfacing is attached or laundered. To make it easier to select a correct interfacing, refer to Table 1.4.

- **Weft interfacing—A weft interfacing is a combination of a woven and knit process.** The knit weave is woven loosely in the weft direction, and a traditional weave is the warp direction. These weft interfacing have been used in the garment industry for the past several years and is slowly being introduced into the home sewing market. Open-weave wefts are used primarily to reinforce coat and suit fronts. The tighter and lighter wefts work primarily with silks and synthetics. Weft interfacings are rapidly replacing canvas hairs.

- **Weft insertion interfacing—A weft insertion is a nonwoven interfacing with a weft insertion in the crossgrain.** The nonwoven fibers are placed on the grain, and a tricot knit is woven loosely in the weft direction. Weft insertion interfacing has been used in the garment industry for the past several years and is slowly being introduced into the home sewing market to replace the traditional nonwoven interfacing. A disadvantage of weft insertion interfacing is that it tears easily.

TABLE 1.4 GUIDE TO SELECTING INTERFACINGS

Interfacing Type	Color	Finish	Description
Polyester/Rayon Blend Weft	White and black	Fusible	Use for women's wear front jacket applications and with dress-weight fabrics. Offers a soft, lightly resilient, round hand.
Non-woven All-purpose polyester/nylon	White and charcoal	Fusible	Works with almost any fabric, especially 100% rayon, cotton, or challis. Gives a softer tailoring hand. Has special glue designed for rayon and other hard-to-fuse fabrics.
Tricot for knits 100% Nylon	White and black	Fusible	Offers a unique softness and drapability to a wide range of knitted fabrics. Fuses easily and performs well with most knitted fabrics.
100% Polyester tricot	White and black	Fusible	Designed for sheer fabric, georgette, and very light-weight fabric. Offers a soft, stable, and sheer polyester tricot designed for today's fashion fabrics used in blouses and dresses.
100% Woven cotton	White and black	Fusible	An excellent woven fusible for light-weight to medium-weight fabrics that can be used with a wide range of woven fabrics, including pure worsteds and blends. Not suitable for fine fabrics or 100% filament synthetics, such as acetate and nylon. Both machine washable and dry-cleanable.

- **Woven interfacing**—Woven interfacing fabrics have a warp and weft construction. Woven interfacings include various types of fabrics such as lawn, batiste, net, siri, organdy, and canvas. A wide selection of weights and colors are available.

- **Nonwoven interfacing**—Nonwoven interfacings are considered bonded fabrics. This means that they are created by thermally bonding, or heat pressing, crosslaid fibers into a finished fabric that gives cross-section stretch and recovery. Nonwoven interfacing has a look and feel similar to woven goods. When using nonwoven interfacing, all interfacing pattern pieces must be laid out, following the grainline, to be sure they also perform in the same manner as woven goods with regard to grainline, crossgrain, and bias. Non-woven interfacings range from fine-transparent to firm and are available in many colors and brand names. They are also engineered to work with medium-weight to light-weight fabrics.

- **Tricot knit interfacing**—Tricot interfacings are usually 100% nylon warp knit and tend to be run resistant. They are very comfortable to the touch and are light-weight. Tricot knit interfacings, such as fusible tricot, or "easy knit" are used with knits. Tricot knit interfacings can stretch in all directions and are more flexible than other wovens and nonwovens. The majority of knit interfacings are fusible.

Finish

Deciding whether to use fusible or nonfusible interfacing can be difficult because of the scientific breakthroughs in fusible interfacing in the past several years.

Nonfusible, or sew-in, interfacing is fabric without any glue. You attach it by machine basting or surging it onto the garment.

Fusible interfacing has a heat-sensitive adhesive on one side, which is ironed onto the fabric. Different fusible interfacings react differently, depending on the amount and type of glue distributed on the surface. For example, the number of dots and the size of the dots varies. A fine dot may be referred to as *30 mesh* and a larger dot may be referred to as *17 mesh*. The 30 mesh has a greater number of dots per inch, but a much finer dot. This is usually used on a finer, lighter-weight fashion fabric. The 17 mesh has larger and fewer dots, and is usually used on heavier to medium-weight fabrics.

On some fusible interfacings, the glues may harden the garment fabric and leave spots. Other glues

react well with fabrics, maintaining the quality and adding body necessary for the finished garment. Therefore, it is important to test a fusible interfacing with a small piece of the garment fabric.

It is important to note that many home sewers have problems with fusible interfacing because they do not apply them to the fabric correctly. For more information, see Chapter 17, "Facings and Interfacings."

Weight

You must consider weight when selecting an interfacing fabric for a garment. *Weight* refers to the texture, body, or drape of fabric. The various fibers used, the methods in which these fibers are put together, and the amount and type of glue used for press-on create weight differences among interfacings.

Preshrinking Interfacing

If you carefully follow the advice in Table 1.4, you probably don't need to worry about preshrinking interfacing. Because there is a small amount of shrinkage in all types of interfacing fabrics, however, you might choose to preshrink interfacing just to be safe.

Remember that heat is the element that relaxes fibers. You should handle both fusible and non-fusible interfacing gently. To preshrink interfacing, carefully fold in half, wrong side to wrong side, and place it in hot water for about 20 minutes. Remove the interfacing from the water and drain it on a towel. Pat out all excess water and place on an airy, dry surface until it is thoroughly dried. If the garment you are making is to be dry-cleaned, simply steaming with the iron may provide sufficient preshrinking. Be careful not to touch the iron to the fabric, however, as it can cause distortion.

CHAPTER 2
The Sewing Machine and Sewing Equipment

SEWING MACHINES

PURCHASING A SEWING MACHINE

A sewing machine uses a needle and rotary hook to interlock threads above (upper thread) and below (bobbin thread) a piece of fabric and produce a "stitch." These stitches can be designed to simply lock two fabrics together, encase the raw edges of a seam, or decorate fabric with a specific pattern. Sewing machine models contain single or multiple stitch functions.

Purchasing a sewing machine can be a daunting task. From older models with basic functions to top-of-the-line models with internal computers and a variety of features, a profusion of sewing machine models are available on the market today. To simplify the decision process, this chapter describes the many attributes of machine types and their usage.

Keep in mind that the machine choice must be suitable with the planned usage. An artistic home sewer might want a machine with many creative stitch functions, while a garment factory would want a machine with basic stitch functions and a stronger motor for faster sewing speeds.

MACHINE CLASSIFICATION

Sewing machines can be classified into two categories, industrial and household. Both categories contain an abundance of model types. However, the difference resides in the intended use. Industrial machines are designed for continuous use at high speeds (1,000s of stitches per minute) and are also typically customized for one specific step in garment construction—such as straight stitching, zipper application, bias binding, buttonholes, or other steps. Household machines have more versatile functions because they are used for many different projects such as clothing repair and construction, quilting, home decorations, and crafts.

INDUSTRIAL MACHINES

All the components of an industrial machine are designed for efficient garment construction, saving time and money. The actual machine, called the "machine head," is configured with a specific stitch for a specific step and can be sized and shaped accordingly. It also typically contains a bobbin system that winds extra bobbins during stitching. The machine head is set into a table that houses a separate clutch motor, a pedal, a thread stand, an automatic lubrication system, a pedal brake that lifts the machine needle when desired, and a knee lift that raises the presser foot so hands can remain free to manipulate the fabric.

HOUSEHOLD MACHINES

Household machines are designed with a variety of stitch functions and come with a variety of accessories (presser feet, etc.). This enables them to perform all the steps needed to complete a project. New models with basic features might cost $100–$300, while computerized models with hundreds of stitch options range from $300–$8,000. To identify which features best suit your needs, study the following pages. Then, visit sewing centers and practice using the machines with the assistance of a knowledgeable salesperson. (See page 23 for a list of sewing machine manufacturers and distributors.)

A good sewing machine should operate smoothly and produce uniformly neat stitches. Basic sewing machines offer a straight stitch (forward and reverse), zig-zag stitch, adjustable stitch lengths, and a buttonhole setting. In general, the more stitch options offered, the higher the cost of the machine. An advanced sewer might enjoy more creative options, but a beginner may appreciate basic features that keep the machine easier to operate.

MACHINE STYLE

Console machines are designed to be set into a table, creating more flat space for sewing—especially useful for larger projects. Portable machines can be set up on any surface and thus travel well for classes and store easily. In the past, all sewing machines were mechanically designed. Dials or levers were provided to change a stitch function, or sometimes a cam disk would need to be changed internally. Today, both mechanical and computerized models are available. Computerized models provide buttons or touch-screens to select stitch settings and generally add to the cost of a machine. Whether to buy a mechanical or computerized version should be based on budget and the desired ease for changing settings.

BOBBIN STYLE—Case or Drop-in/Top-loading

Sewing machines are available in two bobbin designs. In the case style, the bobbin is placed in a bobbin case that is then latched into a compartment beneath the needle plate. In the top-loading style, the bobbin is simply dropped into place under the needle plate. The top-loading design makes changing a bobbin easier on a console model. Both designs have positive and negative attributes, so the choice is left to personal preference.

BASIC STITCH FUNCTIONS NECESSARY FOR FASHION SEWING

(Listed in order of importance—More features included in higher priced models)

- Straight Stitch
- Variable stitch length and stitch width
- Variable needle positions
- Zig-zag Stitch (and variations)
- Buttonhole (single or multiple styles)
- Misc. Sewing Stitches: Hemming Stitches (Blind Hem), Edge-finishing Stitches (overcasting for knits or raveling fabrics)

DECORATIVE/CREATIVE STITCH FUNCTIONS

Decorative stitches vary from brand to brand and model to model. Multiple styles and variations of geometric, floral, and alphabet stitches are available. Decorative stitches are useful to highlight creative and artistic projects. They can also add fun options for beginner sewers, but are not required for basic sewing projects.

NEW TECHNOLOGY/FEATURES

Advanced engineering and modern technology have provided many new features for sewing machines. Again, these add to the cost of the machine, but can assist time efficiency. Listed below are some helpful features.

- Automatic needle threading—a device that hooks thread through the needle eye
- Thread cutter—a button function that clips thread tails
- Speed control—adjusts the maximum speed allowed
- Stitch memory—Similar to speed dialing, it memorizes stitch combinations or settings
- Needle up/down—Sets the needle to stop automatically in the up or down position
- Sensors—Warns when bobbin thread is low/out, advises presser foot choice

Features that cut tail threads or raise/lower the needle with a simple push of a button (instead of turning the hand wheel) can help achieve more efficient sewing. Be aware that new technology can sometimes complicate machine operation. New features sometimes accommodate sewing ignorance and can annoy experienced sewers who wish to manipulate and control the fabric feeding, needle positioning, specific backstitching, etc.

HOUSEHOLD MODEL CATEGORIES

Currently, many household machines are being designed and marketed for specific sewing styles. These machines are customized with various features and stitch options.

Basic Household Sewing ($100–$1,000)—Designed for mending, alterations, home decorations, and beginner to basic sewing, these machines are typically portable and offer basic stitch functions in mechanical or computerized styles. Some higher priced models offer a few decorative stitches as well as needle threading and other new technology.

**BERNINA 1008
BASIC NON-COMPUTERIZED**

	Basic Household Sewing
Babylock	BL6300, Design Pro, Denim Pro
Bernina	1008, Bernette Series
Brother	PS Series
Elna	2000 Series, 3200
Husqvarna/Viking	Lena, Prelude Series, Scandinavia 100, Huskystar Series
Janome	Classmate, Schoolmate, 405, 415, 419, Jem Series
Juki	HZL-E61, HZL-E50, HZL-E40, HZL-30Z, HZL-60
Pfaff	Select Series
Riccar	Utility Series, Rotary Series
Sears/Kenmore	Mini Ultra Series, 15208, 15218, 15202, 15212, 505S
Simplicity	Creative Spirit, Pioneer, Sew Precious, Quilt 'n' Craft, Deco Mate, American Denim, Liberty
Singer	Featherweight II, 1120, 1525, 1725, 4830, 132, 140Q, 6038, 5160, 2950
White	700 to 1800 Series, 2037, 4042

Creative Fashion and Hobby Sewing ($300–$3,000)—These machines offer multiple stitch options (basic and decorative) customized for specific hobbies such as quilting, home decorating, fashion, and crafts. Depending on the price ranking, new features such as needle threading, thread cutting, stitch memory, and specialized decorative stitches are available.

	Creative Fashion/Hobby Sewing
Babylock	Quilter's Choice, Decorator's Choice, Crafter's Choice, BL6800
Bernina	Bernette Series, Activa Series, Virtuosa
Brother	NX Series
Elna	6000 Series
Husqvarna/Viking	Lena, Platinum Series, Interlude Series, Scandinavia 200
Janome	423S, 2003P, Jem Series, Decor Series, Sewist Series, Memory Craft 3000-4000
Juki	HZL-E61, HZL-E70, HZL-E80, HZL-E100
Pfaff	Select Series, Quilt Expression, Expression, Performance
Riccar	Rotary Series
Sears/Kenmore	16231, 19233
Simplicity	Denim Star, Fashion Pro, Quilter's Choice, American Quilter
Singer	2732, 5050, 2662, 3962
White	2037, 1780, 1740

**JUKI HZL-E80
COMPUTERIZED CREATIVE SEWING**

High Fashion/Artistic Sewing ($800–$8,000)—For serious fabric artists and advanced fashion sewing, these machines are computerized models with multiple stitch options, including many decorative stitches. Most models also include top-of-the-line features such as thread cutting, needle threading, stitch memory, sensors, and many adjustable settings. Models in higher price brackets offer embroidery functions, built-in or attached. These models use external and internal computer software to stitch simple to elaborate embroidery patterns.

BERNINA ARTISTA SERIES
HIGH FASHION SEWING/EMBROIDERY MACHINE

	Serious Fashion/Artistic Sewing
Babylock	Ellegante, Ellageo 3, Ellure, Esante, Intrigue, Espire
Bernina	Virtuosa, Artista Series, Aurora
Brother	NX600, Innov-is, PC Series, PE Series
Elna	Envision Series, Xquisit
Husqvarna/Viking	Designer Series, Rose, Iris, Platinum, Scandinavia 300
Janome	Memory Craft 5000 to 10001 series
Pfaff	Creative Series
Sears/Kenmore	19606, 851S
Singer	Quantum Series, Futura

Small Business/Industry Sewing, Embroidery-Only Machines ($1,000–$10,000)—Some smaller-scale industrial machines are available with streamlined features and stronger motors for extended use and faster speeds. These machines provide industrial features in smaller console and portable styles. Embroidery-only (E) machines are also available for smaller businesses or for a serious sewer who would like a separate embroidery machine.

SINGER INDUSTRIAL MODEL #2491D300A

BROTHER PR-600
SMALL COMMERCIAL EMBROIDERY ONLY

	Small Business/Industry Sewing, Embroidery Only
Babylock	Embroidery Professional (E), BL60E, Quilter's Choice Pro
Bernina	Deco (E), 950 Industrial
Brother	PR600 (E), ULT Series
Janome	1600 Professional Series, Cover Pro, 6000QC Series
Juki	TL98Q
Singer	CG Series
White	W3300 (E)

Overlock Machines

This special purpose machine is becoming an increasingly popular second machine for many home sewers. It sews 1,500 or more stitches per minute, approximately twice the speed of a conventional sewing machine. It stitches, overcasts, and trims seam edges in one step. Seams are narrow and have a very professional look. Blindstitch and rolled hem functions are also available.

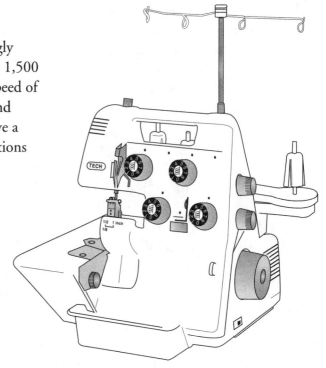

PURCHASING A SERGER (OVERLOCK)

Many different models of sergers (or overlock machines) are available. The main function of a serger is to trim the seam edge and overcast the seam to finish the edge to create a clean inside finish and to prevent the fabric from raveling. (For more information on using a serger, refer to the Bibliography in the next column for a list of books explaining the method of serging.)

A serger performs several functions, including stitching a seam and at the same time overcasting (or marrowing) the edge of the fabric for a decorative outside finish, and sewing a flat, nonbulky, stretchable seam on knits using the flatlock stitch. The function you use depends on the number of threads and needles on the machine:

- A *three-thread serger* has two loopers and one needle. It is used primarily to overcast seams.

- A *four-thread serger* has two loopers and two needles. This type is used to sew and overcast seams at the same time.

- A *five-thread serger* has three loopers and two needles. This machine can chain stitch a seam, overcast seams, and create a rolled hem look.

Because of the many functions and features available on sergers, it is important to comparison shop for price and quality.

REFERENCE BOOKS FOR A SERGER/OVERLOCK

The following books provide further information on sergers:

Baker, Naomi, and Tammy Young. *Distinctive Serger Gifts and Crafts: An Idea Book for All Occasions.* Radnor, PA: Chilton Book Company, 1989.

————. *Simply Serge Any Fabric.* Radnor, PA: Chilton Book Company, 1989.

Bottom, Lori, and Tammy Young. *Innovative Serging.* Radnor, PA: Chilton Book Company, 1991.

Drellich, Karen, and Sue Green. *Singer Sewing Reference Library's Sewing with Sergers.* Available from Cy DeCosse, PO Box 3040, 5900 Green Oak Drive, Minnetonka, MN 55343.

McMakin, Kathy. *French Sewing by Serger.* Huntsville, AL: Albright & Co., Inc., 1988.

Palmer, Pati, Gail Brown, and Sue Green. *Creative Serging Illustrated.* Radnor, PA: Chilton Book Company, 1992.

Sieman, Nancy. *The Busy Woman's Sewing Book.* Menlo Park, CA: Open Chain Publishing, 1988.

MANUFACTURERS OF SEWING MACHINES AND SERGERS

These manufacturers produce sewing machines and sergers in a variety of models with many features and in different price ranges.

Bernina of America
3702 Prairie Lake Court
Aurora, IL 60504-6182
www.berninausa.com
www.bernina.com

Brother International Corporation
(Industrial and Household Machines)
100 Somerset Corporate Blvd
Bridgewater, NJ 08807-0911
www.brothersews.com
www.brother.com

Husqvarna/Viking
31000 Viking Parkway
Westlake, OH 44145-8012
www.husqvarnaviking.com
—**White** (a division of Husqvarna/Viking)
31000 Viking Parkway
Westlake, OH 44145-8012
www.whitesewing.com

Janome America, Inc.
(FORMERLY NEW HOME)
10 Industrial Avenue
Mahwah, NJ 07430
www.janome.com

Juki Union Special Inc.
(Industrial and Household Machines)
8500 NW 17th Street
Suite 100
Miami, FL 33126-1008
www.juki.com

Pfaff Sewing Machines
P.O. Box 458012
Westlake, OH 44145-8012
www.pfaff.com
www.pfaffusa.com

Sears (Kenmore Sewing Machines)
Sears National Customer Relations
3333 Beverly Road
Hoffman Estates, IL 60179
www.sears.com
www.kenmore.com

Singer Sewing Company
(Industrial and Household Machines)
1224 Heil Quaker Blvd.
P.O. Box 7017
LaVergne, TN 37086
www.singerco.com

Tacony Corporation
(Industrial and Household Machines.
Distributers of brands listed below.)
1760 Gilsinn Lane
Fenton, MO 63026
www.tacony.com
—**Babylock**
www.babylock.com
—**Elna**
www.elna.com
—**Riccar Sewing Machines**
www.riccar.com
—**Simplicity Sewing Machines**
www.simplicitysewing.com

Identifying Parts on the Sewing Machine

The principal parts of an average sewing machine are illustrated below. Although your sewing machine may differ slightly, there are many similar features.

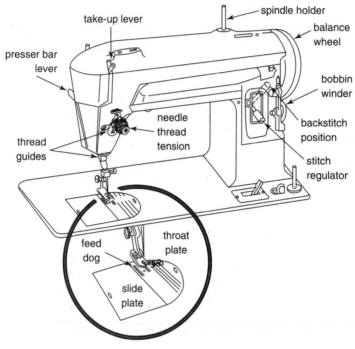

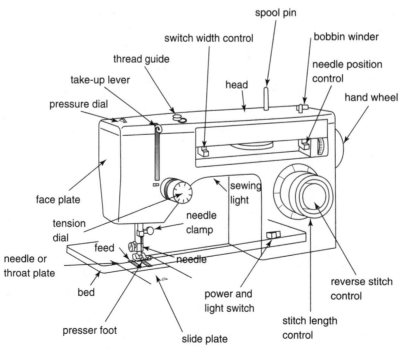

THREADING A FRONT–MOUNTED MACHINE

When threading the machine, you are concerned with three operations: (1) winding the bobbin, (2) threading the bobbin case, and (3) threading the machine. The following instructions illustrate the threading of an average front-mounted sewing machine. However, remember to read the instruction book accompanying your machine.

1 Place a spool of thread on the spindle holder.

2 Lead the thread across the top of the machine into the first thread guide hook.

3 Guide the thread down to the right of the tension disk.

4 Guide the thread around the tension disk, making sure the thread falls between the two disks.

5 Continue around the tension disk, and lead the thread into and under the tension spring lever.

6 Lead the thread back up and through the hole (front right to left) of the take-up lever.

7 Lead the thread down and through the thread guides.

8 Guide the thread into the clamp near the needle holder.

9 Guide the thread through the eye of the needle. (Refer to the section "Threading the Machine Needle.")

Note: *If the sewing machine is incorrectly threaded, the thread of the stitch will loop on the bottom layer of fabric, the machine will skip stitches, or the needle will unthread after you sew a few stitches.*

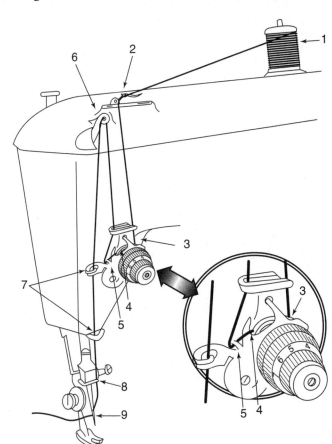

THREADING A SIDE-MOUNTED MACHINE

Many power machines are threaded with this side-mounted style.

1 Place a spool of thread on the spindle holder and lead the thread across the top of the first thread guide.

2 Continue the thread across the top of the machine into the second thread guide.

3 Guide the thread down the beginning of the tubing hole.

4 Continue to lead the thread through the tubing hole.

5 Guide the thread around the tension disk, making sure the thread falls between the two disks and up and over the take-up hook.

6 Lead the thread under the take-up spring.

7 Continue to guide the thread up and through the slot of the take-up disks.

8 Pass the thread down and through the thread guides.

9 Lead the thread into the clamp near the needle holder.

10 Guide the thread through the eye of the needle. (Refer to the section "Threading the Machine Needle.")

Note: *If the sewing machine is incorrectly threaded, the thread of the stitch will loop on the bottom layer of fabric, the machine will skip stitches, or the needle will unthread after you sew a few stitches.*

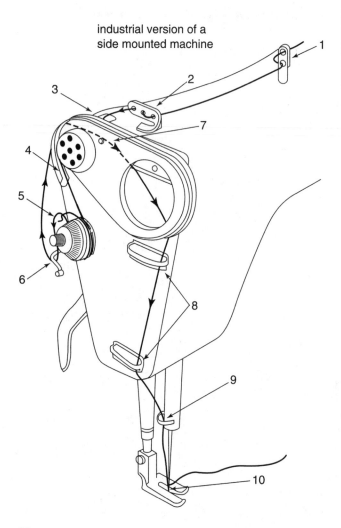

industrial version of a side mounted machine

THREADING A MACHINE NEEDLE

Depending on the sewing machine, the thread could pass through the eye of the needle in one of the following three directions:

1. Front to back
2. Right to left
3. Left to right

Helpful Sewing Hint: *If the needle thread is inserted in the wrong direction, it will unthread, or the top thread will skip stitches, or both.*

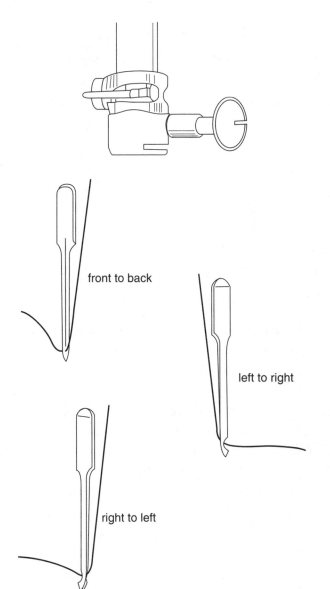

front to back

left to right

right to left

WINDING A BOBBIN

Many machines have the conventional bobbin winder on the righthand side. Refer to the instruction book accompanying your machine. Here are the basic steps:

1 Place an empty bobbin on the bobbin disk holder.

2 Place a spool of thread on the spindle holder.

3 Place the thread through the tension disk.

4 Continue to follow the thread to the empty bobbin. Wind the thread by hand around the bobbin three times.

5 Release the balance wheel tension disk. (This step is not needed on some models.)

6 Push the bobbin winder against the balance wheel.

7 Run the machine. The bobbin winds.

Helpful Sewing Hint: *To ensure that the needle does not break, make sure the presser foot is in the down position.*

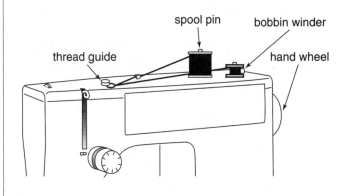

spool pin

bobbin winder

thread guide

hand wheel

THREADING A BOBBIN CASE

Before threading your bobbin case, refer to the instruction book accompanying your machine. The method varies from machine to machine. The following are the basic steps for threading a bobbin case:

1 Place the bobbin into the bobbin case so that the bobbin thread is in a clockwise direction.

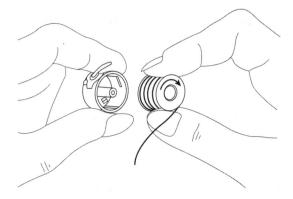

2 Lead the bobbin thread into the slot (1) and under the tension spring (2).

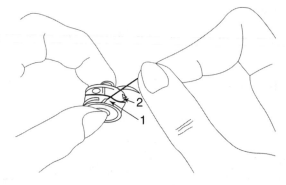

3 Continue to pull the thread around and into the notch (3) at the end of the spring. Leave about 3 inches of thread hanging from the bobbin case.

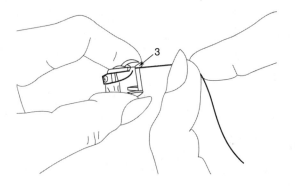

PLACING A BOBBIN CASE INTO A SIDE-MOUNTED MACHINE

1 Hold the bobbin case latch, and position the bobbin case onto the stud of the machine.

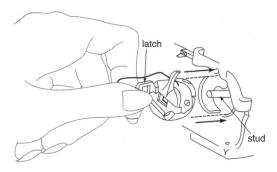

2 Release the latch and push the bobbin case into the machine until you hear the bobbin case click into place.

3 To remove the bobbin case, hold the latch and pull the bobbin case out of machine.

PLACING A BOBBIN CASE INTO A FRONT-MOUNTED MACHINE

1 Hold the bobbin case latch and position the bobbin case flat into the bobbin case area of the machine.

2 Release the latch and push the bobbin case into the machine until you hear the bobbin case click into place.

3 To remove the bobbin case, press the bobbin push button to release the bobbin case and pull it out of the machine.

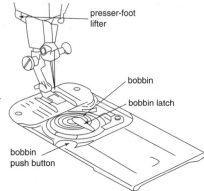

DRAWING UP THE BOBBIN THREAD

1 Hold the needle thread with your left hand and turn the balance wheel with your right hand until the needle is completely lowered into the bobbin area.

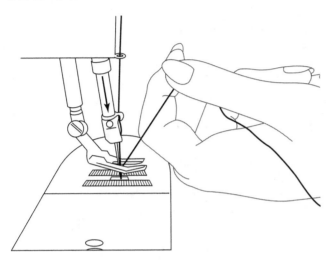

2 Rotate the balance wheel until the needle starts to bring up the bobbin thread. Pull the needle thread toward the front. The bobbin thread loops and automatically follows.

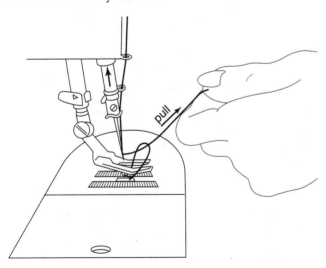

3 Pull the looped bobbin thread toward the front until approximately 3 inches of thread is visible.

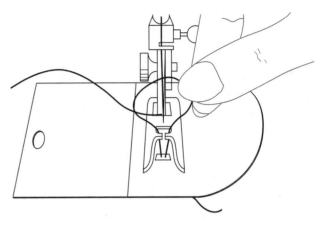

4 Place the needle and the bobbin threads under the presser foot, bringing them behind the foot.

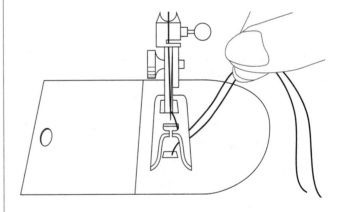

It is not true that sewing machines were designed to confuse the sewer. However, sewing on a machine that is not working properly can be a frustrating experience. Operating a sewing machine is simple when you understand how to use it properly. Be patient and learn how to master your sewing machine. Some common problems and their solutions are outlined below.

Problem	Checklist
Thread looping on the bottom layer of the fabric.	Is the sewing machine threaded correctly? Is the thread around the tension disk correctly?
Skipped or uneven stitches.	Is the machine needle backward? Is the machine needle the correct size? Is the sewing machine threaded correctly?
Needle unthreading or breaking.	Is the thread around the tension disk correct? Is the tension too tight? Is the thread caught on something, such as the thread spool? Is the needle blunt? If so, replace it.
Fabric being pulled down into needle hole.	Are you using the correct throat plate? Make sure you use the straight-stitch throat plate with a small hole, not the zigzag plate with a wide hole.
Puckered seams.	Is the machine threaded correctly? If it is, check the tension. Use a lower number.

The following problems can result from incorrect upper tension:

- Too loose—Stitches appear loose on the top side of the fabric, and links are visible on the underside.

- Too tight—Stitches pull together on the top side of the fabric and create a pinched effect.

- Consult your machine's manual to adjust the tensions correctly.

The following problems can result from incorrect bobbin tension:

- Too loose—Links are visible on the top side of the fabric.

- Too tight—Stitches appear pinched on the underside of the fabric.

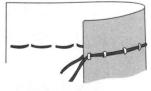

thread looping on bottom layer

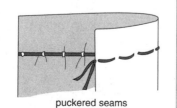

puckered seams

Helpful Sewing Tip: *Rule of Thumb*
If the stitch thread looks incorrect on the bottom layer of your sewing process, usually this means something is wrong with the upper threading, the tension, or the needle.

- *Many beginners experience the machine thread coming out because they have not left at least 5 inches under and behind the presser foot before beginning the sewing process. Also, when starting to sew, the take-up lever should be in its highest position.*

- *If the stitch thread looks incorrect on the top layer, usually this means that something is wrong with the bobbin or the threading of the bobbin.*

Clean the Machine

- *Be sure to clean the machine often to prevent dust build-up and to remove caught thread or fabric pieces.*

SEWING EQUIPMENT AND TOOLS

MEASURING TOOLS

The following are the most common sewing tools for measuring:

- **Tape measure**—A flexible 60-inch reversible tape used to take body measurements.

- **Yard stick**—A 36-inch wooden ruler used to measure hems and grainlines.

- **18-inch clear plastic ruler**—A 2-inch-wide ruler divided into $\frac{1}{8}$-inch grids. A clear ruler is perfect for measuring grainlines and adjusting the pattern at the alteration line. Available through C-thru Ruler Co.

- **Sewing gauge**—A 6-inch gauge with a movable indicator used to measure areas that need a constant measurement such as hem widths, pleats, and tucks.

- **Simflex buttonhole gauge**—An expandable measuring device for spacing buttons and buttonholes quickly and automatically. Available through Brewer Sewing Supplies Co.

- **Clear plastic fashion ruler**—A see-through plastic ruler made by Fashionetics, Inc. Its see-through curved lines allow you to adjust curved lines.

- **Hem marker**—A device used to measure the distance from the floor to the bottom of a garment.

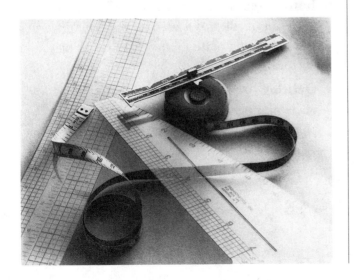

SEWING TOOLS

The following are useful sewing supplies and tools:

- **Straight pins**—Stainless steel or brass silk or dressmaker pins with sharp tapering points that do not rust and are safe for use on all fabrics.

- **Hand sewing needles**—A long, thin steel shaft with an eye at one end. Needles are available in a variety of sizes and types. It is a good idea to purchase a packet of assorted needles. The following are some kinds of needles:

  Sharp needles—These needles are available in sizes 5 through 10; they are all-purpose needles and can be used on sheer, fine, light-weight to heavy-weight fabrics.

  Between needles—These needles are used to sew short, fine stitches for tailoring and hand work.

  Crewel needles—These needles have long oval eyes and can accommodate multiple strands of thread.

- **Thimble**—A lightweight metal (brass or nickel) device with a closed top that snugly fits the middle finger of your sewing hand. It protects the finger as it pushes the needle through the fabric while hand sewing.

- **Pin cushion or pin dispenser**—A sewing tool that keeps pins organized in a convenient place. The most common pin cushion is in the shape of a tomato. However, there are other types and sizes available. Choose a pin cushion that would be easiest to use.

MISCELLANEOUS SUPPLIES

- **Beeswax**—Wax in a holder with grooves. You run thread through the beeswax to strengthen the thread and reduce its tendency to tangle. Be careful when using beeswax on thread that will be used on fabrics that need to be dry cleaned as the wax will melt into the fabric and be visible on the fabric surface.

- **Emery cushion**—A small bag filled with an abrasive material used to remove rust and sharpen needles.

- **Chalk pencils**—Pencils available in pastel colors that are used to transfer markings from the pattern to the fabric. Markings are made on the wrong side of the fabric and do not show on the correct side; they are washable.

- **Loop turner**—A device used to turn bias tubing or belts.

- **Safety pins**—Pins used for stringing cording or elastic, or for turning wider tubing.

- **Tracing paper**—A washable, inked double-coated paper, available in a variety of colors. You slip the paper between the wrong sides of two layers of fabric, and use a tracing wheel to transfer pattern markings to the fabric.

- **Tracing wheel**—A serrated-edge circular wheel with a handle used with or without tracing paper to transfer markings from a pattern to fabric. The wheel portion must be sharp enough to leave an impression, but smooth so it will not snag the fabric.

- **Tailor's chalk**—Washable chalk used to mark fabric at hemlines and other construction lines.

THREAD

Depending on the fabric, garments should be sewn with thread that exactly matches in color. The selection depends on the fabric, the size of the stitch, and the effect desired.

Several types of thread are available for both machine and hand sewing. With all types of thread, the higher the number on the spool, the finer the thread.

The following are some of the most common kinds of thread:

- **Cotton-wrapped polyester thread**—Suitable for most fabrics, thread that has the strength and give of pure polyester, but can take the hot iron required for cotton and linen fabric. It has a coating of cotton around a polyester core and can be used on all types of fabric except fine ones.

- **Spun polyester thread**—A very strong thread that has give and should be used for stretch fabrics and wool fabrics.

- **Mercerized cotton thread**—A thread that has a slight sheen. It comes in number 40 for general use and numbers 50 and 60 for fine fabrics and hand sewing. Use this thread for stitching cotton and linen fabrics.

- **Buttonhole twist**—A thread that is made of polyester or silk and is used for top stitching, for hand-stitching buttonholes, and for sewing on buttons.

- **Quilting thread**—A lustrous, strong thread made of pure cotton or cotton-wrapped polyester. This is ideal for most hand sewing because it does not tangle.

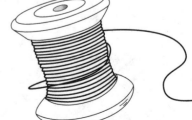

SEWING MACHINE NEEDLES

Sewing machine needle size should coordinate with the type and weight of fabric and size of thread. Needles are available in size 9, for fine and sheer fabrics, through size 16, for heavy-weight fabrics. Most fabrics (medium-weight) require size 10 through 12 needles. This drawing illustrates typical sewing machine needles, which are produced in a variety of lengths and styles by different manufacturers. Check the packaging when purchasing sewing machine needles; the package should list the machine style and the size or sizes of the needles.

Helpful Sewing Hint: *Replace needles if they are dull, bent, or blunt. These needles will cause skipped stitches and may damage fabric. It is a good idea to have extra sewing machine needles on hand.*

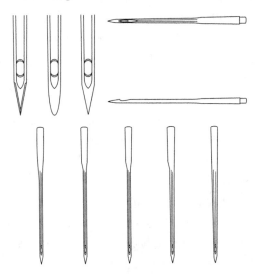

The following are some of the most common types of sewing machine needles:

- **Sharps point needle**—The most common needle type, suitable for most woven fabric. It is available in a variety of needle sizes, from 10 (for light-weight fabrics) through size 19 (for heavy-weight fabrics).

- **Ballpoint needle**—The rounded point on this needle makes it ideal for use on all types of knits or stretch fabrics. It is available in a variety of sizes from 10 through 19.

- **Wedge shaped needle**—A specialty needle used for vinyl, leather, and suede. It is available in sizes 10 through 19.

CUTTING TOOLS

The following are some common cutting tools:

- **Scissors and shears**—Shears are usually 4 to 8 inches long and made of steel; one handle on a pair of shears is larger than the other. Bent-handled shears are excellent for easy and correct cutting. Scissor's are usually smaller than shears, approximately 3 to 6 inches; the handles on a pair of scissors are the same size.

- **Buttonhole scissors**—Small cutting scissors especially designed to cut buttonholes.

- **Pinking shears**—Shears that cut a zigzag edge to prevent fabric from fraying and to create a decorative edge on the seams.

- **Seam ripper**—A small pointed device with a sharp blade. The point helps the sewer to pick up the unwanted stitches, and the blade cuts seam stitches and helps open seams.

- **Thread nippers**—A specially designed nipper that is useful for cutting stray threads and clipping small areas.

- **Trimming scissors**—Scissors that are usually 4 to 6 inches long, with sharp points, and used for clipping threads and trimming or clipping seams.

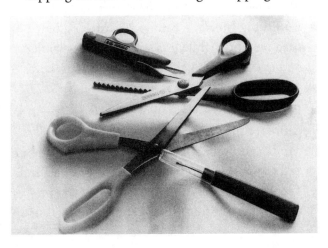

PRESSING EQUIPMENT AND TOOLS

The following are helpful pieces of pressing equipment:

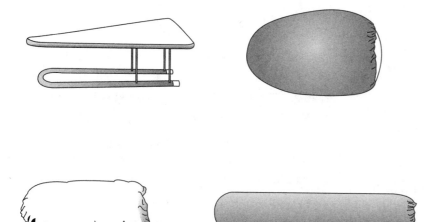

- **Ironing board**—A sturdy surface with a narrow end; it is adjustable to various heights. It should have a clean, finished surface, and is usually covered with an asbestos or a cotton ironing board cover.

- **Iron (steam and dry)**—A steam and dry iron with a wide range of temperature controls, which is the most effective tool for pressing the many varieties of fashion fabrics.

- **Needle board**—A small rectangular board covered with wire needles. This board is used while pressing napped or pile fabric such as velvet and corduroy. The needles prevent the pile from matting.

- **Pounding block**—A smooth hardwood block used on fabric while it is still moist for making strong creases such as on trousers, collars, hems, pleats, and facings.

- **Pressing cloth**—A small open-weave piece of cotton or muslin. The pressing cloth is usually dampened, folded, and placed between the fabric and the iron. While applying some pressure and heat from the iron, the pressing cloth will protect the correct side of the garment from shine and allows a good, clean press.

- **Pressing mitt**—A small padded mitten to press and maintain contoured seams such as sleeve caps and areas that should not be pressed flat.

- **Seam and seam roll**—A small cylindrical, long, firmly padded cushion, covered with heavy cotton on one side and wool on the other. This tool is used to press long narrow seams in hard-to-reach areas such as sleeve seams. The cotton side is used to press most fabrics and the wool side to press woolens.

- **Sleeve board**—A small padded ironing board with different-sized ends. This board sits on top of a regular ironing board and is used to press sleeves and other small areas.

- **Tailor's board**—A wooden tool that tapers to a point, used to press difficult-to-reach areas such as collars, lapels, and other points or corners.

- **Tailor's ham**—A small, oval, lightweight cushion that is firmly padded and covered with heavy cotton on one side and wool on the other. You hold in one hand while pressing contoured seams, darts, collars, and lapels. The cotton side is used to press most fabrics and the wool side to press woolens.

PRESSING METHODS

Pressing is essential to complete a professional looking garment. Using the correct iron temperature, some pressure, and appropriate pressing tools will ensure that all areas are correctly pressed to improve the overall look of the garment.

- **Iron temperature control**—Most irons have a temperature range from cool to hot. If an iron is too hot, it may distort, melt, or scorch the fabric. If it is too cool, it may not press the garment. You can test iron temperature with a small swatch of the fabric selected for the garment.

The following are the steps for **pressing seams and darts:**

1 Press all seams flat to one side. This allows the stitches to settle in to the fabric. Then press the seams open.

2 Press the excess of darts toward the center of the garment or down. A tailor's ham helps to build in the dart excess.

3 Press all the seams and darts from the wrong side of the fabric.

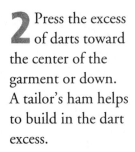

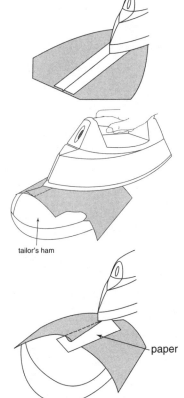

tailor's ham

paper

Helpful Sewing Tip: *When pressing, place a strip of paper between the dart and the fabric to prevent an impression from appearing on the correct side of the garment.*

The following are important pressing techniques:

- Lift and lower the iron. Do not pull the iron back and forth across the fabric.

- Press each area of the garment as it is sewn and before continuing to another sewing step.

- If a flatter, cleaner pressing job is desired, dampen a lightweight towel. Place the damp pressing cloth between the iron and the garment to create more steam. Continue to use the steam setting on the iron and apply a bit more pressure.

- When pressing any napped or pile fabric such as velvet and corduroy, be sure to lay the correct side of the fabric over a needle board and press the wrong side of the garment.

- Use a small seam roll to press long narrow seams. Use a sleeve board.

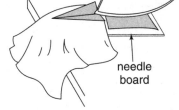

needle board

Helpful Sewing Tip:

If a sleeve board is unavailable, use a towel or a piece of cotton fabric and roll it very tightly into a cylinder. Then tie the two ends with ribbon or yarn and insert it into the sleeve. Press.

seam roll

CHAPTER 3

Body Types and Size Charts

BODY TYPES AND SIZE CHARTS

Understanding body types is important before selecting a pattern size. Body type decribes the height and shape of an individual. The following illustrations and charts represent the various body types for women, children, and men.

After you identify a body type, take accurate measurements to determine the pattern size needed. Underclothes or a leotard should be worn while taking measurements, shoes should not be worn. For a reference point, tie a piece of twill tape around the waistline.

Measure the circumference of the bust, waist, and hips (fuller part). Also measure the length of the center back neck to waist and the sleeve. Record all the measurements.

JUNIOR PETITE, 4'11" TO 5'3"

Small frame, short figure, and small proportions. Usually a young adult.

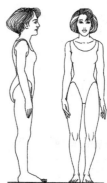

(Measurements in inches)	X-Small	Small		Medium		Large
Pattern & Retail Size	3–4	5–6	7–8	9–10	11–12	13–14
Bust	$30\frac{1}{2}$	$31\frac{1}{2}$	$32\frac{1}{2}$	34	36	38
Waist	23	24	25	$26\frac{1}{2}$	28	30
Hips	$32\frac{1}{2}$	$33\frac{1}{2}$	$34\frac{1}{2}$	36	38	40
Back Waist	$14\frac{1}{2}$	$14\frac{3}{4}$	15	$15\frac{1}{4}$	$15\frac{1}{2}$	$15\frac{3}{4}$

MISSES'S PETITE, 4'11" TO 5'3"

Compared to the junior petite body type, this figure is slightly heavier, fully developed, shorter, has narrower shoulders, higher bust, and thicker waist.

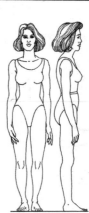

(Measurements in inches)	Small		Medium		Large	
Pattern & Retail Size	5–6	7–8	9–10	11–12	13–14	15–16
Bust	32	33	34	35	36	38
Waist	24	25	26	27	28	30
Hips	35	36	37	38	39	41
Back Waist	$14\frac{3}{4}$	15	$15\frac{1}{4}$	$15\frac{1}{2}$	$15\frac{3}{4}$	16

MISSES, 5'4" TO 5'9"

Fully developed, well-proportioned figure, longer waist length, fuller bust and hips, but generally slim.

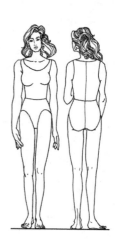

(Measurements in inches)	X-Small		Small		Medium		Large	
Pattern Size—US	6	8	10	12	14	16	18	20
Pattern Size—EU	36	38	40	42	44	46	48	50
Retail Size	2	4	6	8	10	12	14	16
Bust	31	32	33	$34\frac{1}{2}$	36	38	40	42
Waist	23	24	25	$26\frac{1}{2}$	28	30	32	34
Hips	33	34	35	$36\frac{1}{2}$	38	40	42	44
Back Waist	$15\frac{1}{2}$	$15\frac{3}{4}$	16	$16\frac{1}{4}$	$16\frac{1}{2}$	$16\frac{3}{4}$	17	$17\frac{1}{4}$

FULL-FIGURED WOMEN, 5'4" TO 5'9"

A fuller-figured woman with the same proportions as the misses figure. Usually the waist and bust are thicker and heavier.

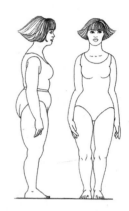

	(Measurements in inches)						
Pattern Size	38	40	42	44	46	48	50
Retail Size	14W	16W	18W	20W	22W	24W	26W
Bust	38	40	42	44	46	48	50
Waist	34	36	38	40	42	44	46
Hips	42	44	46	48	50	52	54
Back Waist	$17\frac{1}{4}$	$17\frac{3}{8}$	$17\frac{1}{2}$	$17\frac{5}{8}$	$17\frac{3}{4}$	$17\frac{7}{8}$	18

HALF SIZE WOMEN, 5' TO 5'6"

More mature, short-waisted woman with a shorter, heavier body type. This is usually a woman who has gone through menopause.

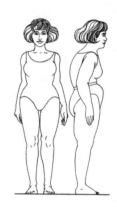

	(Measurements in inches)					
Pattern & Retail Size	$14\frac{1}{2}$	$16\frac{1}{2}$	$18\frac{1}{2}$	$20\frac{1}{2}$	$22\frac{1}{2}$	$24\frac{1}{2}$
Bust	37	39	41	43	45	47
Waist	31	33	35	$37\frac{1}{2}$	40	$42\frac{1}{2}$
Hips	39	41	43	$45\frac{1}{2}$	48	$50\frac{1}{2}$
Back Waist	$15\frac{1}{2}$	$15\frac{3}{4}$	$15\frac{7}{8}$	16	$16\frac{1}{8}$	$16\frac{1}{4}$

PLUS-SIZE WOMEN, 5'4" TO 5'9"

A full-figured woman with rounded shoulders, average shoulder width, fuller stomach, larger biceps, and a larger bust cup. Within this size range, there are the following figure types: Apple Figure—bust and hips are the same width; Rubenesque Figure—hip averages 10" larger than bust; Pear Figure—hip averages 12"+ larger than bust. All three figures have lost a shapely waist.

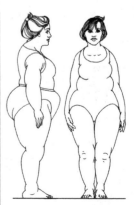

	(Measurements in inches)						
Pattern Size	XL	1X	2X	3X	4X	5X	6X
Retail Size	18–20W	22–24W	26–28W	30–32W	34–36W	38–40W	42–44W
Bust	44–45	46–48	50–52	54–56	58–60	62–64	66–68
Waist	36–37	38–40	42–44	46–48	50–52	54–55	56–58
Hips	50–52	54–56	58–60	60–62	66–68	70–72	74–76
Bicep	18	19	20	21	22	23	24

BODY TYPES AND SIZE CHARTS
FOR CHILDREN

Children's wear is usually sized by the age of the child. However, because children do not grow at the same pace, some children may reach a certain size earlier or later, depending on the rate of growth and development. Therefore, the child must be measured often and those measurements compared to the listing on the pattern.

infant   toddler   little boy   little girl   older child boy   older child girl

INFANTS, 24″ TO 36″

Newborn infant to 18 months. Sizes are determined by the baby's weight and height. Usually the styles for infant boys and girls are similar; color and details are the primary difference.

Pattern Sizes	Newborn to 3 mos	3–6 mos Small	6–12 mos Medium	12–18 mos Large
Weight (lbs)	14	15–20	21–26	27–32
Height (inches)	24	$24\frac{1}{2}$–28	$28\frac{1}{2}$–32	$32\frac{1}{2}$–36

TODDLERS, 31″ TO 40″

Sizes for boys and girls are the same, but the designs vary slightly. Color is the primary difference.

Pattern Sizes	1T	2T	3T	4T
Height	31	34	37	40
Chest	20	21	22	23
Waist	$19\frac{1}{2}$	20	$20\frac{1}{2}$	21
Hips	20	21	22	23

LITTLE GIRLS, 39″ TO 47″

Age ranges from preschool through first grade. The styles are similar to those for boys; color and details are the primary differences.

Pattern Sizes	4	5	6	6X
Height	39	42	45	47
Chest	23	24	25	$25\frac{1}{2}$
Waist	21	$21\frac{1}{2}$	22	$22\frac{1}{2}$
Hips	23	24	25	26

LITTLE BOYS, 39″ TO 49″

Age ranges from preschool through first grade. The styles are similar to those for girls; color and details are the primary differences.

Pattern Sizes	4	5	6	6X
Height	39	42	45	49
Chest	23	24	25	$25\frac{1}{2}$
Waist	21	$21\frac{1}{2}$	22	$22\frac{1}{2}$
Hips	23	24	25	26

OLDER CHILDREN—GIRLS, 50″ TO 61″

Girls are shorter than teen girls, with underdeveloped figures. This size is for girls at the beginning of a growth period that usually represents awkward proportions, and styles are more trendy.

Pattern Sizes	7	8	10	12	14
Height	50	52	56	$58\frac{1}{2}$	61
Chest	26	27	$28\frac{1}{2}$	30	32
Waist	$22\frac{1}{2}$	$23\frac{1}{2}$	$24\frac{1}{2}$	$25\frac{1}{2}$	$26\frac{1}{2}$
Hips	27	28	30	32	36

OLDER CHILDREN—BOYS, 48″ TO 61″

There is a slight difference in height between boys and girls. Boys' styles are patterned after men's clothing. However, some boys' pants styles include slim and chubby variations.

Pattern Sizes	7	8	10	12	14
Height	48	52	56	$58\frac{1}{2}$	61
Chest	26	27	28	30	32
Waist	22	23	24	25	26
Hips	24	27	28	29	31

BODY TYPES AND SIZE CHARTS
FOR ADOLESCENTS

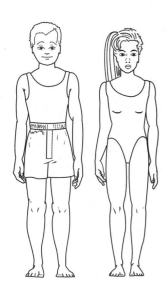

TEEN BOY, 61″ TO 68″

Teen boys are usually between boys' and men's sizes. The preppy look is
most often a choice for this age group.

Pattern Sizes	10	12	14	16	18	20
Neck	$12\frac{1}{2}$	13	$13\frac{1}{2}$	14	$14\frac{1}{2}$	15
Chest	28	30	32	$33\frac{1}{2}$	35	$36\frac{1}{2}$
Waist	25	26	27	28	29	30
Sleeve length	25	$26\frac{1}{2}$	29	30	31	32

YOUNG JUNIORS/TEEN GIRLS, 60″ TO 63″

Young juniors/teen girls have very small bust, thick waists, and fairly small
hips.

	X-Small	Small		Medium		Large
Pattern Sizes	5-6	7-8	9-10	11-12	13-14	15-16
Bust	28	29	$30\frac{1}{2}$	32	$33\frac{1}{2}$	35
Waist	22	23	24	25	26	27
Hips	31	32	$33\frac{1}{2}$	35	$36\frac{1}{2}$	38
Back waist	$13\frac{1}{2}$	14	$14\frac{1}{2}$	15	$15\frac{1}{2}$	16

BODY TYPES AND SIZE CHARTS FOR MEN

MEN, 5′8″ TO 6′0″

Most patterns are for the fully developed male figure. Sizes for men's suits, jackets, and sport shirts are based on the chest measurement. Dress shirts are based on the neck and sleeve measurements. Trousers are sized by the waist measurement.

MEN'S SPORT SHIRTS, DRESS SHIRTS, AND TROUSERS

Pattern Sizes	Small		Medium		Large		X-Large	
Neck	14	$14\frac{1}{2}$	15	$15\frac{1}{2}$	16	$16\frac{1}{2}$	17	$17\frac{1}{2}$
Chest	34	36	38	40	42	44	46	48
Waist	28	30	32	34	36	38	40	42
Sleeve length	$32\frac{1}{2}$	33	$33\frac{1}{2}$	34	$34\frac{1}{2}$	35	$35\frac{1}{2}$	36

MEN'S SPORTS JACKET

Chest Size	38	39	40	41	42	43	44	46
Coat size	38	39	40	41	42	43	44	46
Short (5′3″–5′7″)	—	—	—	—	—	—	—	—
Reg (5′8″–6′1″)	—	—	—	—	—	—	—	—
Long (6′0″–6′7″)	—	—	—	—	—	—	—	—

CHAPTER 4

The Pattern

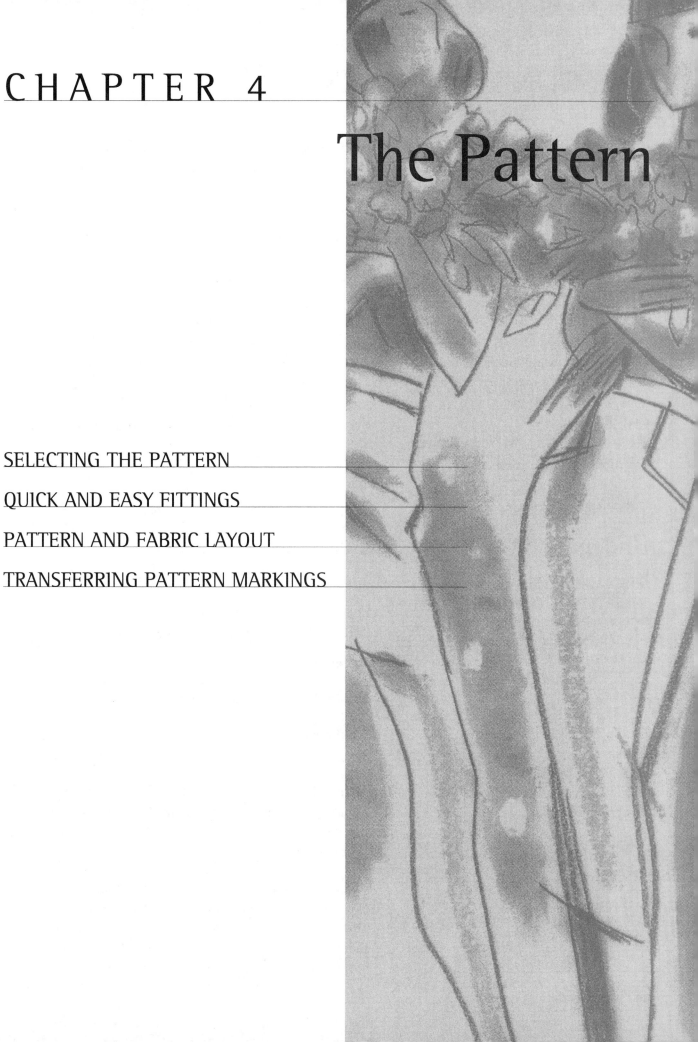

SELECTING A PATTERN

As you select a pattern design, focus on the overall body design and fit. Keep in mind that you can change some simple details such as the neckline shape, the pocket design, the shape of a collar outer edge, the garment length, or the fabric combinations. However, changing major elements that intersect with other garment parts should be left to an experienced patternmaker.

Before purchasing a pattern, you need to measure the person for whom the garment is being made and determine their body type. (Refer to Chapter 3 for Body Types and Size Charts.)

WOMEN

- Use the full bust measurement to select the correct pattern size for a blouse, shirt, jacket, or dress
- Use the hip measurement (widest part) to select the correct pattern size for pants or a skirt

CHILDREN

- Use the chest measurement to select the correct pattern size for a shirt or blouse
- Use the waist measurement to select the correct pattern size for a skirt or pants pattern

MEN

- Use the chest measurement to select the correct pattern size for suits, jackets, or sport shirts
- Use the neck circumference and sleeve length measurements to select the correct pattern size for dress shirts
- Use the waist measurement to select the correct pattern size for trousers

Understanding a Pattern Envelope

Pattern envelopes vary from company to company. The following example illustrates the various features and information included on pattern envelopes.

THE FRONT PATTERN ENVELOPE

Pattern Company Name

Pattern Identification Number

Size Range
The size range notes which sizes are included in the envelope.

Fashion Illustrations or Photographs of the Design
In most cases, patterns are included for all the designs illustrated on the envelope. If a garment is not included, it will be clearly noted.

Level of Difficulty (Front or Back Envelope)
Some pattern envelopes also advise on the sewing skill required to successfully complete the garment. Beginners should choose "Easy-to-Sew" patterns, while experienced sewers might choose "Designer" or "Advanced" patterns.

THE BACK PATTERN ENVELOPE

Pattern Description

This area describes all the styling details of each design. It might also describe the overall fit of each garment (Loose, Semi-fitted, Fitted, etc.). Keep in mind that you can change simple details such as the pocket styling or collar outer edge styling.

Suggested Fabrics

The fabrics suggested exhibit particular drape and hand qualities that are best suited for the specific design. If the pattern is for knit fabric, woven fabrics usually cannot be substituted—they would change the garment fit dramatically.

Company Sizing Specifications

These specifications describe the body size and figure type that the pattern is expected to fit. If your measurements do not seem to line up with their sizing, look for a Finished Measurements section (see below) printed on the envelope or on the actual pattern pieces. Most likely, some alterations will need to be made. Refer to the pattern fitting section at the end of this chapter.

Fabric Amount Required

The fabric amount required is displayed for each design included in the pattern. Fabric amounts are traditionally provided for 45″ (115cm) and 60″ (150cm) wide fabrics. If the fabric you choose is not these widths, refer to the Fabric Yardage Conversion Table in Appendix A (Page 353)

NOTE: *The English section displays yard requirements, the French section displays metric requirements.*

Notions Required

Necessary sewing notions such as buttons, zippers, hooks, elastic, thread, etc. should be listed for each garment.

Finished Garment measurements

If Finished Measurements are included, they are useful for estimating the fitting ease of each garment. They also list the finished lengths and hem circumferences for pants, skirts, and dresses. These are especially helpful for estimating the fullness of a design and whether length alterations will need to be made.

Flat Sketches

Flat sketches are line drawings of the pattern style details. These are useful when pattern details are difficult to see in the front envelope illustrations or photographs. Some pattern companies display only sketches of the back view, others display both the front and back views.

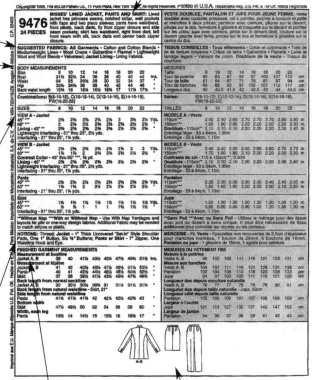

Understanding the Pattern

INSIDE THE PATTERN ENVELOPE

Pattern pieces printed on tissue paper and a pattern guide sheet are included inside of the envelope. The size, style number, and/or letter are printed on each pattern piece.

A guide sheet illustrates the suggested pattern layouts on the various fabric widths, styles, and sizes (see "Pattern and Fabric Layout," page 52). There may also be various versions of layouts for "nap" fabric, which you would follow if you were laying out velvet, corduroy, or one-way prints.

The guide sheet also provides step-by-step sewing instructions for sewing the design selected.

Note: *See "Quick and Easy Fittings," pages 49–51, to fit the pattern pieces.*

IDENTIFYING PATTERN MARKINGS

Pattern markings enable the manufacturer to convey information about the construction of a garment to the fashion sewer. Some markings are accompanied by written instructions, often in several languages.

You should always be able to identify the following markings on a pattern:

- Grainline
- Center front
- Center back
- Darts, tucks, and pleats
- Shoulder markings
- All foldlines
- Single notch in front armhole
- Double notch in back armhole
- Pocket positions
- Alteration lines

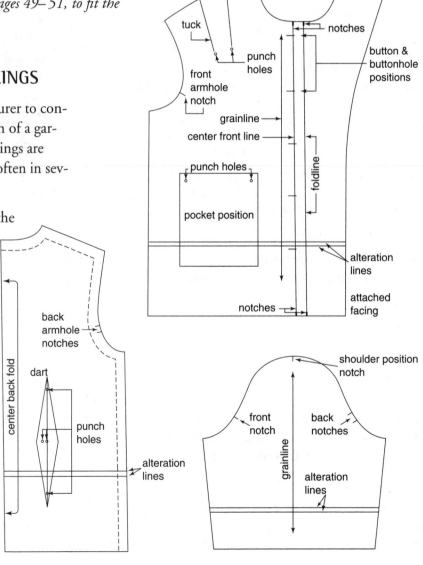

QUICK AND EASY FITTINGS

After you have determined the correct pattern size, you should do a preliminary fitting to check the size and fit of the pattern and make any necessary adjustments.

It is important to have an appropriately fitting garment. All pattern areas have a definite relationship with the figure that enables the garment to be worn and fit correctly. This means that center front and center back of the garment should always be vertical to the floor and hang straight up and down. The grain lines of the garment should be parallel to these lines. Otherwise, the garment will twist or pull. The crossgrains of the pattern should always be parallel to the floor. Otherwise the garment will drag and pull downward.

Garments hang from the shoulder and bust/chest. These pattern areas must be identical to the body shape for correct fit. If the pattern shoulder slope is off just five degrees from the body shoulder slope, the garment will drape incorrectly.

1 Cutting the pattern pieces: Remove from the pattern package all the pieces for the garment being made. Press the pattern pieces to remove all wrinkles. Cut off all excess paper on the main body pieces (front blouse, back blouse, front skirt or back skirt). Do not cut the seam allowances. Clip the neckline and armholes to the stitchline.

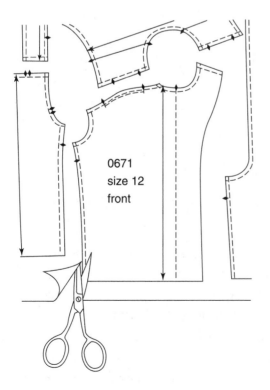

0671
size 12
front

2 Check the pattern side seam balance: Pin the FRONT UNDERARM/SIDE SEAM corner to the BACK UNDERARM/SIDE SEAM corner. From the UNDERARM CORNER PIN, pivot the front pattern until the center front and the center back positions are parallel. The front and back side seams should meet. If not, add to and subtract from the side seams until they match (see illustration).

Also, the front pattern piece should be $\frac{1}{2}$ inch wider than the back pattern. When the side seams are pinned together (before the shoulder seams are pinned), the center front and center back should be parallel. Also, the side seams should be the same shape and length.

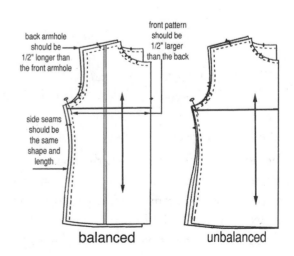

back armhole should be 1/2" longer than the front armhole

front pattern should be 1/2" larger than the back

side seams should be the same shape and length

balanced   unbalanced

3 **Check the armhole balance:** The armholes together must resemble a horseshoe shape. The armholes should also be balanced—the measurement of the back armhole should be $\frac{1}{2}''$ more than the front armhole. The correct armhole shape and balance insures that the sleeve drapes properly.

- Measure the front armhole.
- Measure the back armhole.

The back armhole distance should be $\frac{1}{2}''$ longer than the front armhole measurement. If this is slightly off (within $\frac{1}{2}''$), you can still use the pattern. If, however, the distance is quite a bit off (more than 1 inch), this is a sign of a pattern problem. Using the pattern would definitely result in fitting problems.

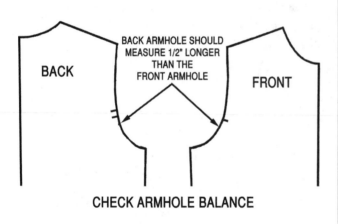

BACK

BACK ARMHOLE SHOULD
MEASURE 1/2" LONGER
THAN THE
FRONT ARMHOLE

FRONT

CHECK ARMHOLE BALANCE

5 **Fitting the pattern:** *Because patterns are made on the half, only one-half of the body will be fitted.* Fit the pattern over tight-fitting clothing or a leotard. Follow this checklist:

- Place the prepared pattern over the body or a custom dress form. Align center front, center back, and the side seam until the pattern hangs perfectly plumb, straight up and down. Make sure the pattern is not twisting or pitching to-

4 **Pin the pattern pieces together:** Pin together the side seams, all style lines, and darts. Because most patterns are made on the half, only one-half of the body will be fitted with the pattern. Pin the blouse front and blouse back together, matching perfectly the shoulder seams and side seams. Do not include facings, collars, or sleeves (unless raglan style or kimono style) in the fitting.

DO NOT PIN THE SHOULDER SEAMS YET.

REMINDER: *Refer to the instructions on the pattern guide sheet to determine which pattern pieces represent a whole pattern and which pieces represent a half. Also, note any pieces that need duplicates, and which pieces are to be placed on a fold.*

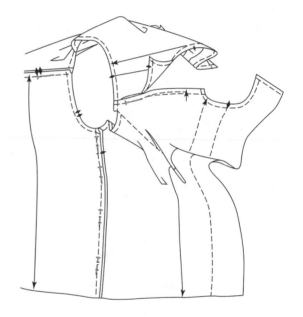

ward the front or back. (Use the backbone as the guide for center back, and use the belly button as the guide for center front.) **The shoulder seams are not pinned at this time.**

- Check for the proper amount of side seam ease. All garments should have some ease for body movement. The amount will depend upon the style of the garment. Readjust the side seam ease by adding to or taking in the side seam.

- Drape, fit and pin the shoulder seams. Smooth the pattern up toward the shoulder. If the seams do not meet, but the pattern is hanging correctly below the bust, add paper extensions to the shoulder seams and pin a new seam. If a collar is included in the design, any adjustments to the shoulder/neck area should be made to the collar also.

- Pin the shoulder seams so that the shoulder seam is on top of the shoulder. It should not slope to the front or to the back.

REMINDER: *Garments hang from the shoulder and bust. These areas must be identical to the body for correct fit and drape. If the pattern shoulder slope is off just five degrees from your shoulder slope, the garment will drape incorrectly.*

- Sometimes adjustments may be needed in the style lines, shoulder widths, and dart positions. Bust darts should point to the fullest part of the bust.

- Adjust the length of skirts, bodices, or sleeves on the *adjustment line* marked on the pattern.

- Necklines should fit snugly without gaping. A badly fitting neckline can be corrected by pinning tiny darts in the neckline. Cut the pattern with the tiny darts pinned in place.

6 Mark the fitted pattern: Using a felt-tip pen, mark all fitting adjustments. Unpin the pattern and lay it flat. Redraw any newly marked lines with a ruler and add new seam allowances to the adjusted areas.

The pattern is now ready to be positioned on the fabric.

CAUTION: *Major adjustments to the shoulder seams or the side seams, may change the shape of the armhole, making it too large or too small. If the problem becomes difficult to solve with a fitting, consider using the next pattern size up.*

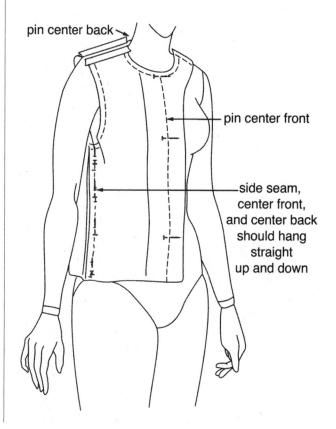

pin center back

pin center front

side seam, center front, and center back should hang straight up and down

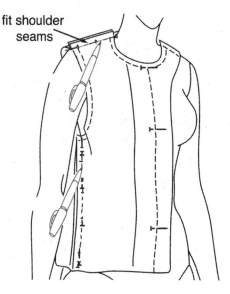

fit shoulder seams

PATTERN AND FABRIC LAYOUT

As discussed previously, every pattern company provides a guide sheet to illustrate the particular pattern layouts for various fabric widths, styles, and sizes. There may also be versions of the layouts for nap fabrics, which have pile or brushed surfaces, such as velvet, corduroy, and one-way prints. These layouts must be followed very carefully. Special considerations are also provided for plaid and most striped fabrics. Review the next several pages before proceeding.

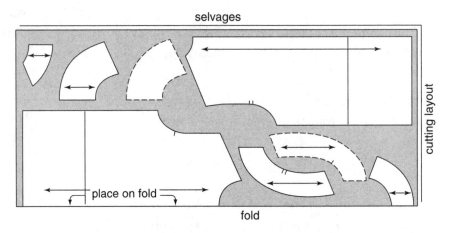

INFORMATION ON GRAINLINES

A line, referred as the grainline, is drawn on each pattern piece to indicate the direction in which the pattern should line up with the fabric.

The most common grainline is a vertical line running from the top to the bottom of the pattern piece. This line indicates that the pattern should be placed on the lengthwise grain of the fabric, which is parallel to the selvage edges. Another popular grainline that is often marked on commercial patterns is the *foldline*. This is also the lengthwise grain of the fabric.

Always plan the layout on the wrong side of the folded fabric with sides together. This makes markings easy to transfer and protects the fabric from soil as the fabric is being handled. Fold the fabric on the lengthwise grain, and align the selvages. For many fabrics, the correct side is obvious because of the nap or print. However, the correct side of the fabric may be difficult to select. In this instance, fold back one corner and compare the two surfaces.

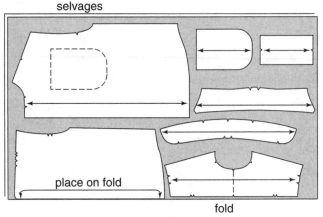

The correct side may have a bright print or a shinier surface. If you can't decide which is intended to be the correct side, select the side you like the best, and be sure to use the same side throughout the finished garment. Mark the wrong side with chalk to help identify the layers.

Helpful Sewing Tip: *To prevent the fabric from slipping as you cut, lay the fabric over a layer of paper, such as shelf paper. Then cut the paper and fabric at the same time. Refer to the following page for more details.*

CUTTING FABRIC ACCURATELY

"GETTING A TRUE CUT"

Stabilizing your fabric with brown craft paper, shelf paper, butcher paper, or unprinted newsprint insures that the fabric will not slip or move during cutting. This is especially vital when cutting any lightweight fabrics such as rayons, linings, chiffons, silks, crepes, knits, or velvets. Cutting with a paper support also helps achieve a clean, more accurate cut and it will not dull fabric scissors or rotary cutters any more than normal use.

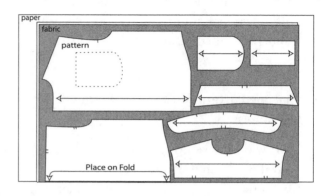

1 Lay out the fabric, matching selvage to selvage, along one paper edge. (Fabric is folded selvage to selvage to keep the lengthwise grain "on fold".) On the paper, draw a crossgrain line perfectly perpendicular to the paper/selvage edge. This insures perfect lengthwise and crosswise grain alignment.

2 Keeping the fabric flat and smooth, align and pin the fabric to the paper edge and crossgrain line. The entire length of fabric can be pinned in place. If you run out of table space, gently fold up the pinned sections until the entire piece is pinned in place.

Press the pattern pieces with a dry iron to remove any creases. Pin all "place on fold" pieces first. Lay out all other pieces, aligning grainlines first, until the entire layout is complete. Pin the remaining pieces to the fabric and paper support.

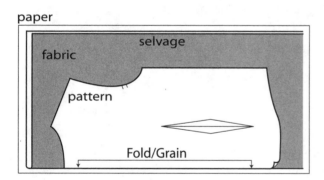

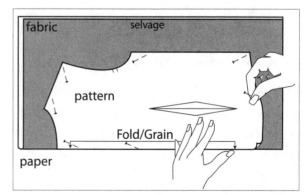

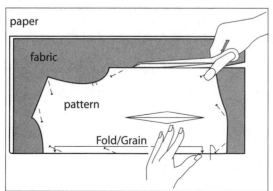

Cut paper, fabric, & pattern at the same time.

3 Cut the paper, fabric, and pattern all at the same time. Use long, continuous strokes to eliminate jagged edges. Do not make short, "choppy" cuts. Notice how the fabric does not move as the scissors cut. The pinned fabric piece can also be moved and adjusted closer to the cutter without distorting the fabric.

TWO-WAY DIRECTIONAL PATTERN LAYOUT

The top and bottom of the pattern pieces may be placed in two different directions (but still following the grain of the fabric) when you are using a solid or multidirectional print fabric. If you are unsure whether the print is multidirectional, you might want to ask the salesperson at the fabric store.

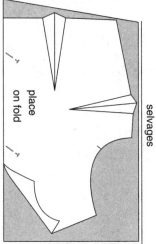

Pinning the Pattern to Fabric Grainlines and Foldlines

1 Start with the pattern pieces that are to be placed on the fold. Pin the pattern foldline exactly on the fabric fold. These pattern pieces should be pinned before all other pieces.

2 Pin one end of the grainline to the straight grain of the fabric. Move the pattern piece until the other end of the grainline measures exactly the same distance from the selvage or fold of the fabric as the first pinned end.

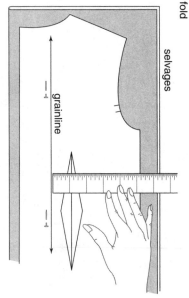

ONE-WAY DIRECTIONAL PATTERN LAYOUT

You use this pattern layout for one-way designs such as nap, pile, knitted, striped, or plain fabrics.

In a one-way directional layout, all pattern pieces are placed facing in the same direction. In other words, the top of each pattern piece will be placed to the right, and the hems will be placed to the left. Be sure to use a one-way directional layout if the fabric has a one-way design, stripe, plaid, or knitted fabric. This will ensure that all stripes and plaids will match, all fabric shading will be in the same direction (nap or pile fabric), and all design features will be in the same direction.

Hint: *When laying out any nap or pile fabric, place the fabric correct side to correct side by gently placing the layers on top of each other. Gently smooth and place the fabric layers on top of each other. Do not smooth out the fabric surface by using the palm of your hand because this stretches the fabric and locks the nap threads to each other, and they will unlock and unstretch after cutting.*

PATTERN LAYOUT FOR STRIPED OR PLAID FABRIC

Preparing Striped Fabrics. When laying out striped fabric on the cutting table, make sure all stripes match on both layers of the fabric.

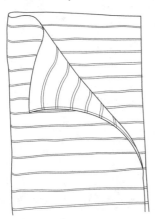

Lay a piece of paper (for example, shelf paper) on the table first. Then, lay the fabric over the paper and pin all the selvages of the fabric to one side of the paper. Next, fold the fabric on top of the first layer (selvage to selvage), pinning and matching all stripes on both layers. Stripes are usually on the crossgrain. If the stripes do not match automatically, the fabric might need to be blocked (see "Blocking," page 10).

Preparing Plaid Fabrics. Plaid fabric must be laid out so that all lengthwise and crosswise stripes of the plaid match on both layers of the fabric.

Follow the same procedure described for preparing striped fabrics, matching both lengthwise and crosswise stripes of the plaid. If the stripes do not match automatically, the fabric may need to be blocked (see "Blocking," page 10).

Note: *When matching lengthwise stripes, the selvages will be parallel, but not necessarily on top of each other.*

Pattern Layout for Striped or Plaid Fabrics. First work with the pattern pieces that require placement on the fabric fold (this varies from style to style). Note and transfer the location of the stripes (both lengthwise and crosswise) from the fabric to the pattern piece. Mark the pattern pieces with pencil at the shoulder, side seams, and armhole notches.

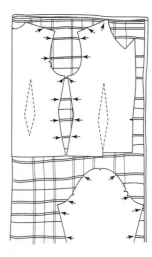

Transfer the same stripe markings to the pattern pieces that are sewn to the seam of the first pattern piece. These markings will help match shoulder seams to shoulder seams, side seams to side seams, and so on. The sleeve cap notches will match to the armhole notches.

Place these marked pattern pieces on the fabric, making sure all stripes of the fabric (lengthwise and crosswise) match the marks on the pattern pieces.

PATTERN LAYOUT FOR INTERFACING

Lay the pattern pieces that need to be interfaced onto the interfacing fabric. Place all pattern pieces following the lengthwise grain of the pattern to the lengthwise grain of the fabric. Place the pattern pieces that need two layers on a double layer of interfacing; place pattern pieces that need one layer of interfacing on a single layer of the interfacing. Pin pattern pieces in place.

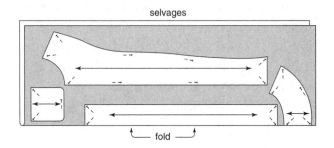

selvages

fold

PATTERN LAYOUT FOR LINING

The layout of the lining pattern pieces also follows the lengthwise grain of the fabric. Place the pattern on a double layer of the lining fabric, on the fold if necessary. Pin pattern pieces in place.

PINNING THE PATTERN TO THE FABRIC

After all pattern pieces have been pinned to the grainline or the fold, you can finish the pinning process. Keep the pins well inside the cutting lines, and place a pin at each pattern corner and every few inches. Be careful not to overpin the pattern as this will distort the fabric. Keep the pattern flat as you pin.

Place pieces as close together as possible. Complete the pattern layout.

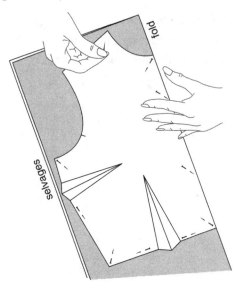

CUTTING THE PATTERN AND THE FABRIC

Keep the fabric flat on the table. Cut with the bulk of the pattern to the left of the scissors (reverse if you are left-handed). Keep one hand on the pattern, close to the cutting line, and manipulate the shears with the other hand.

Use the whole blade and close the scissors to the tips—do not make short, chopping movements.

Hint: *To prevent the fabric from slipping, lay the fabric over a layer of paper. When cutting, cut the paper and the fabric at the same time.*

selvages

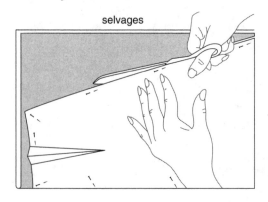

TRANSFERRING PATTERN MARKINGS

Transferring the pattern markings from the tissue paper to the fabric correctly is a very important step for sewing all the design details accurately. Markings include notches, darts, tucks, pleats, foldlines, center front and center back positions, and pocket placements.

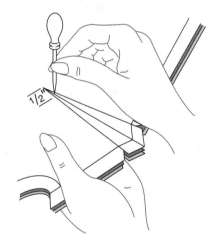

QUICK AND EASY PATTERN MARKING METHOD

1 Snip notches, darts, tucks, pleats, foldlines, and center front and center back positions with the point of the scissors.

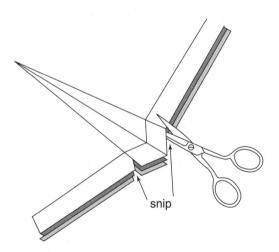

2 Place an awl or a pin through the pattern and both layers of the fabric $\frac{1}{2}$ inch before the end of the dart tip.

3 With a pencil or an awl, mark this position of the dart on the fabric.

PENCIL MARKING METHOD

Insert a pin at each dart point, at each button and pocket placement, and for other pattern symbols that cannot be snipped.

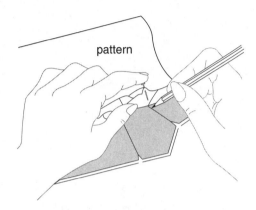

On the wrong side of the fabric, using a pencil or chalk, mark with a dot the position of the pin.

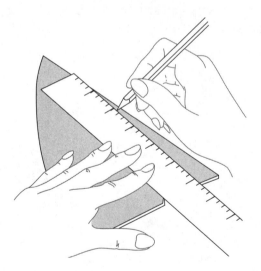

TRACING WHEEL MARKING METHOD

Place dressmaker's carbon paper on the wrong side of the fabric and, using a tracing wheel, trace pattern markings.

Note: *The tracing wheel method may not be accurate. As the pattern is lifted to insert the tracing paper, the fabric and/or pattern may slip out of position. Also, sometimes the marks left by the tracing wheel show through the fabric.*

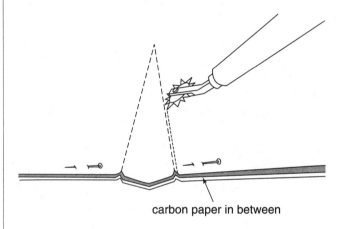

carbon paper in between

CHAPTER 5

Method to This Madness

STEP-BY-STEP SEWING INSTRUCTIONS

ASSEMBLY PROCEDURES

STEP-BY-STEP SEWING INSTRUCTIONS

This chapter, on general sewing steps and assembling a garment, is organized as a logical sequence so that you can understand the method of sewing dresses, blouses, skirts, or pants. You'll learn the theory of accurately sewing together the various parts to complete these garments. It is important that you follow the steps in consecutive order and do not skip around. As you practice these concepts, you can refine the skills presented throughout the text and obtain a greater understanding of how to sew together any garment. Specific sewing instructions for particular garment details are provided in the appropriate chapters in this book.

You should not take the steps in this chapter until you have laid out the pattern on the desired fabric, cut properly, and transferred all pattern markings to the fabric. Refer to pages 52–58 for specific instructions.

Note: *Never proceed to the next sewing step without pressing the garment details or seams that have just been completed.*

STEP 1: DARTS, TUCKS, AND PLEATS

Check each pattern piece for any darts, tucks, or pleats. Regardless of the position of the darts, tucks, or pleats on the garment, they are sewn first. (Refer to pages 107–126.)

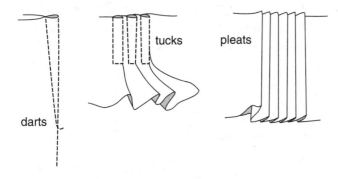

STEP 2: STYLE LINES

A *style line* is any seamline other than shoulder seams, armhole seams, or side seams. A style line usually runs from one point of a garment to another point. For example, a yoke runs from side seam to side seam, and a shoulder princess seam runs from shoulder seam to waist seam.

You should sew all style seamlines after sewing all darts, tucks, or pleats. Also, at this time you should sew a center-front seam or a center-back seam (not a facing area for buttons and buttonholes), and crotch seams on pants or skirt pants.

Do not sew side seams and shoulder seams.

After you finish this step, the result is a complete front of the garment and a complete back of the garment. The front and back of the garment will lie flat. They are not attached at the side seams or at the shoulder seams.

Also, at this point, you should select and sew any specialty seams, such as welt seams, open welt seams, or slot seams. (Refer to "Seams," pages 83–106.)

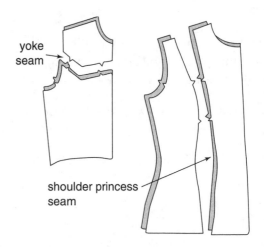

Hint: *If it is part of the design, topstitch all style lines. Topstitching may be done with thread the same color as the fabric or in a contrasting color. For heavier topstitching, use buttonhole twist thread or double-thread the machine. (See pages 25–27.)*

STEP 3: INTERFACING

Regardless of where interfacing is placed on the garment, it should be attached to the garment pieces at this stage of the sewing process. There are many weights of interfacing, so choose a suitable weight for the fabric. Also, interfacing is available in both black and white. Interfacing is also available as woven or nonwoven, and fusible or not fusible fabric. (see "Facings and Interfacings," pages 267–280.)

Most blouses are interfaced on the collars, cuffs, necklines, and other facing areas. Most skirts or pants with a waistband require interfacing.

Hint: *At this stage, side seams and shoulder seams have not been sewn.*

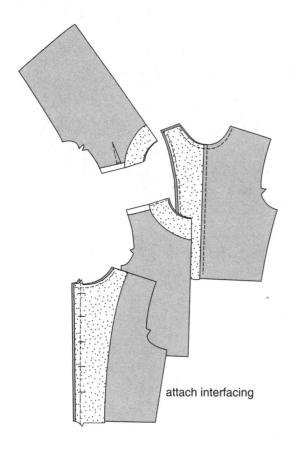

attach interfacing

STEP 4: POCKETS

Attach any pockets. Because the garment is relatively flat, pockets can be attached easily, and if the garment has a pair of pockets, the sides will be balanced perfectly. Pockets are one of the most obvious details on a garment; the time spent on their construction will be evidence of the level of ability and workmanship. (See "Pockets," pages 171–203.)

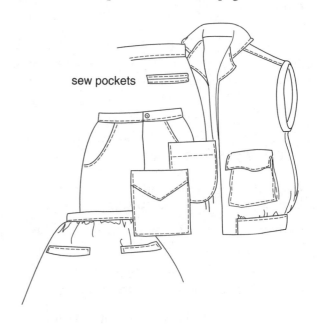

sew pockets

STEP 5: ZIPPERS

Zippers are most often used on skirts, pants, one-piece dresses without skirt seams, and jacket fronts. Most blouses button down the center front or center back and do not need a zipper.

Examine the pattern and determine whether the garment requires a zipper closing and the type of zipper suitable for the garment.

If the design requires a zipper, this is the time to attach it, while the garment is still flat. (See "Zippers," pages 155–170.)

Note: *If the dress has a waist seam, skip this step and proceed to step 6. Zippers on dresses are discussed in step 15. If the garment requires buttons and buttonholes rather than a zipper, skip this step and proceed to the next appropriate step. Buttons and buttonholes are applied when the garment is finished (see step 17).*

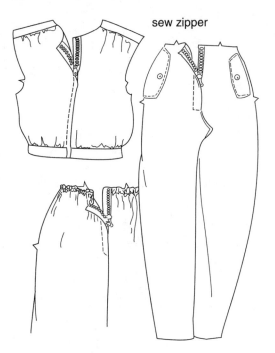

sew zipper

STEP 6: SHOULDER SEAMS

Most dresses or blouses have shoulder seams both in the body of the garment and in the facings. All shoulder seams should be sewn at this time.

Note: *Usually shoulder seams use a plain seam. However, there are exceptions (for example, men's shirts may use a welt seam). (See "Seams," pages 83–106.)*

Note: *This is a good time to stop and make sure all seams are pressed. Never sew without pressing.*

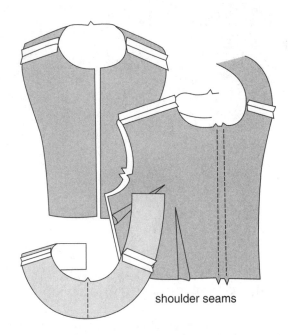

shoulder seams

STEP 7: SIDE SEAMS AND INSEAMS

It is now time to create the garment that goes around the body. Select a seam suitable to the garment design and fabric, and sew all side seams on blouses, bodices, skirts, and pants. Sew all inseams on pants or skirt pants.

Note: *Most garments have side seams; however, some wrap-type designs do not. In this case, skip this step and proceed to step 8.*

Note: *If the dress design has an attached skirt, you should sew the side seams of the skirt at this time, but do not sew the skirt to the bodice yet.*

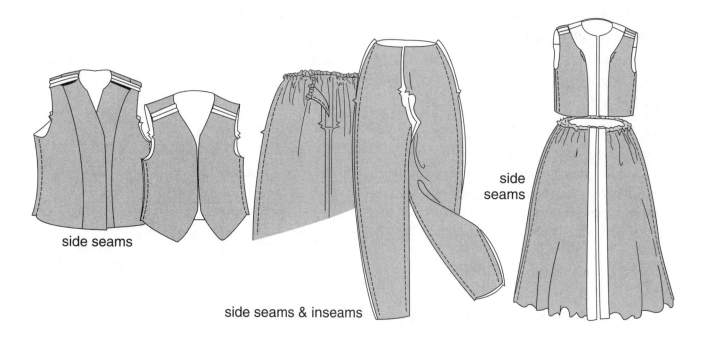

side seams

side seams & inseams

side seams

STEP 8: WAISTBANDS AND/OR FACINGS FOR SKIRTS OR PANTS

Attach waistbands, waist facings, center-skirt facings, and elastic waists. (Refer to "Waistlines," pages 309–326.)

Hint: *If the garment requires lining, follow the same steps as for the outer layer and sew the lining. At this time, attach the lining to the outer layer, wrong side to wrong side, and matching waistlines. Finish the waistband.*

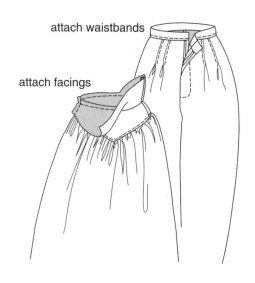

attach waistbands

attach facings

STEP 9: PREPARATION

It is very important to understand that a collar is being prepared at this time, but not being attached to the garment. (Refer to "Collars," pages 229–252.)

Press and set aside the collar until step 10.

Hint: *If the dress or blouse design does not have a collar, skip this step. However, a bias binding or a facing will be necessary to clean-finish the neckline. Facings are sewn in the process.*

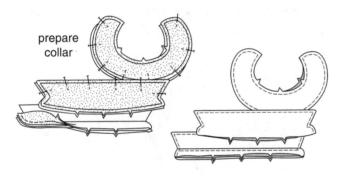

prepare
collar

STEP 10: COLLAR ATTACHMENT

Attach collar at this time.

Note: *Some collars do not require facing, some collars require full facing, and others require partial facing. All three types of facings are discussed on pages 241–246.*

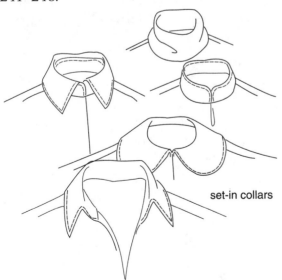

set-in collars

STEP 11: SLEEVE PREPARATION

Attach all detailing such as plackets, cuffs, flounces, gathers, and elastic to the sleeve. (Refer to "Sleeves," pages 205–227.)

It will be easier to maneuver the bodice and sleeve if you complete these details on the sleeve before inserting it into the armhole.

Note: *If your design or blouse is sleeveless, skip this step. However, a bias binding, facing, or hemming edge stitch will be necessary to clean-finish the armhole. Facings are sewn later in the process.*

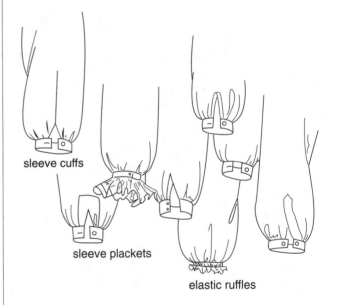

sleeve cuffs

sleeve plackets

elastic ruffles

STEP 12: SLEEVE SET-IN

The garment is now ready for you to set the finished sleeve into the armhole. (Refer to "Sleeve Designs," pages 208–209.)

Note: *If the garment is sleeveless, the armhole will probably need a bias binding, facing, or hem finish. See step 13.*

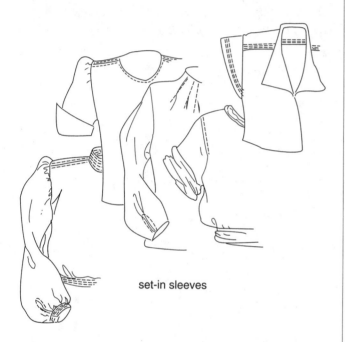

set-in sleeves

STEP 13: BODICE FACINGS (WITHOUT COLLARS AND/OR SLEEVES)

Sew the armhole or neckline facings.

If the garment does not have sleeves or a collar, it is necessary to *clean-finish*, or conceal the raw edges and create smooth, flat edges with facing or bias binding. (See "Facings and Interfacings," pages 267–280 and "Bias and Bias Treatments," pages 127–138.)

Note: *Many blouses and dress bodices have center-front facings. However, this facing is usually attached at the time the collar is attached.*

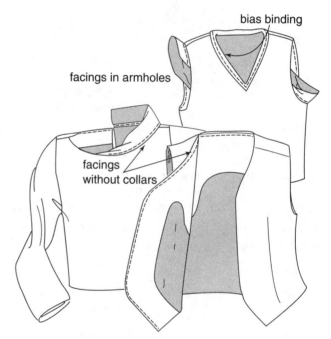

bias binding

facings in armholes

facings
without collars

STEP 14: DRESSES WITH BODICES AND SKIRTS

If you are sewing a dress, sew the bodice and skirt at the waistline to create one unit.

STEP 15: ZIPPERS IN DRESSES WITH WAIST SEAMS

If your dress has a waist seam and needs a zipper, sew the zipper to the garment at this time. As previously discussed, the pattern suggests the appropriate type and size of zipper for the garment.

Note: *Some dresses button down the center front and do not need a zipper. If your design requires buttons and buttonholes, skip this step.*

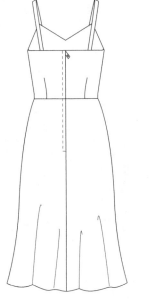

STEP 16: HEMS AND HEM FINISHES

Select a hem suitable to the garment and fabric. (See "Hems," pages 327–333.)

A hem should not be conspicuous, unless it is intentionally decorative. The purpose of a hem is to provide a clean-finished bottom edge, prevent raveling, and add a little extra weight to the bottom of a garment so that it hangs smoothly.

sew hems

STEP 17: CLOSURES

It is important to select the most efficient method of keeping the garment closed. Zippers, buttons and buttonholes, snaps and hooks and eyes are all types of closures. Choose the type of closure most appropriate for the garment, and complete your garment.

If the garment needs buttons and buttonholes, select the type of button for the garment, and consider the placement of buttonholes at this time.

Note: *Make a test buttonhole on a scrap of the garment fabric before constructing the buttonholes on the finished garment.*

Note: *Buttons and buttonholes are placed on the center-front line, not on the edge of the garment. The pattern shows the center-front line and the suggested button and buttonhole placement.*

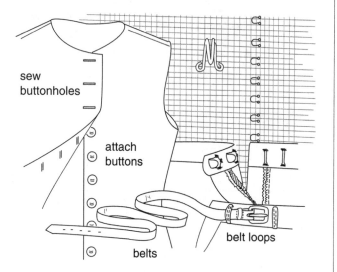

STEP 18: FINISHING TOUCHES

Belts, bows, spaghetti belts, and so on are made as the finishing touches on the garment.

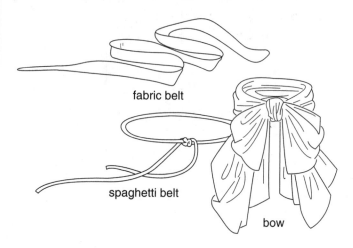

ASSEMBLY PROCEDURES

The *assembly procedures* outlined in this chapter comprise a systematic approach to the construction of a garment. The whole process is an organized method that exists in many sample rooms and is used primarily in fashion production sewing.

Following assembly procedures has several advantages. When you follow these procedures, the complete front and back of the garment sections lay flat as long as possible. In other words, all darts, tucks or pleats, and style seamlines are sewn first to keep these sections laying flat. They are not attached at the side seams or at the shoulder seams until absolutely necessary.

Also, because these sections remain flat, specialty seams and pockets are much easier to complete, and it is easier to manipulate the garment in the machine. It is easier to press each piece of the garment, which creates a more professional look. Each section of the garment is handled less, which keeps the garment looking fresher and saves time.

The next several pages are a simplified summary to guide you through the sewing of various garments, including a pair of pants, a knit t-shirt, a skirt, and a tailored shirt. Specific sewing instructions for particular garment details are provided in the appropriate chapters in this book.

This assembly procedure presents the basic steps in the garment construction procedure. It allows each piece to be kept flat as long as possible as it is being sewn and pressed. This results in less handling of the various pieces of a garment, keeps them fresher looking, and saves time.

ELASTIC-WAISTED PANTS

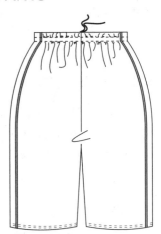

1 Sew front and back crotch seams.

2 Sew outer leg seams.

3 Sew inner leg seams.

4 Insert elastic into waistband.

5 Fold over waistband, and sew it.

SKIRTS WITH SEPARATE WAISTBANDS

1 Gather the front and back skirt sections.

2 Sew front yoke to front skirt. Sew back yoke to back skirt.

3 Sew center-back seam, and insert back zipper.

4 Attach any side-seam pockets, and sew side seams.

5 Sew waistband.

6 Sew hem.

7 Sew buttons and buttonholes.

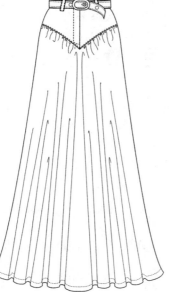

KNIT T-SHIRTS

1 Sew shoulder seams, leaving 1 inch not sewn at one neck/shoulder edge if bias binding will be sewn into the neckline.

2 Sew sleeves to bodice, using the open sleeve method.

3 Sew side seams and underarm sleeve seams, in one step.

4 Sew bias binding and finish neck, or sew in the neckline placket and attach the collar.

5 Sew sleeve details (cuffs or hems).

6 Sew hem.

7 Sew button and buttonholes.

TAILORED-YOKE SHIRTS

1 Sew back yoke.

2 Sew front plackets.

3 Sew front yokes.

4 Sew collar and finish neck.

5 Sew sleeve plackets.

6 Sew sleeves to garment, using the open sleeve method.

7 Sew side seams and underarm sleeve seams, in one step.

8 Sew hem.

9 Sew button and buttonholes.

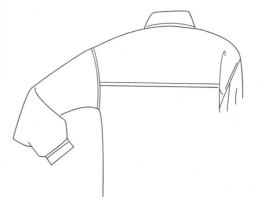

CHAPTER 6

Stitches

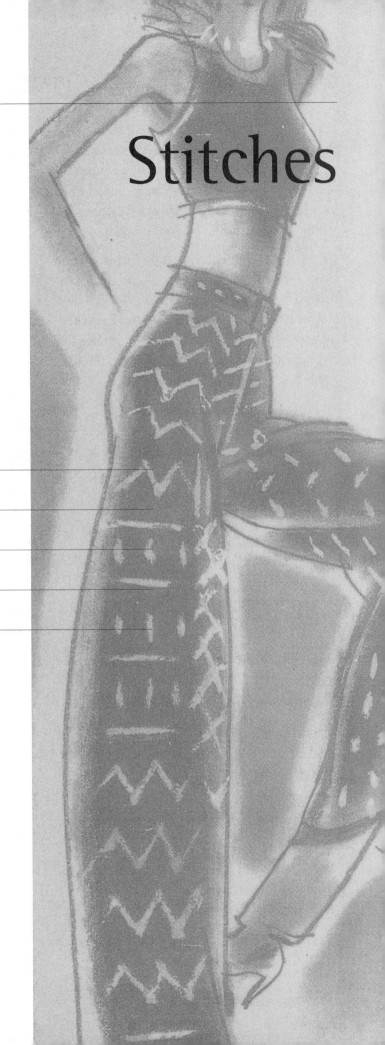

KEY TERMS AND CONCEPTS

Stitches are created in a complete sewing action, using a threaded needle. They may be produced either by hand or machine. Stitches may be functional or decorative, and they may be concealed within or show on the face of a garment.

Permanent Stitches are used for seams, darts, and tucks. The length and tension of the stitch vary, depending on the fabric used. On most medium-weight fabric, there are about 10 to 12 stitches per inch; sheers require a finer stitch length, about 14 stitches per inch; heavyweight fabric generally needs 8 to 10 stitches per inch.

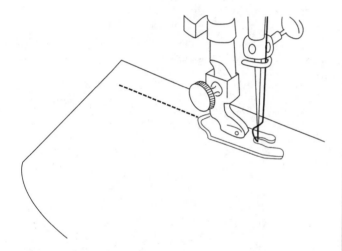

Hint: *Place a piece of tissue paper under fabrics such as sheers, or smooth, slippery fabrics to prevent slipping. After stitching, tear the tissue away.*

Hint: *When sewing velvet or pile fabrics, hand baste along the seam line to prevent the fabric from slipping. Stitch the seam in the direction of the pile.*

Hint: *Areas where there is strain or a need for reinforcement, such as points of collars, cuffs, and pointed faced openings of necklines, need a finer, tighter stitch, usually 16 to 18 stitches per inch.*

Regular stitch is a straight, consistant, even length stitch used as a permanent stitch.

Basting stitches are long temporary stitches made by hand or machine, approximately 6 stitches per inch. Ends are not fastened or backstitched. Before basting stitches are removed, threads are snipped every few inches to facilitate removal.

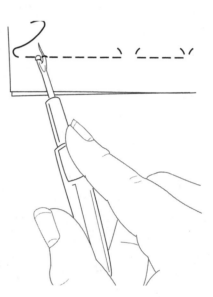

Hint: *In* pin basting, *pins are used to hold fabric pieces together, placed so that they can be easily removed as stitched. You use as many pins as necessary to keep the layers of fabric from slipping.*

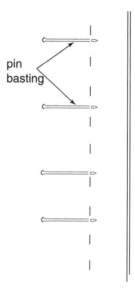

pin basting

Stay stitching is plain machine stitching that is done on the stitchline before the garment is assembled. It is used to maintain the original shape of the garment pieces and prevent stretching, which is especially necessary in necklines.

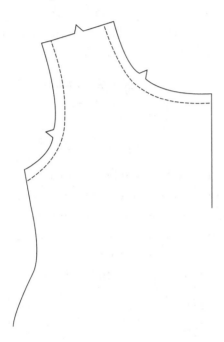

Hint: *Place your index finger behind the foot as you sew to prevent the seam from stretching out the original shape of the fabric.*

Zig-zag stitches are sewing machine stitches that have a saw-toothed shape. Zig-zag stitches are used to join two pieces of fabric together to create a decorative design. The stitch length and width can be varied, depending upon the desired use. Also, when using a zig-zag stitch on the seam edge this will prevent raveling.

Top Stitching is a single or multiple rows of machine stitching made on the outside of the garment, through all layers of the garment. Top stitching is used to outline seams; attach pockets, plackets, or yokes; and add stability to a garment. It is mainly used as a decorative stitch. Usually top stitching is done $\frac{1}{4}$ inch from the edge.

Top stitching is usually done with a longer-than-usual plain stitch. The stitch length should be set to 6 to 8 stitches per inch so that it appears uniform.

Top stitching is a smart and practical way to accent the seams of a fashion garment. It is usually done with thread the same color as the fabric. However, to accentuate the decorative effect of top stitching, a contrasting thread or buttonhole twist may be used as the upper thread. Because top stitching is visible on a garment, it requires careful placement and execution.

When positioning top stitching, always follow a guide. The edge of the presser foot is the most common guide used to apply straight and accurate top stitching. Other guides include a strip of masking tape, lines marked on the machine, and a guide attached to the throat plate or presser foot of the machine, such as a quilting guide.

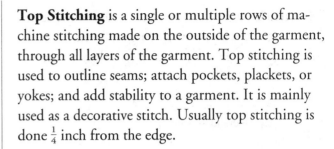

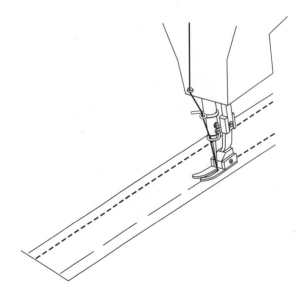

Edge stitching is stitching that is close to the seamline. Edge stitching should be right on the edge. If stitching is more than $\frac{1}{16}$ inch from edge, it is considered top stitching.

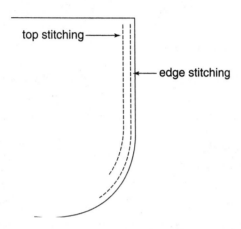

Understitching is a row of stitching on the facing or under layer that keeps the facing, under layer, or seam edge from rolling to the outside of the garment.

When understitching, you press the facing away from the garment and position all the layers of the seam allowance to the facing side. On the correct side of the facing, you machine stitch close to the seam edge. While stitching, gently pull the facing and the garment sections on both sides of the stitch line to help make both pieces lay flat.

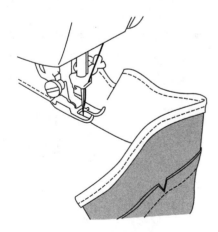

Stitching in the ditch is sewing in the ridge of a previously stitched seam, on the correct side of the garment. Because it is sewn into the ridge of a seam, it is an inconspicuous stitch. It is used to complete waistbands, cuffs, collars, and French bias binding, when you don't want the stitching to be obvious. You use a regular stitch length and thread, whose color matches the fabric.

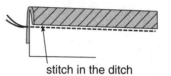

Directional stitching refers to the rules you should follow on the direction of your seam stitching. In general, shoulder seams are stitched from the neckline to the armhole; side seams from the underarm to the waistline; sleeve seams from the underarm to the wrist; and skirt seams from the hem to the waistline.

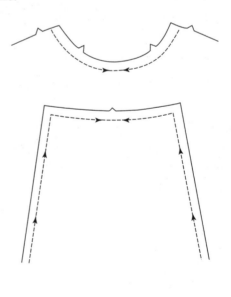

CRIMPING AND EASE STITCHING

Crimping and ease stitching are stitching methods used when one edge of a garment is slightly longer than the matching edge that is to be sewn to it. In order for the seam to appear smooth and not pucker or pleat, the longer piece must be crimped, or ease-stitched, to the shorter piece.

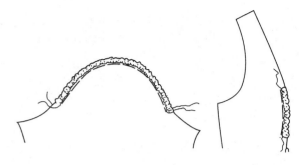

Crimping and ease stitching are most commonly used on sleeve caps, neckline edges that have been stretched out, princess seam curves over the bustline, and turned hems on slightly flared skirts.

CRIMPING

1 Place your left index finger tightly behind the presser foot, and machine-stitch a single row of stitching on the stitchline. Allow the fabric to flow freely under the presser foot, and machine stitch a single row of crimping on the stitchline. Fabric will pile up between your index finger and the presser foot. This puckers and crimps in the fabric.

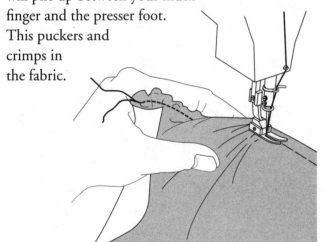

2 Distribute the crimping evenly. Placing the right sides of the fabric together, and pin the shorter seam to the crimped seam, placing a pin approximately every $\frac{1}{2}$ inch.

3 Keeping the crimped seam on top, stitch along the stitchline. Sew the two seams to each other, using a regular machine stitch. Be careful not to sew in any folds or gathers.

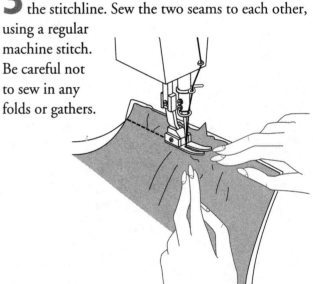

EASE STITCHING

Sew a double row of basting stitches close to the seamline, and pull the threads to the desired fullness (it should be a minimal amount of fullness). Refer to "Plain Seam Using a Basting Stitch," pages 88–89 and "Stretching and Sewing Elastic," pages 78–79.

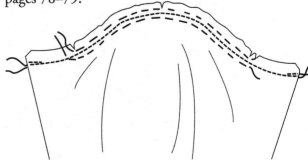

GATHERING

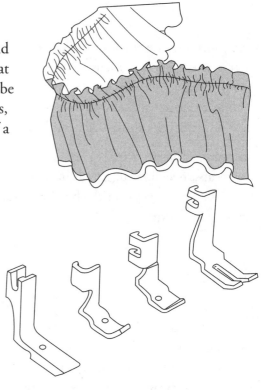

Gathering means drawing up fabric fullness along the stitchline and distributing the fullness where desired. Many garments require that pieces be gathered before they are sewn into a seam. Gathers may be used in a garment section or design detail, such as ruffles, ruchings, and flounces; dirndl skirts; full or puffed sleeves; and style lines of a dress or blouse.

Most sewing machines include a *gathering foot,* which will automatically sew a single row or multiple rows of gathers quickly and evenly. Because the foot is designed to lock fullness into every stitch, it ensures evenly spaced gathers. The shape of this foot varies from machine to machine, but it usually has a "hump" on the bottom.

1 Place your left index finger tightly behind the gathering foot, and machine stitch a single row of gathers on the stitchline, from the beginning to the end of the area that needs to be gathered. Allow the fabric to flow freely under the gathering foot. Fabric will pile up between your index finger and the presser foot. Lift your finger to release some fabric. Replace your finger near the back of the gathering foot, and repeat until the entire area is gathered.

Note: *The stitch length on the sewing machine controls the amount of fullness. A longer stitch length creates more fullness, and a shorter stitch length creates less fullness. Also for maximum fullness on heavier fabrics, it might be necessary to tighten the tension.*

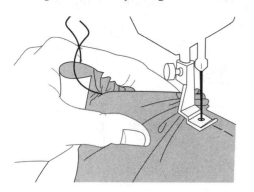

2 Distribute the gathers evenly. Placing correct sides of the fabric together, and pin the shorter seam to the gathered seam. Place the gathered garment section on top. Pin approximately every $\frac{1}{2}$ inch.

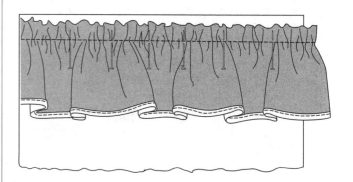

3 Keeping the gathered section on top, stitch along the stitchline. Sew the two seams to each other, using a regular machine stitch. Be careful not to catch any folds.

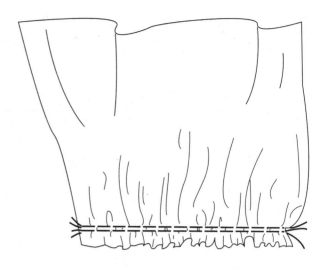

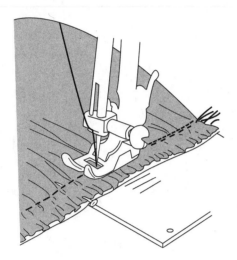

Hint: *Another method of making gathers is to sew a double row of basting stitches and pull the bobbin threads until you achieve the desired fullness.*

STRETCHING AND SEWING ELASTIC

Elastic is often used to gather a ruffle or the bottom of a sleeve, or to introduce fullness to a fitting area in a garment (such as the waist seam).

1 Distribute the elastic in half (and in quarters, if needed), and mark with a pin. Divide the garment area requiring the elastic, and mark with a pin.

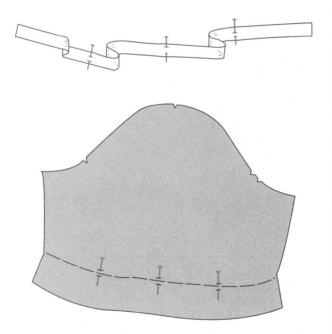

2 Place the elastic on top of the wrong side of the garment, noting divided positions. Starting from the edge of the garment, tack the end of the elastic to the edge of the garment area requiring the elastic.

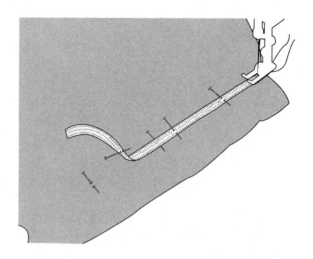

3 With the machine needle in the down position, stretch the first portion of the elastic to the first divided position. Stitch the elastic to the garment until the first divided position is reached. Repeat this stretching and sewing technique until the elastic is completely attached.

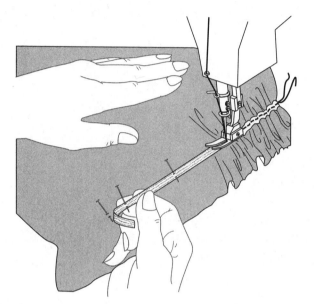

Note: *The garment will look gathered; however, it will stretch when needed to put the garment on.*

Hint: *Use elastic thread in the bobbin to give gathered effects in garment pieces. Wind elastic thread on the bobbin by hand. Be sure not to stretch the elastic. Use regular thread as the upper thread.*

HAND HEMMING STITCHES

Several stitches can be used to hem a garment. Select thread to match your garment. Fullness should be eased in and distributed evenly for a flat, smooth finish. Hem stitches should also be spaced evenly and inconspicuously sewn to the fabric. Choose one of the following stitches, as appropriate for your garment and fabric.

PICK STITCH

A *pick stitch* is a small durable backstitch to hand finish a hem or a zipper application. Also called hand pick stitch.

1 Pick up a small stitch of the garment with the needle.

2 About $\frac{1}{4}$ inch from the hem edge, pick up another stitch.

3 Continue to stitch, taking a stitch first in the garment and then in the hem edge, until the hem is finished.

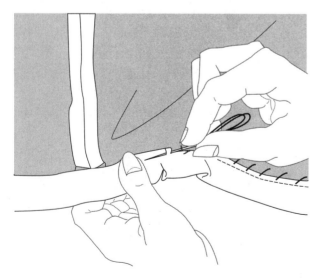

CATCH STITCH

A *catch stitch* is a hand-worked, short backstitch, taken alternately from left to right, ply to ply, to form a close cross-stitch. It is used especially for hemming.

1 Take a small, horizontal stitch in the garment, from right to left, near the edge of the hem.

2 Pick up a thread of the garment diagonally, below and to the right of the first stitch.

3 Continue to stitch in this zig-zag pattern until the hem is finished.

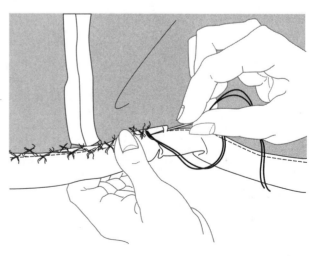

SLIPSTITCH OR BLINDSTITCH

A *slipstitch* or *blindstitch* is a small hand stitch used for hemming that is almost invisible. You conceal the thread by slipping the needle through a fold in the cloth with each stitch.

1 Pick up a small, inconspicuous stitch of the garment with the needle.

2 Take another small stitch in the hem edge, diagonally.

3 Continue to stitch, taking a small stitch first in the garment and then in the hem edge, until the hem is finished.

blindstitch

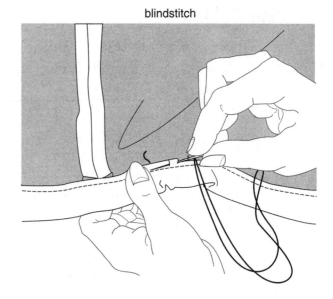

slipstitch

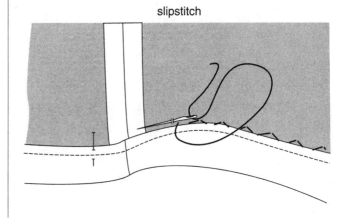

Machine Hemming Stitches

Many garments can be hemmed with a machine stitch. The bias-cut edge, the serged/overlocked hem, and the narrow hem are some of the choices for finishing a garment by machine.

BIAS-CUT EDGE HEM

For bias-cut edges of hems, use a picot hem stitch or a rolled hem, or simply overcast and stitch with a $\frac{1}{4}$ inch hem.

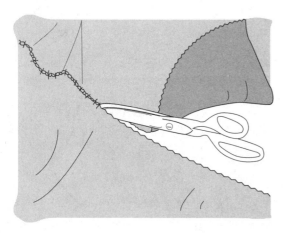

SERGER OR OVERLOCK HEM

You can use a narrow stitch on a serger to clean-finish a hem. It will not need any further turning or stitching.

NARROW STITCH HEM

A *narrow stitch hem* is a narrow hem used on the bottom of shirts, blouses, and some skirts.

1 Fold the garment edge under $\frac{1}{4}$ inch, and fold the hem allowance (usually $\frac{1}{2}$ inch) up along the stitching line.

2 Machine stitch the folded edge in place.

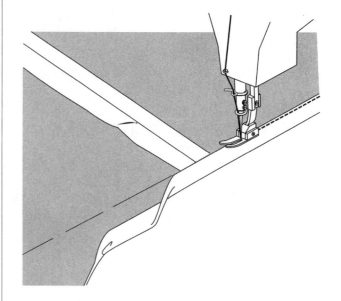

CHAPTER 7

Seams

KEY TERMS AND CONCEPTS

Seams are created in the process of matching and sewing two or more pieces of fabric together to form a finished edge. The type of seam selected should be appropriate for the fabric, type of garment, and location of the seam in the garment.

Seams are stitched in the following direction:

■ Shoulder seams—from the neckline to the armhole.

■ Bodice side seams—from the underarm to the waistline or hem.

■ Sleeve seams—from the underarm to the wrist.

■ Skirt seams—from the hem to the waistline.

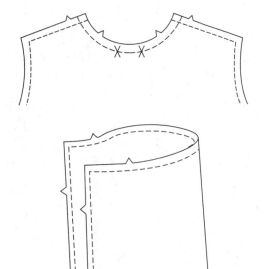

The **seam allowance** is the excess fabric needed to sew a seam, usually $\frac{1}{2}$ inch or $\frac{5}{8}$ inch.

Backstitch is the reverse stitch on the machine. You backstitch by sewing backward and forward to reinforce the stitching at the beginning and end of a seam.

The **seamline** is the line on a pattern along which you sew.

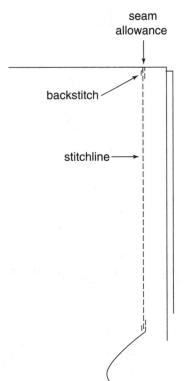

The **length of the stitches in a seam** depends on the type of stitch needed for a garment area:

■ A **permanent machine stitch in a seam** uses stitches, meaning 10 to 12 stitches per inch. Ends are not backstitched, so the seam can be removed easily.

■ A **reinforced stitch in a seam** uses very short stitches, 16 to 18 stitches per inch, and reinforces an area subject to strain, such as corners.

The **seam guidelines** help you guide the stitching so that it is straight and parallel to the seam edge. The seam guidelines are usually marked on the throat plate of the sewing machine. The lines, which are usually numbered in $\frac{1}{8}$ inch increments, indicate the width of the seam allowance desired for the garment pieces.

Hint: *Place a strip of masking tape along the chosen seam guideline on the throat plate to provide a seam guideline all the way across the sewing area of the machine.*

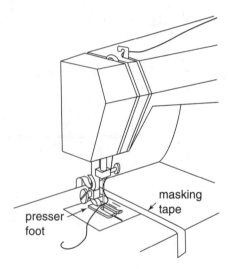

The **presser foot** is the attachment on the sewing machine that holds fabric steady at the point where it is being advanced, while the needle is stitching. The all-purpose foot is used for most stitching.

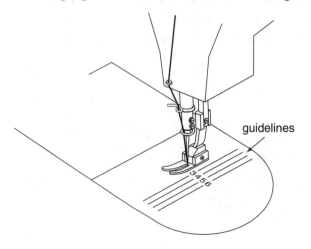

SEWING GUIDELINES

Always start and finish stitching with the needle and foot in the up position. There should be 5 inches of the thread behind the presser foot.

Place the fabric under the presser foot so that the cut edges are to the right of the needle and are lined up with the seam allowance guideline on the throat plate. This should position the seamline directly under the needle.

Drop the presser foot, and lightly hold the fabric as it passes under the needle. At the same time, guide the fabric parallel to the seam guidelines on the throat plate.

Look at the cut edge of the garment—not at the needle—as the fabric moves through the sewing machine. Stitch forward $\frac{1}{4}$ inch, and then backward to the edge of the fabric and forward again along the stitchline to complete the plain seam. At the end of the stitchline, backstitch $\frac{1}{4}$ inch, and then stitch forward to the edge of the fabric.

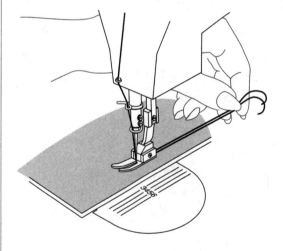

SEAMS

Plain Seam

The plain seam is the most common seam used to sew two garment pieces together. It is used on side seams, shoulder seams, and style lines. The plain seam is used on most fabrics, except knits. The length of the stitch is between 10 and 12 stitches per inch for most fabrics. (Refer to Chapter 6 for more detailed information.) The width of the seam allowance is usually $\frac{5}{8}$-inch for fashion sewing and $\frac{1}{2}$-inch for industry sewing.

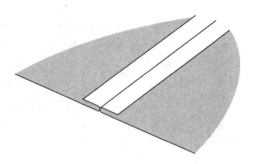

1 Place one piece of fabric on the sewing table, with the correct side up.

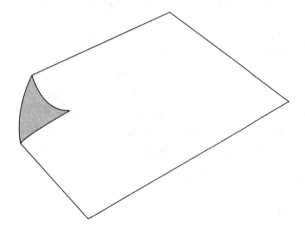

2 Place the second piece of fabric on the first piece, with correct sides together.

3 Pull both the bobbin and needle threads under and behind the presser foot.

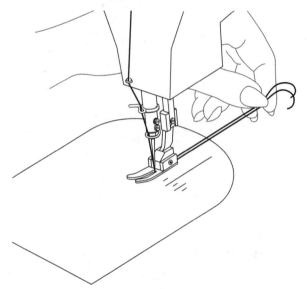

4 Place both pieces of fabric under the presser foot at the beginning of the garment piece stitchline, with the edge of the fabric on the seam guidelines on the sewing machine throat plate.

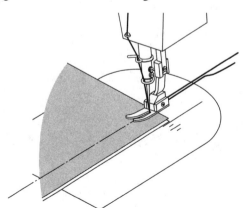

5 Stitch forward ¼-inch, then backward to edge of fabric, and then forward again along the stitch-line to complete the plain seam. Follow the seam guidelines on the sewing machine throat plate.

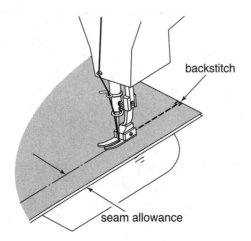

backstitch

seam allowance

6 At the end of the stitchline, backstitch ¼-inch, and then stitch forward to edge of fabric.

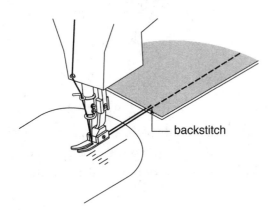

backstitch

7 Pull the fabric and the attached threads behind the presser foot and clip the threads close to the fabric.

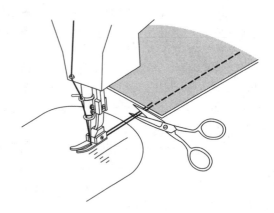

8 Press the seam open.

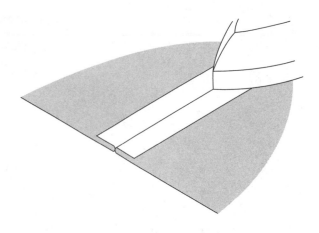

Plain Seam Using a Basting Stitch

A basting stitch is used to sew two pieces of fabric together when a temporary seam is needed. This may be in the slot seam, an open welt seam, or the preliminary seam for setting a railroad zipper. It may also be used in seam areas of the garment for preliminary fittings. The length of the stitch is about 6 stitches per inch and is generally the longest stitch on the machine. The width of the seam allowance is the same as that of the plain seam.

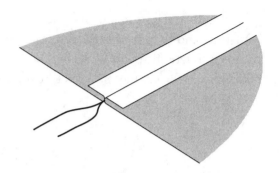

1 Place one piece of fabric on the sewing table, with the correct side up.

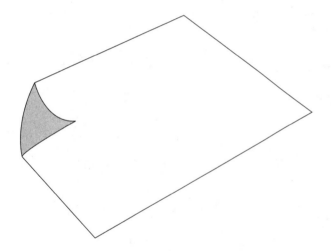

2 Place the second piece of fabric on the first piece, with the correct sides together.

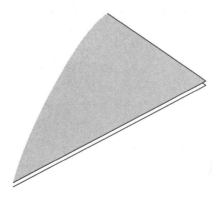

3 Pull both the bobbin and needle threads under and behind the presser foot.

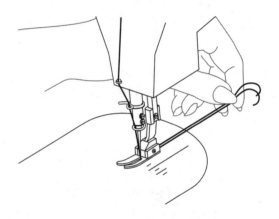

4 Place both pieces of fabric under the presser foot at the beginning of the garment-piece stitchline, with the edges of the fabric on the seam guidelines.

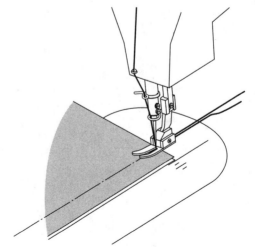

5 Following the seam guidelines, use the longest stitch. Do not backstitch. Continue sewing along the stitchline to complete the seam.

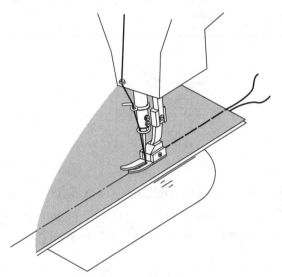

6 Pull the fabric and the attached threads behind the presser foot, and slip the threads halfway between the fabric and the needle.

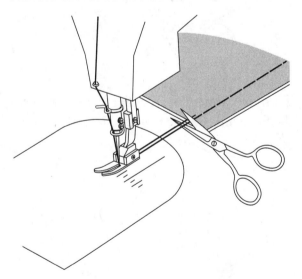

7 Press the seam open.

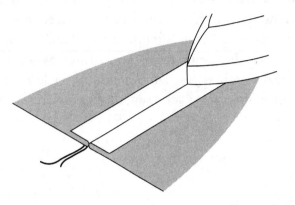

Slot Seam

A slot seam is desirable when a strip of lace fabric or a matching or contrasting strip of fabric is added to the underlay area of the seam. After the basting stitch is removed from the stitched seam, the backing strip shows between the finished seam edges. This seam can also add a bit of spice to an otherwise plain seam, used mostly in yoke seams.

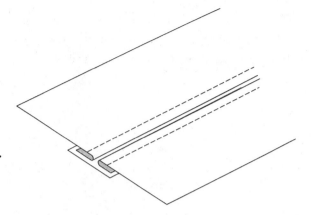

1 Sew a plain seam using a basting stitch. Refer to "Plain Seam Using a Basting Stitch," pages 88–89.

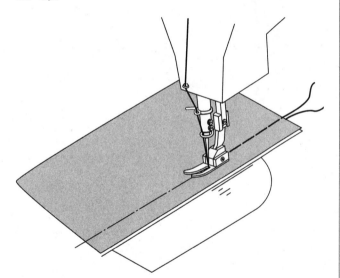

2 Press the seam open.

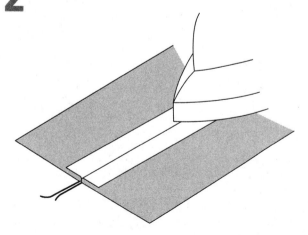

3 Cut a strip of matching or contrasting fabric the same width as the two seam edges. Lay the strip in place as illustrated. Pin if necessary.

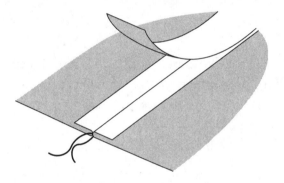

4 Turn the garment over, with the correct side of the fabric up and the strip still in position.

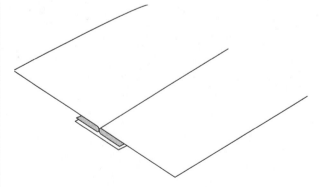

5 Using the presser foot as a guide, stitch $\frac{1}{4}$ inch away from the seamline with a straight machine stitch.

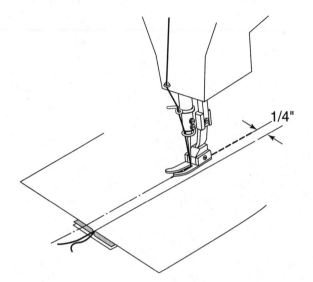

6 Repeat on the opposite seamline, and press in place.

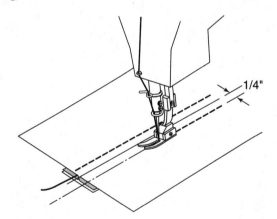

7 Remove the basting stitches.

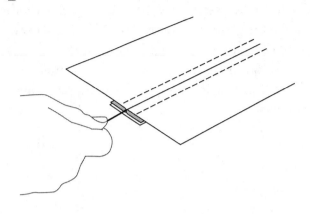

Flat-Felled Seam

The flat-felled seam provides a clean finish to both sides of the garment. Two rows of stitching show on the outside of the seam. This type of seam is usually used for sports clothes to give strong, nonfraying, durable construction for sportswear and reversible garments.

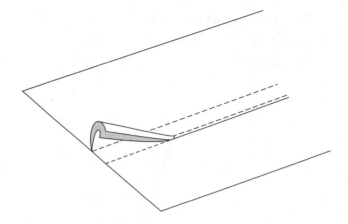

1 Place the garment pieces on the sewing table, with wrong sides together.

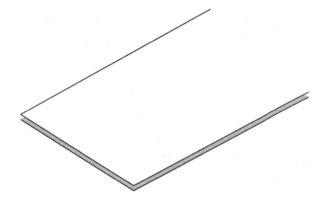

2 Sew a plain seam (refer to "Plain Seam," pages 86–87). Press to one side.

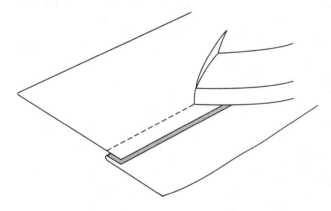

3 Fold over both edges of the seam $\frac{1}{4}$ inch.

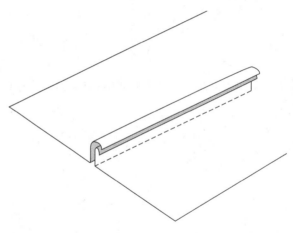

4 Lay seam allowance flat, as illustrated.

5 Using the needle as the sewing guide, stitch the edge of the fold through all the layers of fabric.

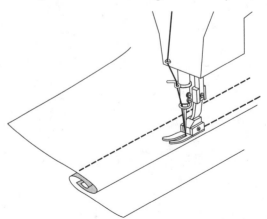

French Seam

The French seam is a narrow seam within a seam that encloses the raw edges of fabric so that fraying does not occur. This seam is used on sheer fabrics and lingerie to conceal the raw edges of see-through fabrics. This seam gives a finished seam look from the outside of the garment, as well as from the inside. It is not recommended for curved seams because they tend to buckle.

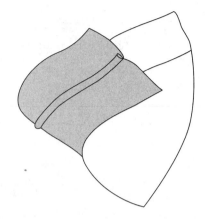

1 Place the garment pieces on the sewing table, with the wrong sides together. Follow the seam guidelines on the throat plate, and stitch with a $\frac{1}{4}$- inch seam allowance. Backstitch as illustrated for a plain seam (page 87).

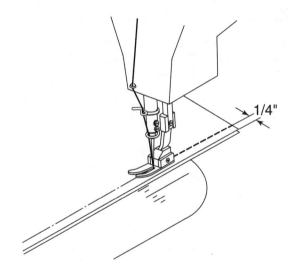

1/4"

2 Trim the seam allowance to $\frac{1}{8}$ inch.

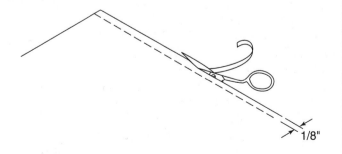

1/8"

3 Press the seam allowance open.

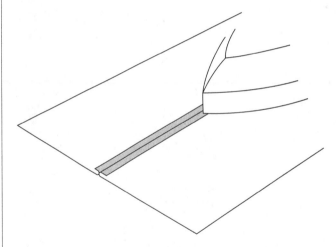

4 Fold the fabric so that the correct sides are together.

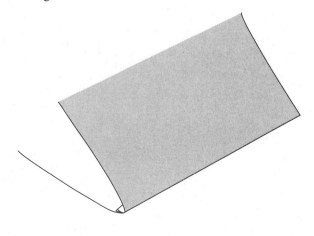

5 Stitch a new $\frac{1}{4}$-inch seam allowance. Backstitch as illustrated for a plain seam (page 87).

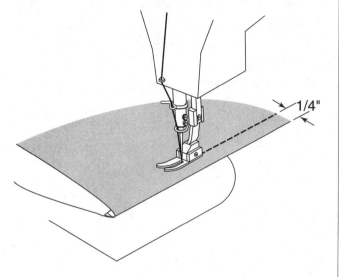

1/4"

6 Turn the garment over, to the correct side. Press the seam flat to one side. Notice that the seam is now enclosed, which gives a finished seam look from the outside of the garment and an enclosed seam on the inside of the garment.

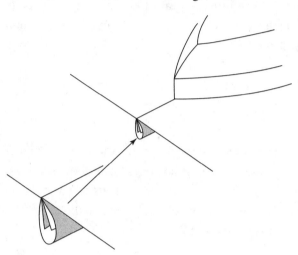

Corded Seam

The corded seam is a decorative seam or edge and can be used as a design feature on garments or home fashion accessories, such as throw pillows. Corded seams are used in necklines, collar edges, and pocket edges to accentuate the outer edges of these pieces. A corded seam gives a stiff finish and should be used in medium-weight fabrics.

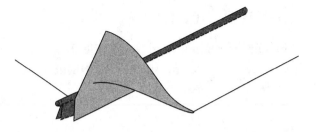

1 With a piece of fabric correct side up, place the raw edge of the cording even with edge of fabric. Baste stitch the cording to the seam.

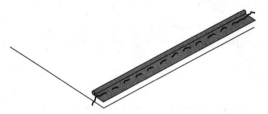

2 Place the second piece of fabric, with the correct side down, over the cording. Make sure all the edges are even.

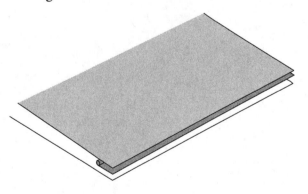

3 Using a cording foot or a zipper foot, stitch along the edge of the cording on the seamline.

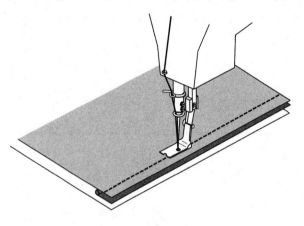

Hint: *For an outside curved seam with cording, stretch the seam allowance around the outside curve and ease the cording. For an inside curved seam with cording, stretch the cord and slightly ease in the seam allowance.*

Curved Seam

The curved seam is used to provide shaping, usually in a style line of a garment, such as on a princess seam, bodice yoke, or skirt yoke.

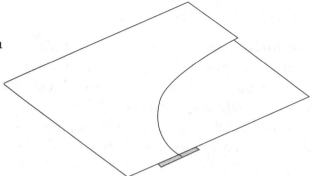

1 Place a garment piece with a concave curve on the sewing table, with the correct side up.

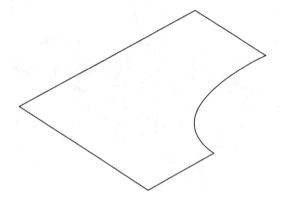

2 Place a garment piece with a convex curve on the first piece, with the wrong side up, as illustrated.

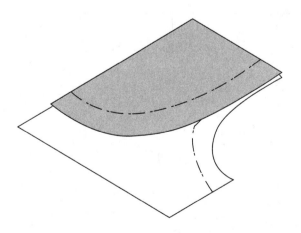

3 Start stitching the same as for a plain seam (pages 86–87).

4 Continue sewing to the point where the stitchline (or the edges of the fabric) begin to diverge.

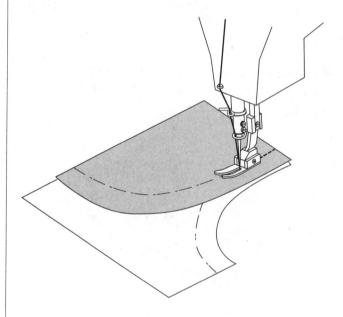

5 Turn the needle down into the fabric, and raise the presser foot.

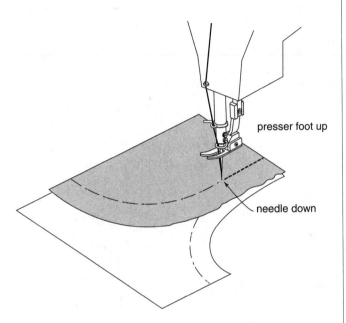

presser foot up

needle down

6 Pivot the top fabric around the needle, until the stitchline (or fabric edges) converge.

7 Continue stitching.

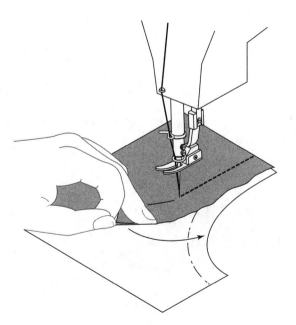

8 Repeat this procedure until the seam is completed.

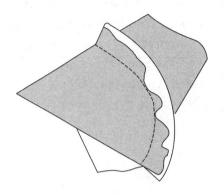

9 Press the entire seam to one side.

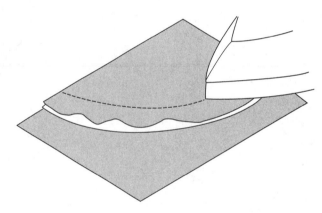

Corner, or Pointed, Seam

A corner, or pointed, seam is a seam featured in a V or square yoke or style line, or in a V neckline. The sewing method used to turn the corner of the seam is a bit tricky because the corner must be pivoted exactly on the stitchline of the corner or V. The sewing method used to turn a corner can be applied to any angular seams, such as those in godets or pointed yokes.

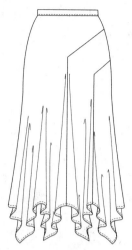

1 Place the first garment piece of fabric (usually the larger piece) on the sewing table, with the correct side up.

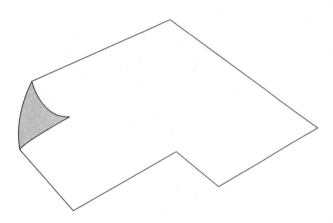

2 Place the second garment piece on top of the first piece, with the correct side down (that is, correct sides together), matching stitchlines. (The angles will not meet.)

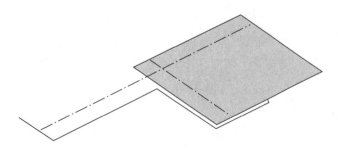

3 Stitch, on the stitchline, to the corner.

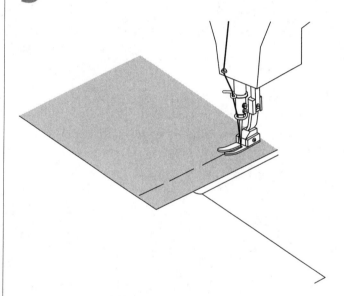

4 Carefully clip the bottom layer of fabric, into the corner.

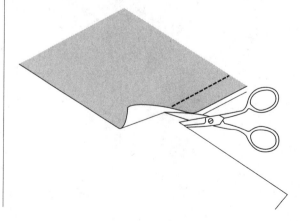

5 With the needle down and the presser foot up (at the stitchline corner), pivot the top layer of fabric.

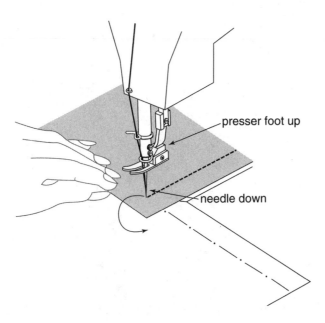

presser foot up

needle down

6 Continue pivoting the top layer until it meets the seamline on the bottom layer.

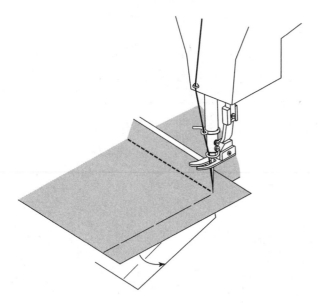

7 Continue to sew on the stitchline until the seam is completed.

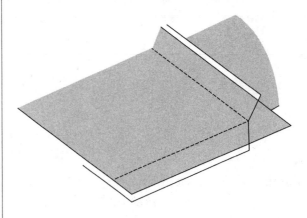

Ruffle Applied in a Seam

This technique illustrates when a purchased gathered decorative trim or a prepared gathered piece is sewn into the style edge of a collar, cuff, or blouse facing.

1 Pin the ruffle to the outer edge of the garment piece. The correct side of the ruffle should be placed facing the correct side of the garment edge.

2 Baste the ruffled edge in place.

3 Place and pin baste the facing layer on top of the ruffled layer.

4 Stitch the outer layer seam along the stitchline, for the entire length of the outer seam.

5 Turn the garment piece correct side out. Press the outer edge flat.

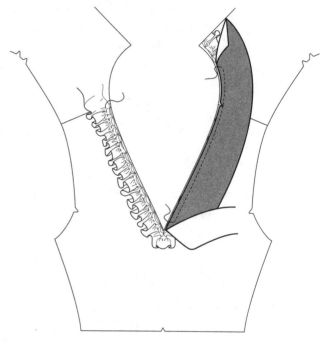

Shirt Yoke Seam

The traditional shirt yoke seam can be designed with a variety of yoke styles and center-front plackets, both as a dress shirt or sport shirt for women, men, and children. The yoke is usually fully lined with the same fabric as the garment. However, on a quilted flannel shirt, the yoke is usually lined with lining fabric.

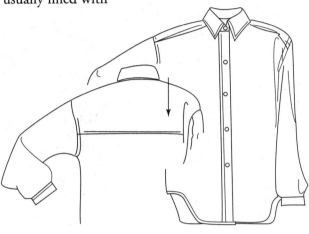

1 Sew all tucks and pleats. Notice the pleats in the back shirt piece (sometimes there is only one, at the center back).

2 Sew the outside yoke piece and the lining yoke piece to the back shirt piece, sandwiching the shirt piece between the yokes.

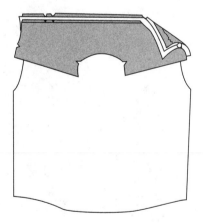

3 Match the right and left front shirt pieces to the yoke lining (one layer only).

Note: *The correct side of the yoke lining will match to the wrong side of the front shirt pieces that is, correct side to wrong side.*

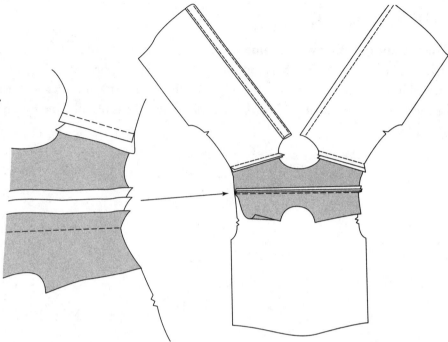

4 Press the yoke seams toward the yoke. Press the seam allowance of the top yoke, and pin baste the yoke over the stitchline of the front yoke seam. Edge stitch the top layer of the yoke to the garment.

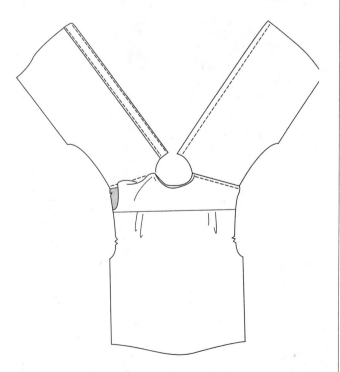

5 Press the yoke pieces up, and top stitch this back yoke seam.

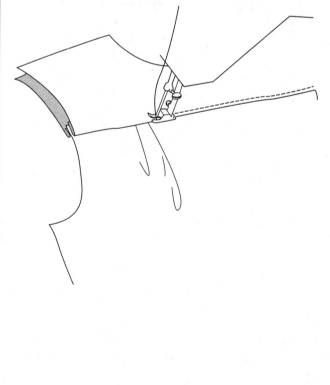

SEAM FINISHES

Plain Seam with a Self, Clean-Edge Finish

The self, clean-edge seam is a quick and neat method of finishing a plain seam. This finishing method prevents the cut edges of the seams from unraveling on certain fabrics, such as course weaves and tweeds. It also helps to give a more finished look in garments such as jackets.

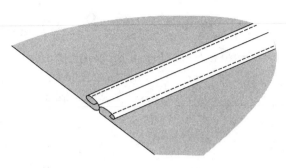

1 Sew a plain seam. Refer to "Plain Seam," pages 86–87.

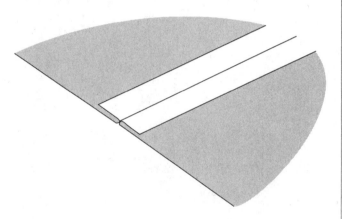

2 Place the garment seam on the sewing table, with the wrong side up and with one seam allowance folded under, as illustrated.

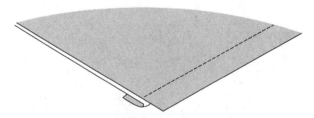

3 Fold over the edge of the exposed seam allowance $\frac{1}{8}$-inch.

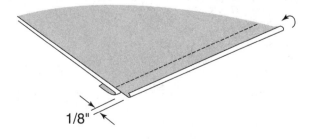

1/8"

4 Stitch close to the folded edge.

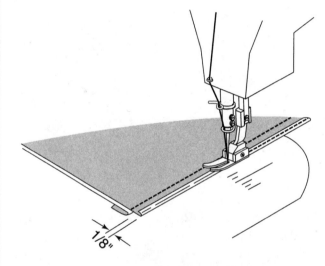

1/8"

5 Repeat on the other seam allowance.

6 Press the seam open.

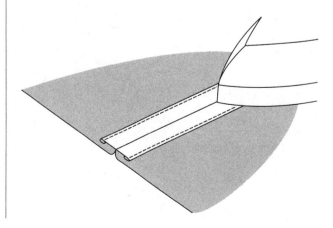

Plain Seam with Bound Edges

A bound-edge seam requires bias tape to finish the raw edges of the seam. This method is desirable when sewing with fabric such as coarse weaves or loosely woven woolens that fray easily. It is also used on fake furs or unlined jackets to give a finished look.

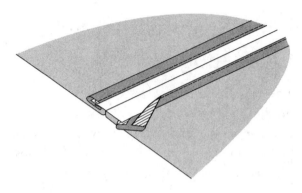

1 Sew a plain seam. Refer to "Plain Seam," pages 86–87.

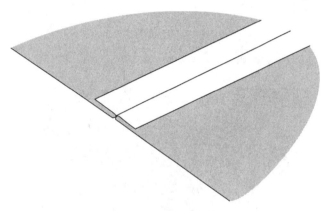

2 Place the garment on the sewing table, with the wrong side of the fabric up, as illustrated.

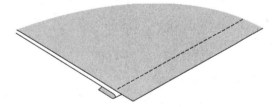

3 Slip purchased bias over one edge of the seam allowance.

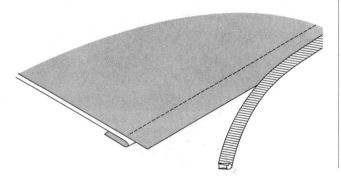

4 Edge stitch along the fold of the bias tape.

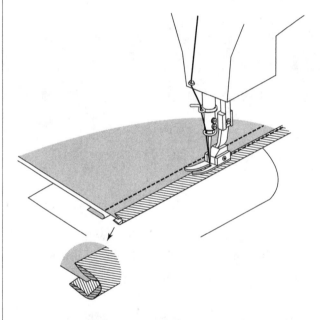

5 Repeat this procedure on the opposite seam allowance, and press the seam open.

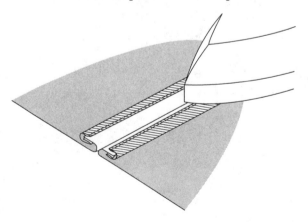

Welt Seam Finish

A welt seam finish allows the plain seam to be "detailed" with top stitching in thread the same color as the garment or in thread of a contrasting color. This seam finish is used most often in princess-style seams and yoke seams, often with firm fabrics. This seam provides a strong seam construction and gives a decorative effect.

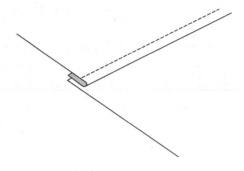

1 Sew a plain seam. Refer to "Plain Seam," pages 86–87.

2 Press the seam allowance to one side.

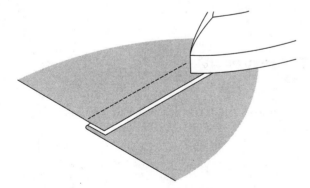

3 Turn both pieces of the fabric over so that the garment is correct side up.

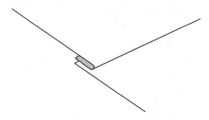

4 Using the presser foot as a guide, stitch $\frac{1}{4}$ inch away from the seamline with a straight machine stitch.

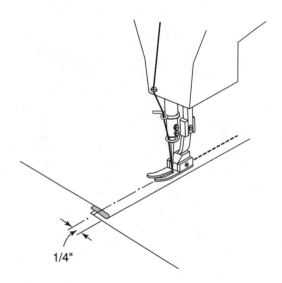

1/4"

5 Press in place.

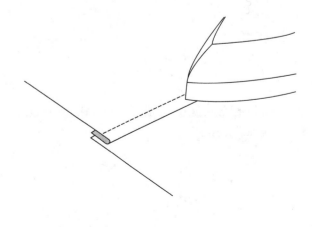

Open Welt Seam Finish

An open welt seam finish is decorative. The seam forms a small tuck and emphasizes a construction detail. This adds interest to a garment and is suitable for almost all fabrics, except sheer fabrics.

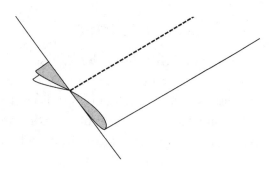

1 Sew a plain seam, using a basting stitch. Refer to "Plain Seam Using a Basting Stitch," pages 88–89.

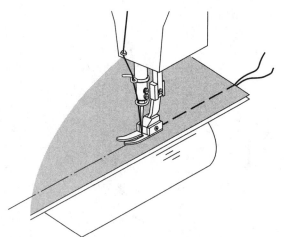

2 Press the seam allowance to one side.

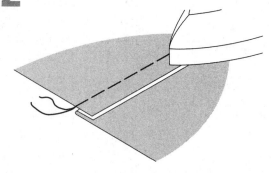

3 Turn both pieces of fabric over so that the correct side faces up.

4 Using the presser foot as a guide, stitch $\frac{1}{4}$-inch away from the seamline with a straight machine stitch.

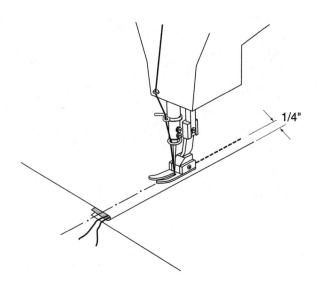

1/4"

5 Press in place.

6 Remove the basting stitches.

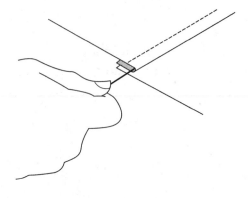

CHAPTER 8

Darts

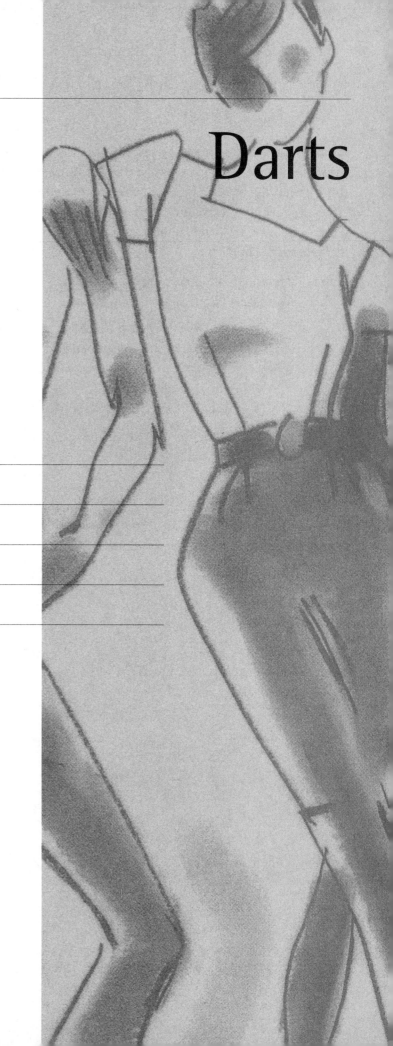

KEY TERMS AND CONCEPTS

A **dart** is the take-up of excess fabric, of various widths, at the edge of the garment and converging to a diminishing point. There are several types of darts, as shown in this chapter. Darts must be positioned and sewn accurately in order to emphasize the lines on the body.

Darts are the most basic structural elements in sewing and are used in

- The front bodice section, to contour the body.
- The front bodice section, from any perimeter point, toward the apex, to shape the fabric over the bust, to contour the body.
- The back bodice waist, to fit fabric to the waistline.
- The back neck or shoulder seam, to shape the fabric over upper shoulder and allow ease over the shoulder blade.
- Fitted sleeves, to allow for elbow movement.
- The pants front and back sections of skirts and pants, to shape fabric to the waistline and allow ease over the hips.

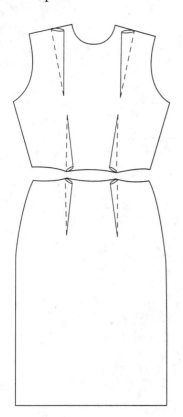

Dart legs are the stitch lines on both sides of the dart.

The **dart point** is the vanishing point and the small end of the dart.

The **wide end of the dart** is the widest end of the dart legs.

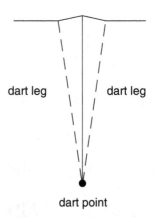

Bust darts help the garment fit over the bust area. They usually begin at the shoulder or side seam and finish 2 inches from the bust point (that is, apex).

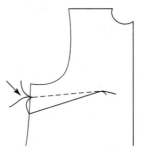

Skirt and pants darts bring in the waist of a skirt or pants. The front darts are usually shorter than the back darts.

Fisheye darts are most often used on garments without a waistline seam, such as blouses, dresses, vests, or jackets, to bring in fullness at the waist area. They allow the garment to curve smoothly in at the waistline and create ease at hip areas.

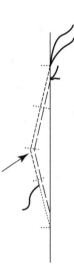

The **French dart** is a diagonal dart originating from any point between the hipline to 2 inches above the waist, along the side seam and tapering to the apex.

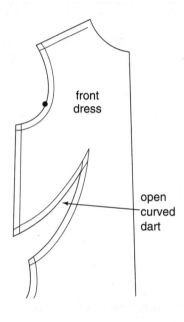

front dress

open curved dart

STRAIGHT TAPERED DART

The straight tapered dart is the basic dart used in a bodice, skirt, or sleeve, to give a smooth, rounded fit. This dart creates a rounded fullness at the fullest part of the body.

TRANSFERRING STRAIGHT TAPERED DART MARKINGS

Transfer the dart marking from the pattern to the wrong side of the fabric. Refer to Chapter 4 for specific directions.

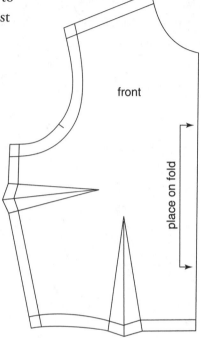

1 With the correct sides of the fabric together, fold the dart so that the snip ends match.

2 Continue to fold the dart (along the center line) to the punch hole or pencil mark.

3 If necessary, pin and pencil in the stitchline. Refer to Chapter 4 for detailed instructions.

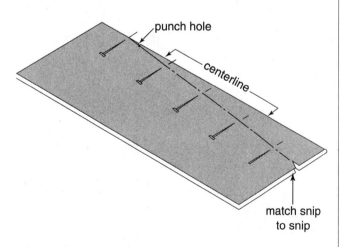

4 Start to sew (and backstitch) from $\frac{1}{2}$ inch beyond the punch hole or pencil mark to ensure that the hole is caught. Make sure the needle enters the fabric exactly on the fold at the stitchline for a couple stitches.

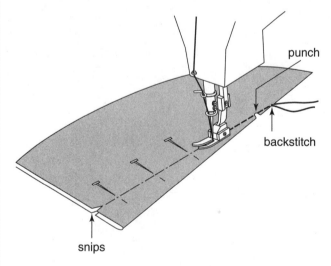

5 Following the stitchline exactly, continue to stitch the dart from the narrow end to the wide end (toward the snips). Backstitch and clip the threads.

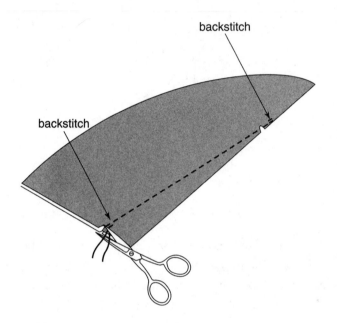

backstitch

backstitch

6 Press the dart excess toward the center or down. Press from the wrong side only. You can use a tailor's ham to build in the dart area. Refer to Chapter 2 for detailed pressing techniques.

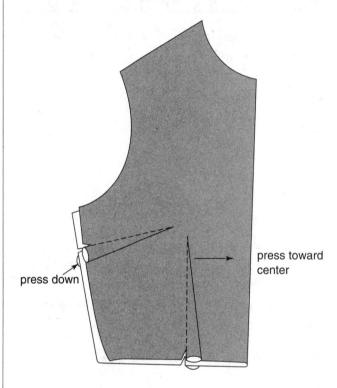

press down

press toward center

SHAPED TAPERED DART

The shaped tapered dart is a single dart that usually allows more contouring fit in a torso bodice or a halter bodice, on woven fabrics.

TRANSFERRING SHAPED TAPERED DART MARKINGS

Transfer dart markings from the pattern to the wrong side of the fabric by following the pencil method.

1 With the correct sides of the fabric together, fold the dart so that the snip ends match. Continue to fold the dart (along the center line) to the pencil mark or punch hole, being certain that the shape of the dart is maintained exactly.

2 If necessary, pin and pencil in the stitchline.

3 Start to sew (and backstitch) the dart $\frac{1}{2}$-inch beyond the punch hole or pencil mark (this is to ensure that the hole is caught). Make sure the needle enters the fabric exactly on the fold at the stitchline for a couple inches.

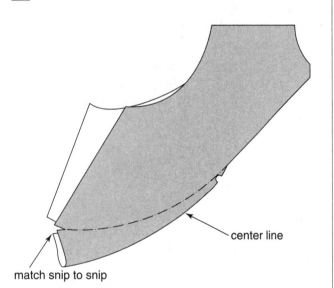

center line

match snip to snip

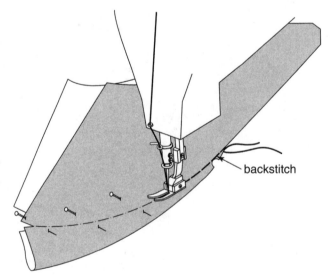

backstitch

4 Following the stitchline exactly, continue to stitch the dart from the narrow to the wide end (toward the snips). Backstitch and clip the threads.

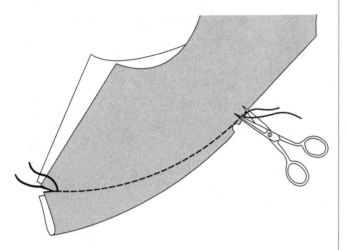

5 Clip excess of fold to relieve strain, allowing dart to curve smoothly.

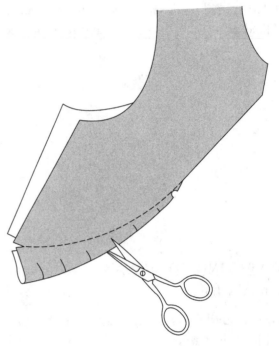

6 Press dart excess toward the center or down. Press from the wrong side only. You can use a tailors ham build in the dart area.

Hint: *When pressing, place a strip of paper between the dart and the fabric to prevent an impression from appearing on the correct side of the garment.*

CUT-AWAY DART

A cut-away dart is used in garments that require extremely wide darts (primarily bodice fronts). A cut-away dart reduces bulk in the finished dart area because the excess amount in the middle of the dart has been cut away. This style of dart is used in woven fabric blouses and dresses that have large shaped darts. The dart is stitched in a seam and then pressed.

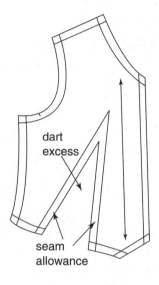

TRANSFERRING CUT-AWAY DART MARKINGS

Transfer dart markings from the pattern to the wrong side of the fabric:

1. Eliminate the dart excess by cutting along the cutting line of the pattern.

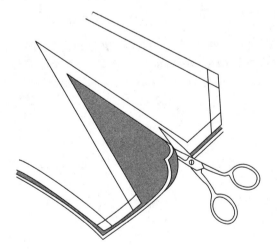

2. Snip the ends of the dart lines.

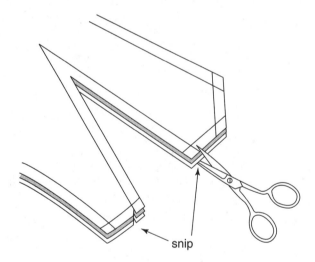

3. Punch a hole or pencil mark $\frac{1}{2}$-inch before the end of the dart tip.

1 With the correct sides of the fabric together, fold the dart so that the snip ends match. Continue to fold the dart, following the seam allowance of the dart to the punch hole or pencil mark.

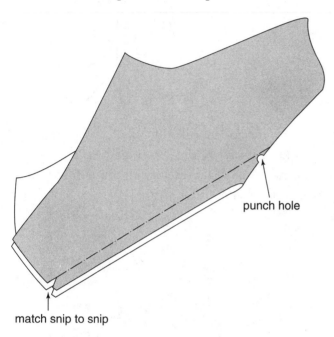

punch hole

match snip to snip

2 If necessary, pen and pencil in the stitchline.

3 Start to sew (and backstitch) the dart $\frac{1}{2}$-inch beyond the punch hole or pencil mark to ensure that the hole is caught.

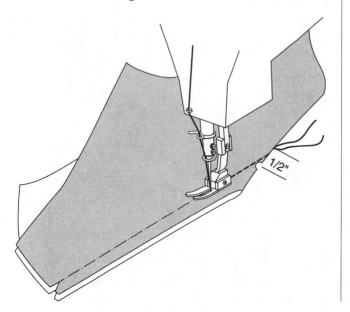

1/2"

4 Following the seam allowance and the stitchline exactly, continue to stitch the dart toward the widest end and the snips. Backstitch and clip the threads.

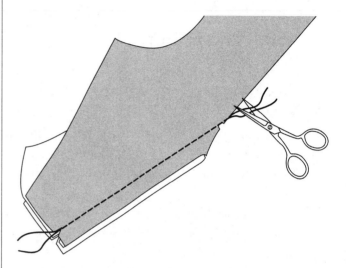

5 Press the dart excess open, over a tailor's ham.

FISHEYE DART

A fisheye dart is a double-ended dart formed to fit the body contour at the waistline area. This dart varies in size and length.

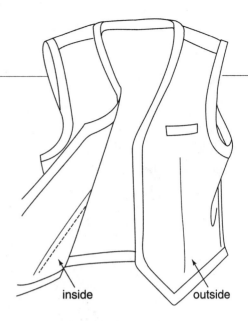
inside   outside

TRANSFERRING FISHEYE DART MARKINGS

Transfer dart markings from the pattern to the wrong side of the fabric:

1. Place a pin through the pattern and both layers of the fabric ½-inch from each end of the dart. Mark with a pencil or punch a hole with an awl.

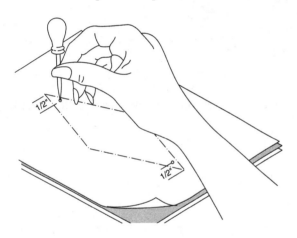

2. Pencil mark (or punch a hole) at the center of the dart and ⅛-inch in from the widest point of the dart.

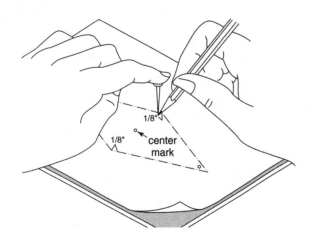

1 With the correct sides of the fabric together, fold the crease of the dart so that the top, bottom, and center marks are in one continuous fold. (This is the center of the dart.)

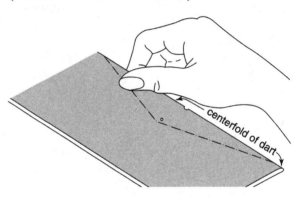

2 Start to sew from ½-inch beyond the top mark to ⅛-inch beyond the center mark, to ½-inch beyond the bottom mark.

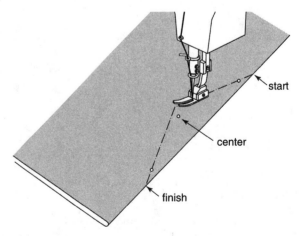

3 Press the dart with the wrong side of the fabric up. Snip the fold at the center of the dart. Press the finished dart toward the center of the garment.

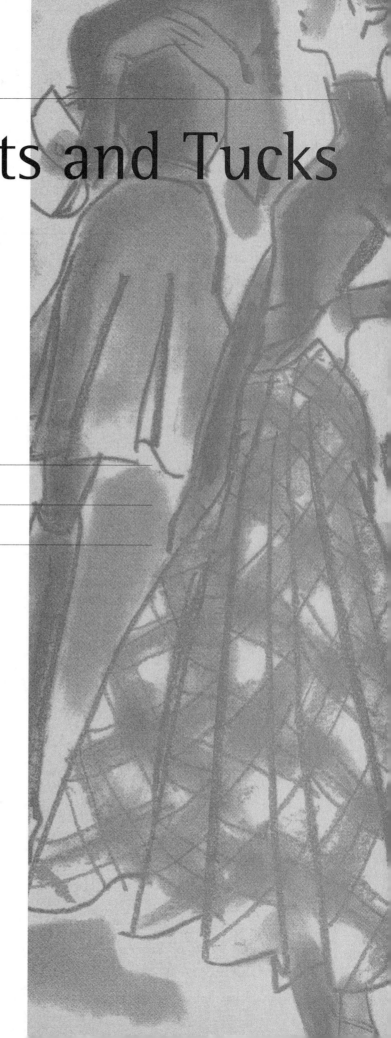

CHAPTER 9
Pleats and Tucks

KEY TERMS AND CONCEPTS

A **pleat** is folded excess fabric at the edge of a garment. It is created by doubling the fabric ply on itself, producing a fold and forming an underlay of $\frac{5}{8}$-inch to 2 inches. Pleats can be used

- Singly or in a series
- At the waist, shoulder, or hipline
- Below a bodice yoke seam or skirt yoke seam
- To fit the lower edge of a sleeve into a cuff
- At a sleeve cap as a design feature
- On a blouse, bodice, or jacket to release fullness over the bust or across the shoulder

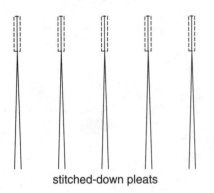

stitched-down pleats

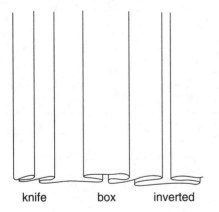

knife   box   inverted

Pleats are either pressed or unpressed and stitched to one side. They create a softened effect at points of release, which aids in fitting the garment over body curves.

Pressed pleats have the crease line firmly pressed in position the entire length of the pleat. They may be evenly spaced pressed folds or part of a seam, stitched and pressed in place. The most common types of pressed pleats are

- Accordion pleat
- Box pleat
- Crystal pleat
- Inverted pleat
- Kick pleat
- Knife pleat

Unpressed pleats are those that do not have the pleat crease line pressed in place and are used to create a rather soft effect, such as in the lower edge of the sleeve.

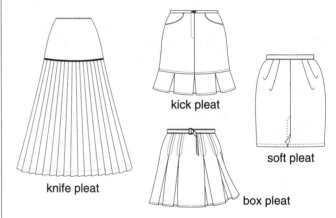

knife pleat   kick pleat   box pleat   soft pleat

A **tuck** is the take-up of excess fabric of a determined amount, at the edge of the garment and converging toward a point or points of release.

There are two basic styles of tucks:

- Dart tuck
- Pin tuck

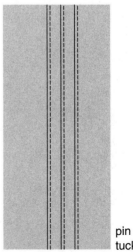

pin tucks

Dart tucks are used to control and release fullness as well as to create design details for some garments. Pin tucks are evenly spaced parallel folds, $\frac{1}{8}$-inch or less, and stitched to be released. Both styles can be formed on the inside or outside of the garment.

Tucks can be used

- To hold fullness in place or for a decorative effect

- On the front bodice at the waistline, shoulder, or center front to release fabric to conform to the bust shape

- On the back bodice at the waistline or shoulder, to release fabric to conform to the body contour.

- On the waistline of a skirt, pants, or shorts, to allow ease over the hips and abdomen.

- On one-piece garments at the waistline, to release fullness above and below a fitted area.

- Instead of darts, to create a softer design effect.

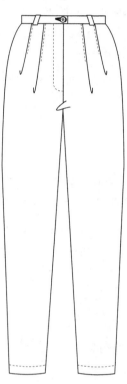

PLEATS

In-Seam Pleat

An in-seam pleat is an extra fabric ply added to the seam, usually lengthwise, pressed and held in place by top stitching. After the seam is stitched, different styles of pleats are created by the direction of the pressed pleat:

- Box pleat—spaced folds doubled over to face away from each other.
- Inverted pleat—spaced fold doubled over to face each other (opposite direction of the box pleat).
- Kick pleat—spaced folds pressed in one direction.

1 With the correct sides of the fabric together, match the pleat seams to each other.

2 Machine stitch a regular stitch from the top of the seam to the bottom of the pleat seam.

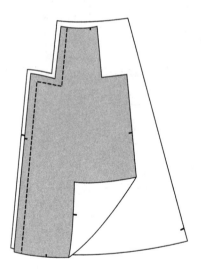

3 Press the seam allowance and the pleat in the direction desired for the pleat.

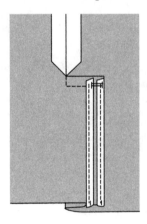

4 On the correct side of the garment, top stitch or edge stitch.

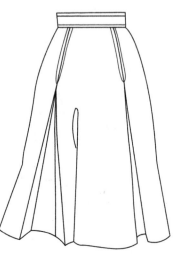

Knife Pleat

A knife pleat is a fabric ply pressed in a series of folds forming underlays permanently pressed to lie in one direction. They may be planned in groups or as an evenly spaced series around the circumference of a garment.

Each pleat in the pattern is marked with two vertical lines from the waistline or a style line to the lower edge. One line designates the top fold of the pleat, and the other designates the position of the fold forming the pleat. Each pleat is made proportionately deeper at the waistline or style line.

TRANSFERRING KNIFE PLEAT MARKINGS

1. Snip the ends of each pleat.
2. Mark the foldlines with a hand thread basting stitch. Take small stitches every 3 inches. Clip the thread between stitches. Use one color thread for the foldline and another color for the placement line.

   OR

   Pull the pattern away from the fabric. Using a ruler and chalk pencil, mark the pleat lines, using the snips as a guide.

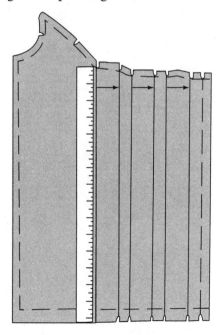

Hint: *Hem the lower edge of a knife-pleated garment before forming the pleats. This make's the hemming process much easier. The finished length of the garment must be accurately known if this technique is used.*

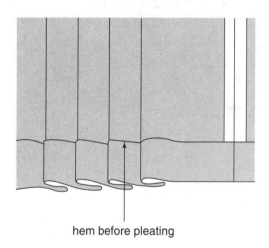

hem before pleating

1 Form each pleat by folding the fabric along each foldline, bringing the fold over to meet the placement line. Pin and baste each pleat the length of the fold.

2 Baste across the top of the pleated section to hold the pleats in place.

3 Press pleats from the correct side, using a pressing cloth. Press lightly for a soft look. Use more pressure for a sharp finish. Turn the garment over, and press again.

4 Attach the adjoining garment piece (for example, bodice, yoke, or waistband).

PLEAT VARIATION

To make stitched-down pleats, top stitch close to the folded edge, from the hem to where the pleat is to be stitched to the skirt.

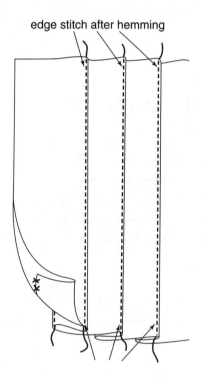

edge stitch after hemming

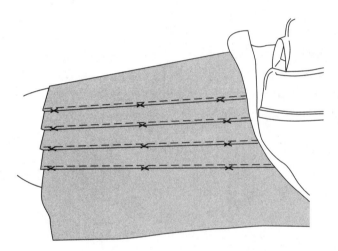

Box Pleat

A box pleat has two folds of equal width turned toward each other, forming two unpressed soft pleats that add extra fullness in a garment section. The pleats are secured with a stitch across the end of the pleat. The box pleat is located in yoke style lines, waist seams of pants or skirts, and the lower edge of sleeves.

1 With the correct sides of the fabric facing up, crease both pleat foldlines to each other, meeting at the center.

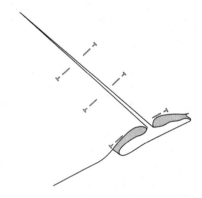

2 Baste across the top of the pleated section to hold the pleats in place.

3 Press the pleat flat.

TUCKS

Pin Tuck

Pin tucks are permanently stitched narrow folds of fabric that are stitched partway or the entire length and add design interest. They can run the full length of a garment piece or end at various points. The width of the tucks and the spacing between the tucks can vary, depending on the design.

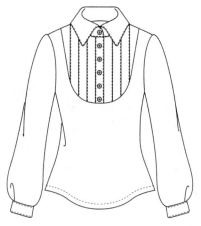

1 Mark the stitching lines of each tuck on the side of the fabric that will be stitched. If the tucks will be stitched from the correct side, use thread basting.

2 Fold and press each tuck, matching stitching lines.

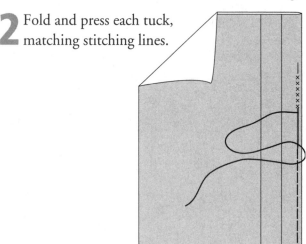

3 Stitch each tuck from the side of the tuck that will be seen. Stitch the tucks along the stitching line, using the foldline of the tuck as a guide.

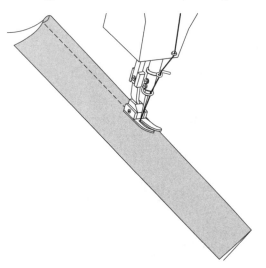

4 Press each tuck flat. Then press each tuck to one side as desired for the design.

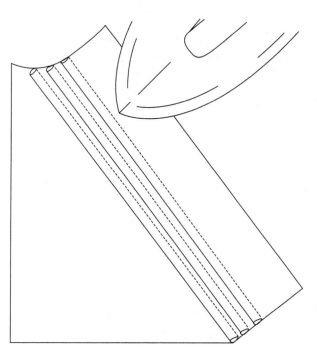

Hint: *You can add tucks to a garment by tucking the fabric before cutting out the pattern pieces.*

Release Tuck

Release tucks are used to control fullness and then release it at a desired point, such as at the bust or hips. Sometimes, fullness can be released at both ends of the release tucks. The spacing between the tuck's depends on the effect desired in the finished garment. The most common place for release tuck's is at the waist areas of skirts or pants and the shoulder areas of bodices.

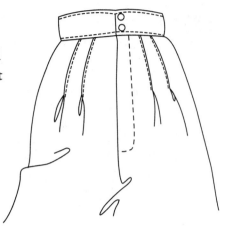

TRANSFERRING RELEASE TUCK MARKINGS

Transfer tuck markings from the pattern to the wrong side of the fabric as follows:

1. Snip the ends of the tuck lines.

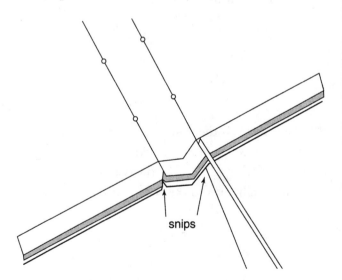

snips

2. Place a pin through the pattern and both layers of the fabric. With a pencil, mark the desired stitchline.

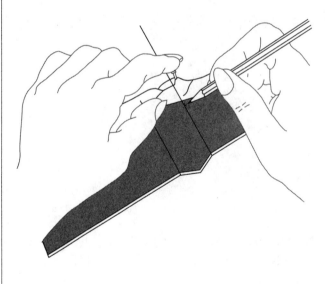

1 With the correct sides of the fabric together, fold the tuck so that the snip ends match.

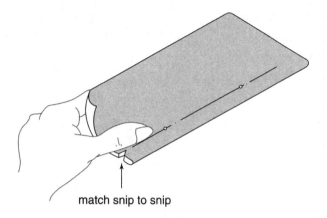

match snip to snip

2 Continue to fold (and pin, if necessary) to the end of the tuck.

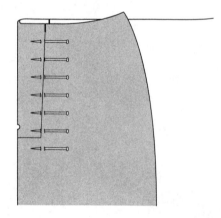

3 Start to sew (and backstitch) from the snipped ends to the release point (the end of the tuck).

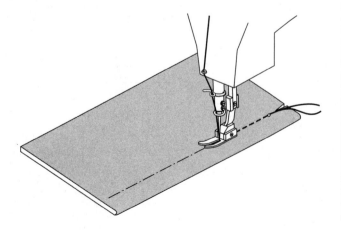

4 If desired, stitch across to complete the tuck.

snips

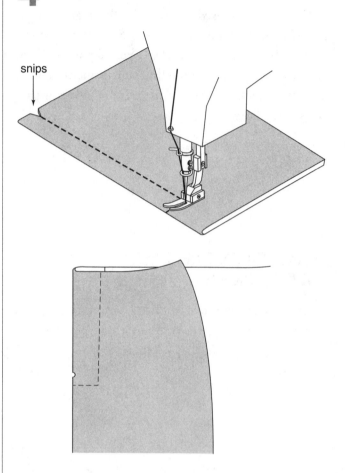

5 Press tucks in the same direction in which they are stitched. Do not allow the iron to go beyond the stitching. Press the tucks in the direction desired, usually toward the center of the garment.

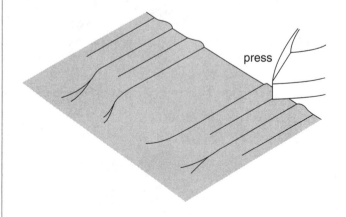

press

CHAPTER 10

Bias and Bias Treatments

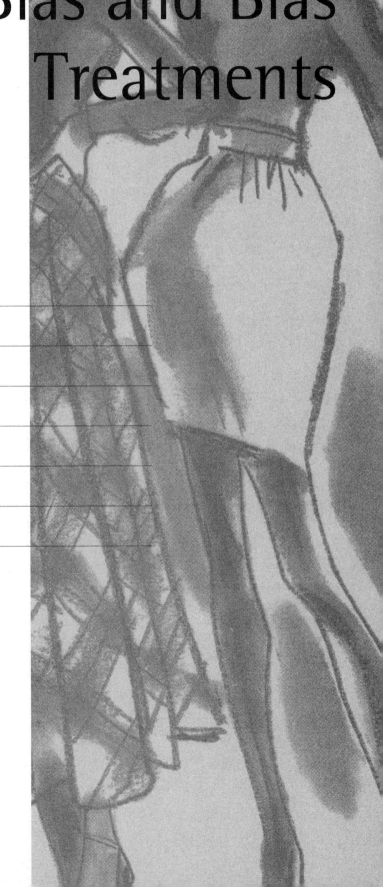

KEY TERMS AND CONCEPTS

Bias is a line diagonally across the grain of the fabric. True bias is at a 45-degree angle. Fabric cut on the true bias has the maximum give and stretchability of woven fabric.

Bias can be a commercially or self-prepared bias strip of fabric, approximately 2 inches in finished width, of matching or contrasting fabric.

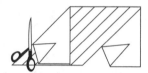

A **bias strip** is fabric used to finish and strengthen a raw edge. The bias strip is folded so that it encases the edge and shows on both the right and wrong sides.

Commercially prepared bias is precut and folded bias binding, also known as bias tape. It is available in a variety of widths and in fabrics of cotton, silk, synthetics, and blends.

Bias binding is single or double-fold (French bias binding) strips cut on true bias, one edge of which is stitched to the garment edges as a finish or trim.

BIAS USES

Bias strips or bindings can be used to:

- Finish and strengthen a raw edge such as in necklines and sleeveless garments. Add a decorative trim or band to a garment
- Replace facings, such as at the edge of necklines, sleeves, or armholes
- Replace or enclose a hem edge
- Make a casing for elastic and drawstrings
- Conceal collar edges
- Stay and reinforce curved seams of crotch and sleeve underarm
- Create tubing for button loops, spaghetti strips, belts, or ties

FINISHING BIAS-CUT GARMENTS

Bias-cut garments are inherently stretchable. Bias-cut designs require special sewing techniques if you don't want the bias garment to continue stretching. There are several sewing solutions to prevent further stretching.

PREVENTING BIAS STRETCH ON TRUE BIAS NECKLINES

Sew a narrow on-grain folded strip (1 inch wide, folded in half) to the neckline, and then turn back the garment onto the strip (see illustration).

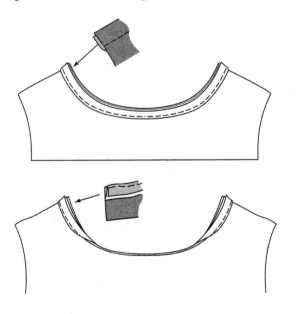

PREVENTING BIAS STRETCH IN A NECKLINE WITH A CONCAVE CUT

Carefully fold the neckline over twice and stitch in place. Because the cut outer edge is shorter than the stitchline, this folding and stitching process holds the neckline in place.

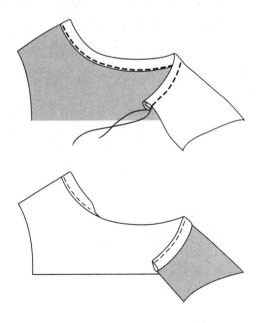

CUTTING BIAS STRIPS

Bias strips are cut from fabric, following lines established on the true bias. Bias strips are more pliable and can be easily shaped to all edges. Therefore, it is necessary to cut and join strips of bias fabric accurately.

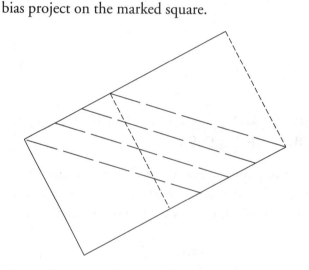

1 Fold the fabric with the lengthwise grain parallel to the crosswise grain. The folded edge is the true bias.

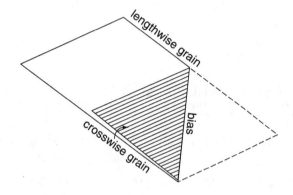

2 Another method of determining the true bias and preparing the fabric to cut strips is to draw a perfect square on the fabric with a pencil.

3 Draw a straight line diagonally from one corner to the other.

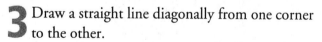

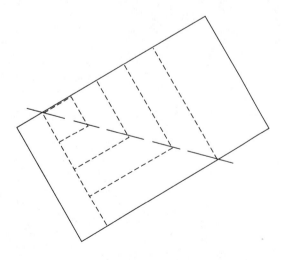

4 After locating the true bias, draw the desired width and the number of strips needed for the bias project on the marked square.

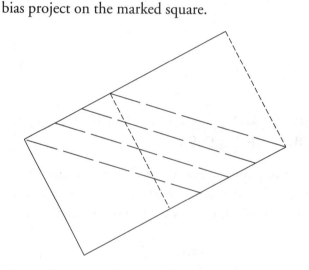

5 Cut the desired number of bias strips.

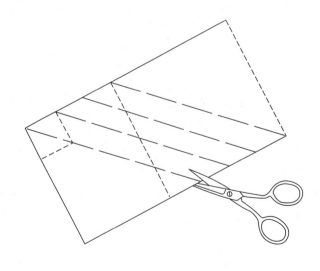

JOINING BIAS STRIPS

You must cut and join an adequate number of bias strips to create the continuous length needed before starting to sew bias binding, facing, spaghetti tubing, and so on.

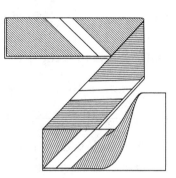

1 Place the bias strips at right angles, correct side to correct side.

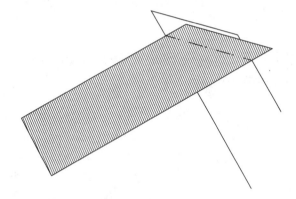

2 Stitch bias strips with a $\frac{1}{4}$-inch seam allowance at angles, as illustrated in step 1.

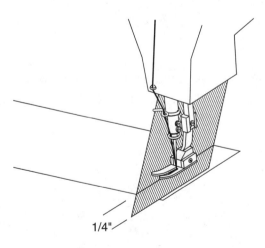

1/4"

3 Continue to join bias strips as needed for the desired length.

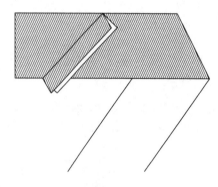

4 Press all seams open and snip extended points.

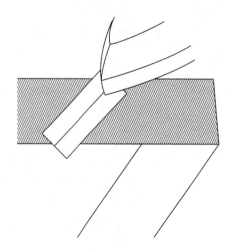

SINGLE BIAS BINDING

Single bias binding is used to finish and strengthen a raw edge and also to add a decorative trim to a garment. In some cases, it can replace a facing at the neckline, sleeve, or armhole edge.

PREPARING SINGLE BIAS STRIPS

Use a $1\frac{1}{2}$-inch wide strip of bias (either in the same color as the garment or a contrasting color) or purchase a commercially prepared double-fold bias tape. Refer to pages 130–131, "Cutting Bias Strips" and "Joining Bias Strips."

1 Place the garment on a sewing table, with the wrong side up.

2 Place the bias strip on the garment, with the correct side down—raw edge to raw edge.

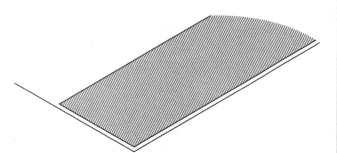

3 Stitch with a $\frac{1}{4}$-inch seam allowance.

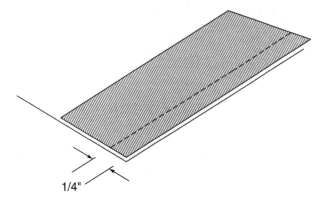

1/4"

4 Fold the unsewn edge of the bias strip over $\frac{1}{4}$-inch and press down.

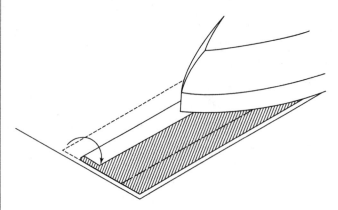

5 Fold the bias binding out and away from the garment edge, along the stitchline, and press down.

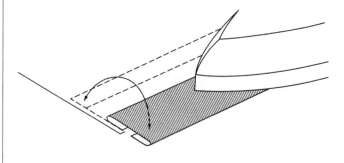

6 Turn the garment over, so that the correct side is up.

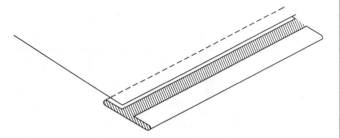

7 Fold the bias strip in half, to the correct side of the garment, just covering the stitchline.

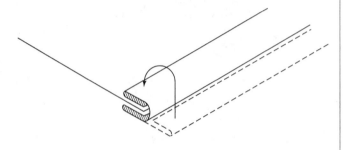

8 Stitch along the edge of the bias binding.

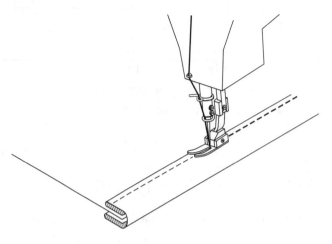

FRENCH BIAS BINDING

French bias binding is similar to single bias binding in that the final appearance is the same. The difference between the two bias treatments is that a single bias binding starts as a single layer of fabric, and French bias binding starts on the fold. A single bias binding is suitable for most fabrics; however, the French bias binding is appropriate for sheer fabrics to conceal raw fabric edges and add thickness to the neckline or armhole edge.

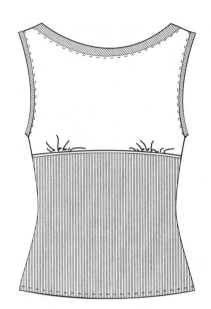

PREPARING FRENCH BIAS STRIPS

Use a 2-inch-wide strip of bias (either in the same color as the garment or a contrasting color) or purchase a commercially prepared single-fold bias tape. Refer to pages 130–131, for "Cutting Bias Strips" and "Joining Bias Strips."

1 Fold the bias strip in half, wrong side to wrong side, and press.

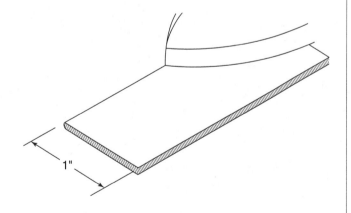

2 Place the garment on a sewing table, correct side up.

3 Place the folded bias strip on the garment, with the correct side down—raw edge to raw edge. Stitch with a $\frac{1}{4}$-inch seam allowance.

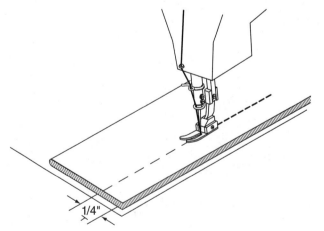

4 Fold the bias binding to the wrong side of the garment, just covering the first stitchline. Press down.

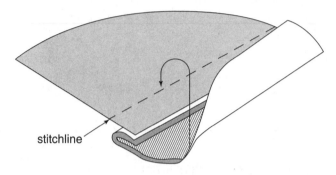

stitchline

5 From the correct side of the garment, stitch in the ditch. Be sure to catch the folded edge of the bias binding on the opposite side.

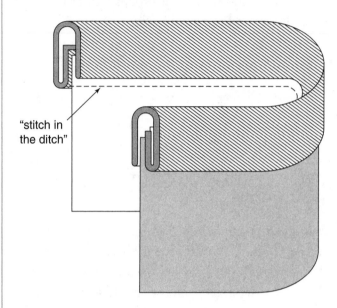

"stitch in the ditch"

SPAGHETTI TUBING

Spaghetti tubing is a self-prepared bias strip, stitched and turned to produce a self-stuffed, clean-finished tubing. Spaghetti tubing can be used to make button loops, spaghetti straps, thin, round belts or ties, and fashionable trims.

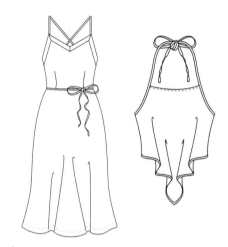

PREPARING SPAGHETTI TUBING BIAS STRIPS

Join the bias strips and cut to the desired length. To determine the width, cut the bias strip either $1\frac{1}{2}$-inches wide or, for wider spaghetti tubing, 2 inches wide. Refer to pages 130–131, for "Cutting Bias Strips" and "Joining Bias Strips."

Note: *The width of the finished spaghetti tubing depends on the distance between the stitchline and the folded edge of the bias strip. When spaghetti tubing is turned correct side out, the seam allowance becomes the filler of the tubing. Heavier fabrics require wider strips than do lighter-weight fabrics.*

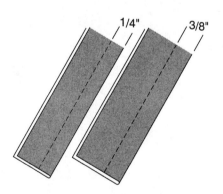

USING A LOOP TURNER

A loop turner, which you can purchase in most fabric stores, is a necessary tool for turning spaghetti strips correct side out. This tool has a latch on one end to catch and pull the fabric through the tubing.

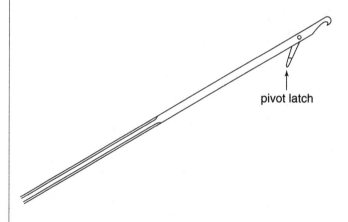

pivot latch

1 Fold the bias strip in half lengthwise, correct side to correct side.

2 Stitch the strip ¼-inch from the folded edge (⅜-inch for heavier fabric), stretching fabric slightly as you sew.

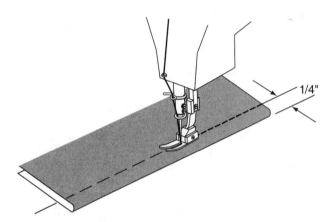

3 Remove the sewn strip from the sewing machine and cut one end of the bias strip at a sharp angle, as illustrated. Do not trim the seam allowance.

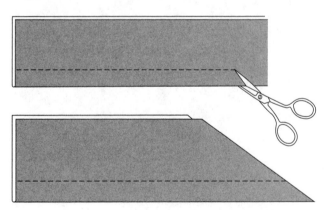

4 Insert the loop turner into the uncut end of the bias.

Note: *Before inserting the loop turner into the bias tubing, position the hook and latch as illustrated.*

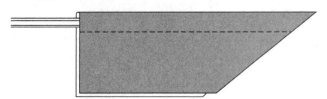

5 Slide the loop turner through the bias tubing until the hook appears at the cut end.

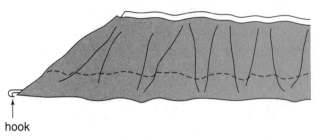

hook

6 At ¼-inch from the end of the bias strip, insert the pivot latch through the fabric. Close the latch over the hook.

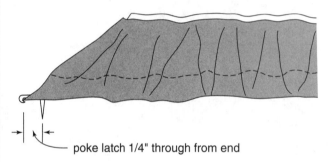

poke latch 1/4" through from end

7 Start turning the bias strip inside-out by gently working the fabric over the hook.

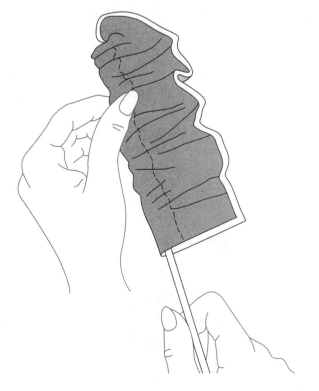

8 Place the ring end of the loop turner over the spool holder on the sewing machine or over another convenient anchor.

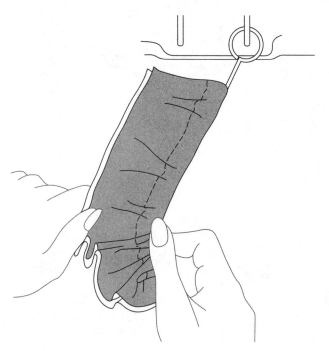

9 With the hook end of the loop turner toward you, work the fabric over hook a little at a time. Continue reversing the bias strip.

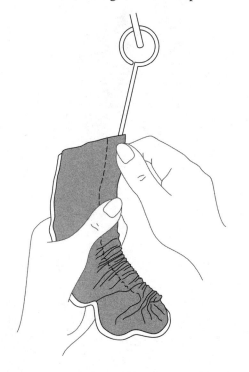

10 When the loop turner emerges from the bias strip, remove the turner and continue the procedure using your hands.

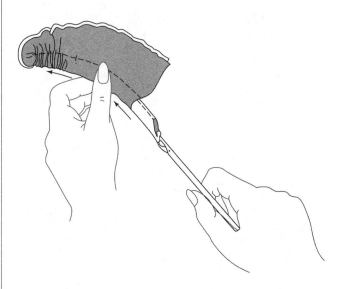

Hint: *If you are using spaghetti tubing for a tie or belt, you can knot the ends, snipping excess fabric from the ends.*

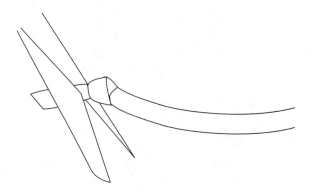

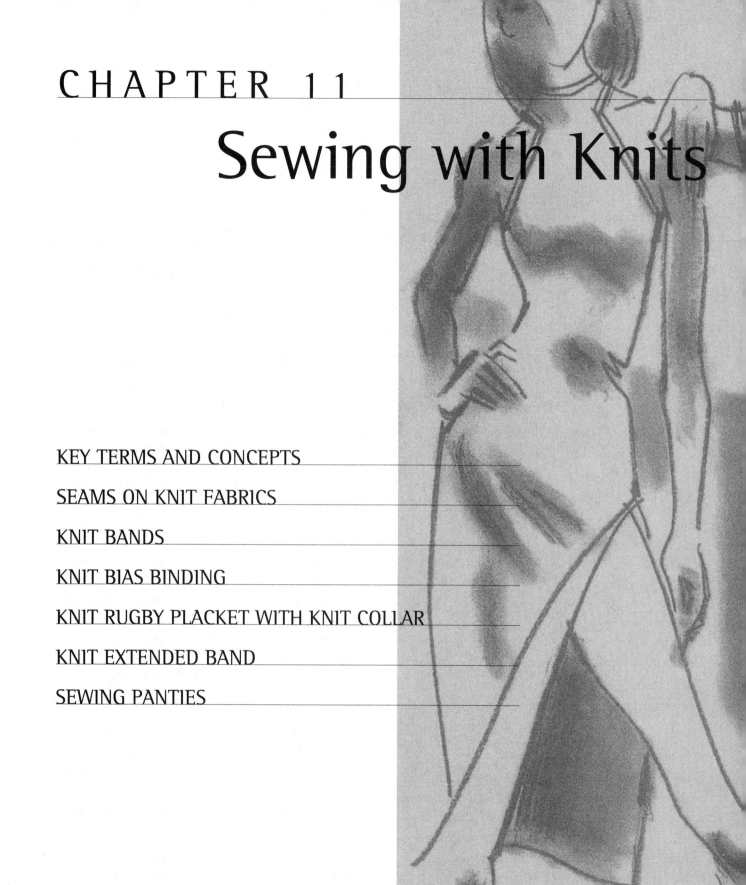

CHAPTER 11
Sewing with Knits

KEY TERMS AND CONCEPTS

Knit fabric is a fabric structure constructed through the process of interlocking loops. It is divided into two general types:

- **Weft knitting** is identified by one continuous yarn forming **courses** across the fabric.
- **Warp knitting** is identified by a series of yarns forming **wales** in the lengthwise direction of the fabric.

Variations in the pattern of knits are achieved by changing the arrangement of the basic stitch or loop.

The important characteristic of a knitted fabric is its capacity to change its dimensions through stretching. The amount and direction of stretch varies according to the knitting process used, the gauge (that is, the size of the stitch), and the denier (that is, the weight of the yarn).

Knitting machines produce either tubular or flat knits in a variety of widths, depending on the type of machine and the specifications of manufacturers.

Knits can be made to stretch in either the course or wale direction, or both, depending on elasticity desired.

The type of knit fabric to use for a sewing project depends on

- The particular properties of the knit fabric
- The desired degree of stretch or stability
- The type and the design of the garment

Double knit is suitable for styled t-shirts and easy dresses. It is firm, flat, and stable. It is the easiest of the knits to sew because it reacts similarly to woven fabrics. It falls into moderately soft flares, and retains its shape in a garment. The fiber content could be polyester, cotton, wool, or wool jersey.

Interlock knit is suitable for styled t-shirts, elastic-waist pants, elastic-waist skirts, and easy dresses. It is flat and slippery smooth, and it has the same appearance on the face and the back. It can accommodate fullness if it is gathered or used with elasticized shirring. Its fullness retains a soft graceful fall. The fiber content could be nylon, polyester, or cotton.

Jacquard knit is suitable for styled t-shirts and fitted dresses with few seams. It can be shaped and molded by stretching, and it falls close to the body contour. The fiber content could be polyester or a nylon or polyester blend.

Jersey knit is suitable for styled t-shirts and easy dresses. It falls into moderately soft flares, and it retains its shape in a garment. The fiber content could be polyester, cotton, wool, or a polyester blend.

Milanese knit is suitable for sweater-look tops, sweater-look dresses, and elastic-waist skirts. It is silky and slippery soft. It has controlled stretch in the crosswise direction and no stretch in the lengthwise direction. It does not curl at the edges. It can accommodate fullness by being gathered or with the use of elasticized stirring. Its fullness retains a soft, graceful fall. The fiber content is usually nylon.

Raschel knit is suitable for loose, easy, swing-type jackets. This knitted fabric imitates crochet or net. It falls into wide cones, its fullness maintains a lofty effect, and it follows the silhouette of the garment. The fiber content could be acrylic, wool, cotton, or polyester.

Rib knit is suitable for necklines, cuffs, and jacket hem bands. It can be shaped by stretching and has high stretch and recovery properties in the crosswise direction. It consists of groups of alternate knit and purl stitches. The fiber content could be acrylic, cotton, or polyester.

Tricot knit is suitable for panties, slips, nightgowns, and pajamas. It falls into soft flares. It can accommodate fullness by being gathered or using elasticized shirring or smocking. It is available in sheer to medium weights. The fiber content is usually made of nylon.

Single knit is suitable for styled t-shirts and easy dresses. It is a flat-surfaced knit fabric with a smooth face and a looped reverse. It stretches in the crosswise direction and has controlled stretch in the lengthwise direction. It falls into soft flares, and its fullness retains a moderately soft fall. The fiber content is usually cotton or a cotton/poly blend.

Spandex, or Lycra yarn, knit is suitable for activewear sports clothing and bathing suits. It has an elastic-like ability to stretch and recover, and can be molded and shaped by stretching. It is made of spandex, or Lycra, combined with nylon.

Knit interfacing is used in collars, cuffs, pocket flaps, and front facing areas. "Easy knit" interfacing is a popular tricot knit interfacing used with knit fabrics.

Needle and Thread Selection

Use the strongest fine thread available and a fine needle. Silk, nylon, spun polyester, and polyester-core threads (mercerized cotton with a polyester wrap, in fine or all-purpose weight) are considered strong, fine threads.

The choice of needle is especially important when sewing with knits. You should use a ballpoint sewing machine needle. The rounded tip of the ball point needle separates rather than punctures the fibers during the stitching process. The needle size depends on the fabric thickness. The needle should be large enough, and therefore strong enough, to penetrate seam layers without being deflected; also, it should have an eye large enough to allow the thread to pass through freely.

Ballpoint needles include sizes 9, 11, 14, 16, and 18, and are available from a variety of manufacturers, such as Dritz, Singer, and Schmetz.

TABLE 11.1 NEEDLE AND THREAD SELECTION CHART FOR KNITS

Knit Fabric	Thread	Ballpoint Needle Size	Stitches per Inch
Very sheer type knit: ■ Nylon tricot	Finer than all-purpose thread—silk or nylon	9	12
Lightweight knit: ■ Lingerie and tricot ■ Lightweight single knit, jersey, or raschel	General-purpose spun silk, nylon, or polyester	11	12
Medium-weight knit: ■ Double knit ■ Spandex ■ Tricot ■ Rib knit	General-purpose spun polyester	14	12
Heavyweight knit: ■ Double knit ■ Velour ■ Bulky knits ■ Stretch denim	General-purpose polyester/cotton	16 to 18	12 to 14

Hint: *Knits with such a sharply pressed fold should be cut to avoid letting the fold fall within a pattern section. The original pressed fold from the bolt of knit fabric can seldom be pressed out. When parts of the pattern must be placed on a fold, it is best to create a new fold and place the pattern fold on this new fabric fold rather than use the origianl bold fold.*

SEAMS ON KNIT FABRICS

Seams on stretch fabric need to be sewn with a stitch that allows the seam to give; otherwise, the stitch might break during wear. Using the following stitches ensures that the stitches remain permanent and produces smooth, strong seams that elongate slightly as the fabric stretches:

- Regular stretch-and-hold seams
- Zig-zag seams
- Straight stitch with zig-zag stitch seam
- Automated stretch stitch seam
- Reinforced taped seams

The method you select for creating seams with knits depends on the characteristics of the fabric and the style of garment you are making.

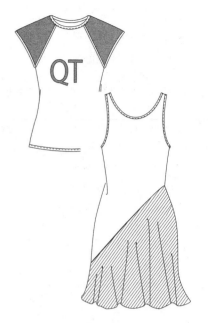

REGULAR STRETCH-AND-HOLD SEAM

When sewing knits, hold the seam on one end and stretch the other end. This stretches the fabric in the same manner as it will stretch when the garment is worn. On most knits, use a regular stitch with nylon or polyester thread, and apply this stretch-and-hold technique. This allows the seam to stretch and not break with the motion of the body. This stretch-and-hold method is used with other stitching methods as well.

Note: *The systematic approach to the construction of a knit t-shirt is illustrated in a simplified summary on page 70 of Chapter 5.*

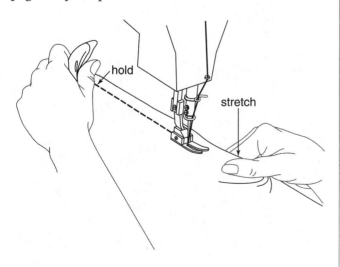

ZIG-ZAG SEAM

A single, narrow zig-zag stitch can also be used. The seam will not lay flat after it is processed. It is suitable for double knits and rib knits.

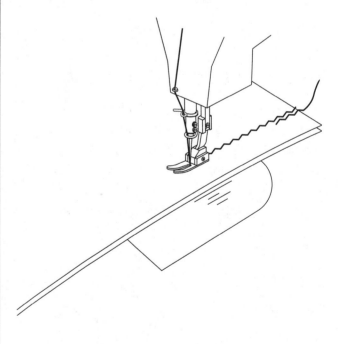

STRAIGHT STITCH WITH ZIG-ZAG STITCH SEAM

A straight stitch (created using the stretch-and-hold technique) along the stitchline, and a zig-zag stitch on the seam allowance side next to the regular straight stitch allows the seam to lay flat. This is used on sportswear and activewear garments made of lycra, fiber, or stretch denim. It is a strong seam because of the zig-zag stitch.

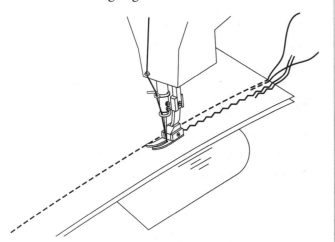

AUTOMATED STRETCH STITCH SEAM

Some sewing machines have a built-in stitch for knit fabrics that can be used in lieu of the regular zig-zag stitch. This stitch usually consists of two stitches forward and one stitch backward, repeated along the stitchline. This stitch can be used on most knits, except very lightweight stretch knits.

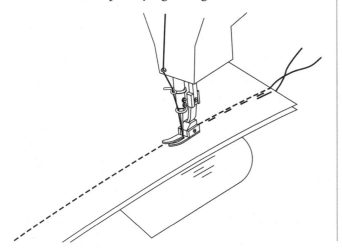

REINFORCED TAPED SEAM

Reinforced taped seams maintain the shape and control the stretching of knit seams, such as armholes, shoulders, and necklines. Choose seam binding or twill tape the color of the fabric, and add it to the seam during the sewing process.

On the wrong side of the fabric, pin baste the seam binding or twill tape to the stitchline of the seam:

- For an armhole seam, stitch the tape and the sleeve to the armhole of the garment when setting the sleeve.

- For a shoulder seam, center and baste the seam binding, and stitch through the seam binding and seam at the same time.

- For a faced neckline that is not being finished with seam binding, baste the twill tape, press, and shape the neckline. Stitch through the twill tape and the facing at the stitchline.

Follow the same technique for any other seam requiring additional reinforcement, such as a zig-zag stitch.

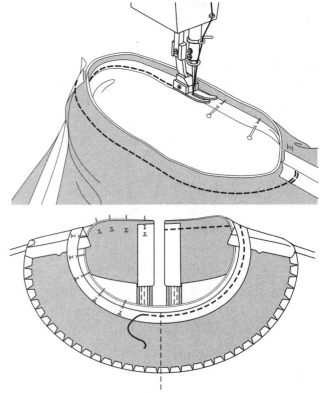

KNIT BANDS

Knit bands are ideal for finishing the neck, wrist, and waist-line edges of garments. These bands give a professional look and provide a comfortable fit to a knit garment.

FIGURING STRETCH ALLOWANCE FOR RIB KNIT

A rib knit, used as a trim, is cut a little shorter than the garment edge and then stretched slightly as it is being stitched to the garment. The following instructions help determine the stretchability of a rib knit being sewn to a traditional knit, such as an interlock knit.

Measure the Desired Length

1 Measure the edge of the garment in which the rib knit is to be sewn.

2 Subtract one third of this measurement.

3 Add a seam allowance ($\frac{1}{2}$ inch or $\frac{5}{8}$ inch) on each end.

Measure the Width

1 Measure the desired width of the rib garment piece.

2 Double this width.

3 Add a seam allowance ($\frac{1}{2}$ inch or $\frac{5}{8}$ inch) on each long end (seam that sews to garment).

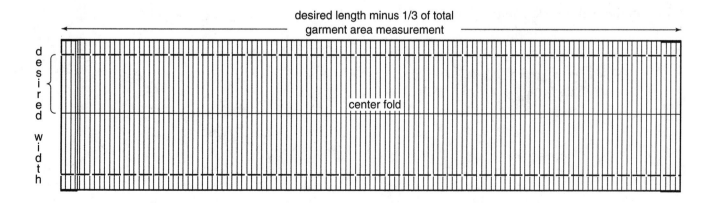

desired length minus 1/3 of total garment area measurement

desired width

center fold

SEWING RIB KNIT TRIM INTO A NECKLINE

1 Cut rib trim (one third less than the actual garment piece measurement), with the stretch going the length of trim.

2 Stitch the ends together, with the desired seam allowance. This will make the piece circular.

3 Press the seam open.

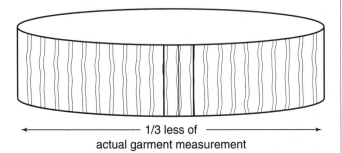

1/3 less of
actual garment measurement

4 Fold the rib trim piece in half lengthwise, enclosing the stitched seam, wrong sides together.

5 Divide the band into four equal sections. Pin mark these divided sections on the open edge of the garment.

6 Place pins on the garment edge at the center front, the center back, and the shoulders (for necklines).

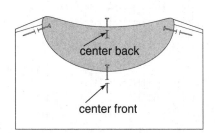

center back

center front

7 With the raw edges of the neckband seam facing up, pin the band to the garment edge. Match all sections previously pin marked.

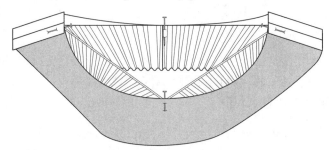

8 Stitch the three raw edges of the neckline seam, with the band side facing up. Start at the center back, and stretch the band as you sew so that the pin marks match up.

9 Stitch a second row. Trim $\frac{1}{4}$-inch away from the stitchline, and overlock this edge if desired.

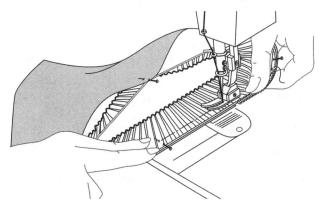

10 Press the entire seam allowance down into the garment, and use steam to shrink out the fullness in the neckband. Press flat.

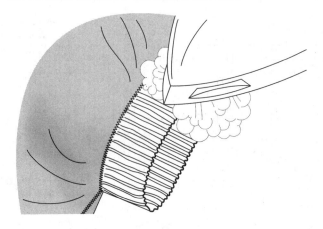

KNIT BIAS BINDING

Knit bias binding is used to finish the raw edges and give a soft roll and decorative trim to the neckline and armholes of knit garments. It replaces facing at the neckline, sleeve, or armhole edges.

The main difference between knit bias and woven bias is that a slight stretch is present in knit bias, which helps to create the soft roll and makes it more appropriate for use with knit fabric.

USING KNIT BIAS STRIPS IN A BODICE

Use $1\frac{1}{2}$- or 2-inch wide strip of bias (either in the same color as the garment or a contrasting color). Also, if the knit fabric stretches a good deal on the crossgrain, you can use the crossgrain in lieu of the bias direction.

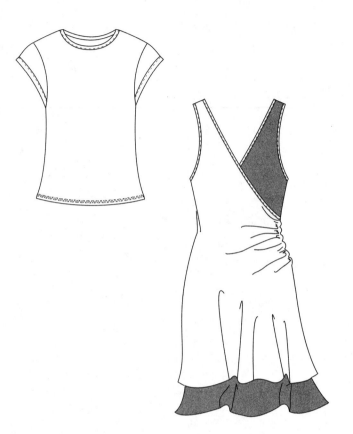

1 Sew the bodice, leaving one shoulder seam not stitched. Place the garment on a sewing table, with the wrong side up.

2 Place the bias strip on the garment, with the correct side down—raw edge to raw edge. Start placing the bias strip at the unstitched shoulder seam.

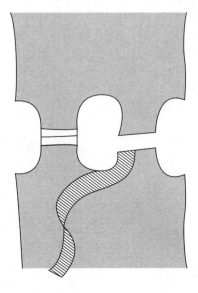

3 While slightly stretching the bias strip, stitch the bias strip to the garment with a $\frac{1}{4}$-inch seam allowance.

4 Turn the garment over so that the correct side is up.

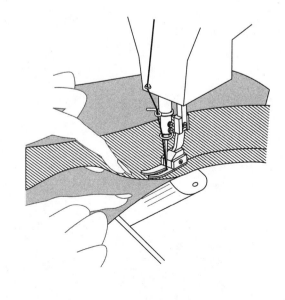

5 Press the entire seam allowance toward the bias strip. Carefully press along the stitchline.

6 Fold the outer edge of the bias strip over $\frac{1}{4}$-inch, and press down.

7 Fold the bias strip in half, to the correct side of garment, just covering the first stitchline.

8 Stitch along the edge of the bias binding.

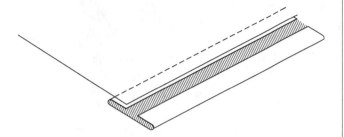

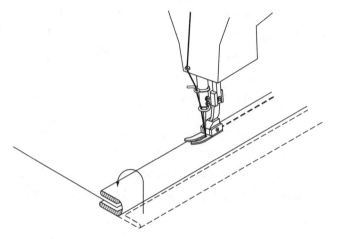

KNIT RUGBY PLACKET WITH KNIT COLLAR

A knit rugby placket with a knit collar is used for a neckline opening. It is usually styled in rugby-type knit shirts worn by men and women. The application of this placket is very similar to the application of the continuous sleeve placket. However, the rugby shirt placket piece is wider, to accommodate buttons and buttonholes.

PREPARING THE GARMENT

Cut the neckline opening, and staystitch the indicated stitchline as illustrated.

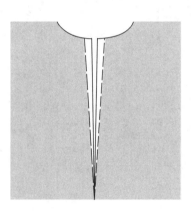

PREPARING THE PATTERN

Use a strip twice as long as the slashed opening and at least $2\frac{1}{2}$-inches wide.

Hint: *To allow greater ease in sewing the placket in place, press all seam allowances and press the placket in half.*

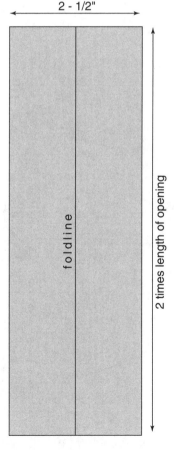

1 Place the front bodice on the sewing table, with the correct side up.

2 Spread the slash open.

3 Place the correct side of the placket to the wrong side of the neckline opening.

Note: *The placket opening of the bodice is placed in a V position to the edge of the placket piece.*

4 Stitch with a $\frac{1}{4}$-inch seam allowance along the entire placket opening.

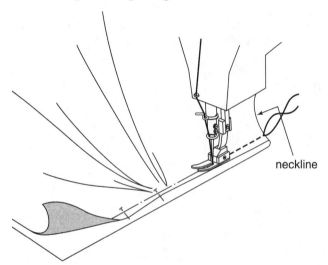

neckline

5 Press under the unsewn $\frac{1}{4}$-inch seam allowance.

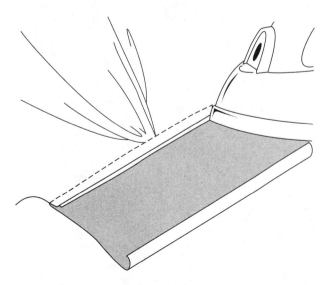

6 Fold over the placket to just past the original stitching, and stitch the placket in place.

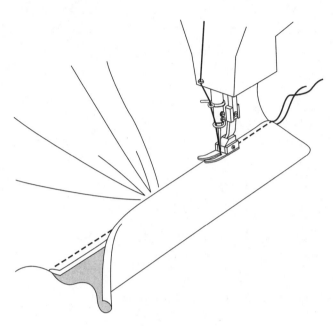

7 Press the placket in the final position. The placket will fold under on the right side of the shirt and extend out on the left side of the shirt (see illustration). Stitch across the bottom of the placket, from the outside of the shirt.

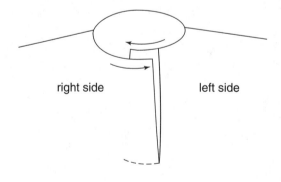

right side   left side

8 Pin a knit collar to the correct side of the neckline (refer to "Collars," pages 229–252). The collar ends should be pinned to each edge of the original stitchline of the placket opening (see illustration).

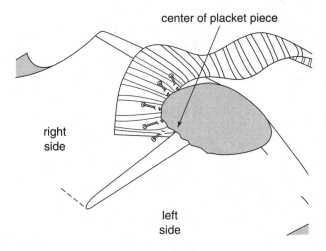

center of placket piece

right side

left side

9 Pin a strip of 1-inch-wide twill tape on top of the pinned collar, around the entire neckline, including the edge of the extended left placket.

10 Stitch along the neck edge.

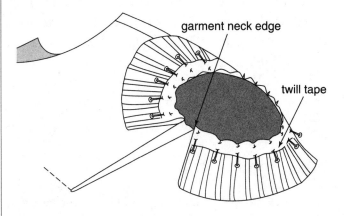

garment neck edge

twill tape

11 Fold the twill tape in place, covering the seam allowance. Stitch across the bottom edge of the tape, along the entire neck edge.

KNIT EXTENDED BAND

The knit extended band is a wide bias piece that extends beyond the garment to form a shaped area around the neckline.

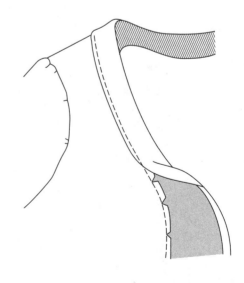

PREPARING BIAS STRIPS

Cut a bias strip the length of the neckline and twice the desired finished width, adding a seam allowance on each side (usually 2 to 3 inches). The bias strip can be either in the same color as the garment or a contrasting color. Also, if the knit fabric stretches a good deal on the crossgrain, you can use the crossgrain in lieu of the bias direction.

JOINING BIAS STRIPS

If the bias cannot be cut long enough for the garment design, it may be necessary to join the bias strips. Refer to "Joining Bias Strips," page 131.

1 Stay stitch the neckline edge.

2 Pin the correct side of the band to the inside of the garment.

3 Stitch the seam, with the band side facing up. Be careful not to stretch the band. Trim the seam allowance to $\frac{1}{4}$-inch.

4 Turn under the seam allowance at the outer edge of the band.

5 Fold the band strip in half, to the correct side of the garment, just covering the first stitchline.

6 Stitch along the edge of the band.

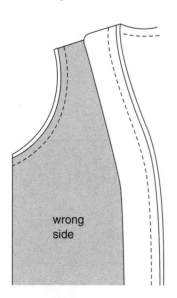

wrong side

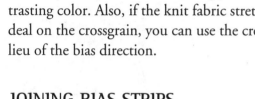

SEWING PANTIES

Panties are sewn with a technique that conceals the crotch seams and creates a double layer of fabric in the crotch area.

1 Cut the panty out of knit fabric that has the same stretch ratio as the desired finished brief.

Note: *It may be preferrable to cut the second layer (lining) of the crotch piece out of cotton knit.*

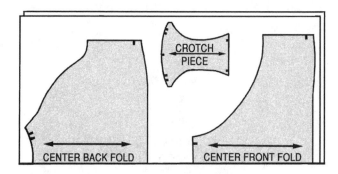

2 Stitch the back crotch seam

A. Sandwich the back seam panty seam between both crotch pieces, matching correct sides and back notches.

B. Stitch the crotch seam and press.

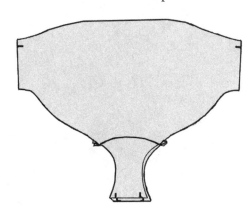

3 Sew the front crotch seam:

A. Pin the front crotch knit piece to the front panty, matching correct sides and notches.

B. Position the wrong side of the panty facing up. Wrap the lining (cotton knit) front crotch piece over the front and back waist and around to the pinned front crotch seam. Match correct side to correct side. Stitch the front crotch seam.

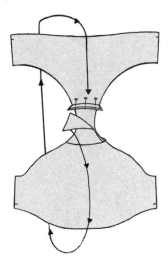

4 Pull the panty correct side out through one of the leg areas.

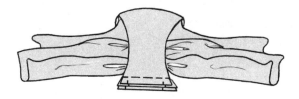

5 Sew the side seams. Match the front and back panty sections to each other, correct side to correct side. Stitch the side seams.

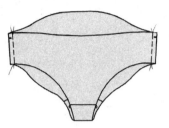

6 Sew the elastic.

A. Stretch elastic to a comfortable fit for the waistline and each leg, subtract 2 inches from each piece.

B. Using a stretch and sew method, single-needle stitch, serge, or zig-zag stitch the elastic to the wrong side of the waistline and the two legging areas.

Note: *Stretch the elastic more in the lower back legging area to create a secure back fit.*

To conceal the elastic, fold the elastic to the wrong side and top-stitch in place using the stretch and sew method.

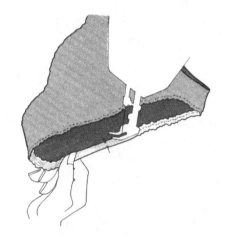

CHAPTER 12

Zippers

KEY TERMS AND CONCEPTS

Zippers provide a convenient access for opening and closing a garment. Several types and lengths of zipper closures exist, and a variety of methods can be used to insert zippers. The type selected depends on the location of the zipper in the garment, the type of fabric, and the design of the garment.

A zipper is a fastening device made with metal teeth or synthetic coils that make a complete closure by interlocking. There are three basic types of zippers:

- The **conventional zipper** opens at the top and has a stop at the bottom. This style is available in a variety of lengths, and is used for garment styles that require a top opening and a bottom closure. This zipper is used on

  - Skirt and neckline openings
  - Trousers, slacks, and pants
  - The finished edges of fitted sleeves
  - The center seam of a hood to convert a hood to a collar
  - Long sleeve openings
  - Horizontally for design detail, such as in pockets

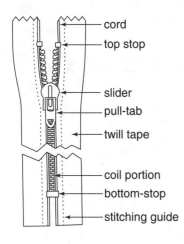

cord
top stop
slider
pull-tab
twill tape
coil portion
bottom-stop
stitching guide

- The **invisible zipper** is similar to the conventional zipper, but because of its special coils is concealed in the seam and is applied using a special sewing foot and instructions. The invisible zipper is used

  - Where any other zipper application would detract from the finished appearance of the garment, such as on matte jersey, velvet, or lace.
  - To give a smooth, continuous seamline.
  - On the lower edge openings of fitted sleeves.

- The **separating zipper** is open at both ends. This type is available in lightweight to heavyweight coils and can be inserted as a decorative zipper where tape and teeth will show on the face of the garment or be concealed beneath the seam folds. This zipper is available in a variety of lengths. The separating zipper is used

  - Wherever two sections of a garment separate completely, such as on a jacket, coat, vest, or parka
  - On detachable hoods
  - To separate linings from dual-season coats and jackets
  - On snowsuits and leggings
  - As a design detail on those listed above.

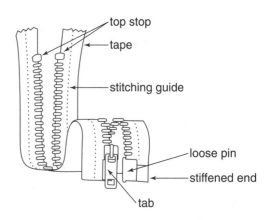

top stop
tape
stitching guide
loose pin
stiffened end
tab

An **adjustable zipper foot** for home machines is a single-toed presser foot that is notched on both sides. It is designed with a shank that is fixed to an adjustable horizontal slide bar to accommodate the needle and facilitate stitching for left and right construction, close to the raised edges of a zipper.

A **half zipper foot or slit foot for industrial machines** has a narrow two-toed base to accommodate the needle. This foot permits sewing close to the raised edge of the zipper teeth or coil. It is used in applications for heavyweight fabrics, or any centered, lapped, or fly-front zipper insertion.

A **cording foot** is a metal presser foot, notched on one side only, to permit sewing close to the raised edge of zipper teeth or coil. Some seamstresses prefer to use the cording foot instead of the adjustable zipper foot.

PREPARING A SEWING MACHINE WITH A ZIPPER FOOT

For all zipper applications, attach the zipper foot to the sewing machine. Position the foot so that the needle is to the side of the zipper being sewn—usually the right side. On an industrial machine, use the half foot to insert zippers.

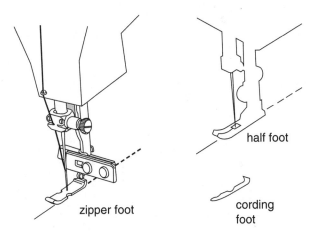

zipper foot

half foot

cording foot

ZIPPER APPLICATIONS

There are several methods of inserting zippers, depending on the placement of the zipper in the garment, the type of zipper, and the type of garment. Popular zipper applications are

- Hand-stitched zipper application, which is used on sheer or couture fabrics, or garments not subject to hard wear or laundering.

- Railroad, or centered, zipper application, which is used on center-front or center-back seams at a neckline or waistline.

- Lapped zipper application, which is used on necklines of dresses and back openings of skirts and pants.

- Fly-front or mock fly zipper application, which is used on men's, women's, or boys' trousers.

- Invisible zipper application, which is concealed in the seam and is applied using a special sewing foot and instructions.

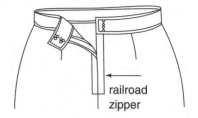

railroad zipper

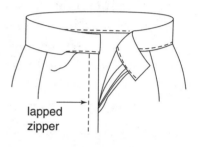

lapped zipper

fly front zipper

RAILROAD, OR CENTERED, ZIPPER APPLICATION

The railroad, or centered, zipper application is the application most commonly used. It is used in center-front or center-back seams at a neckline or waistline. The stitching is visible on both sides of the zipper and is an equal distance from the center.

With the basted seam method, you insert the zipper while the zipper seam allowance is sewn together with a basting stitch.

1 Baste stitch the seamline for the zipper opening. Press the seam allowance open.

Note: *Home sewing patterns usually allow a $\frac{5}{8}$-inch seam allowance for zippers. Industry patterns allow a $\frac{3}{4}$-inch to 1-inch seam allowance.*

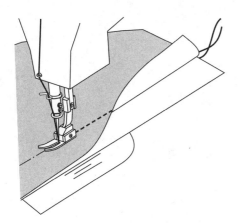

2 Open the zipper and place the correct side of the zipper to the wrong side of the garment, with the zipper teeth against the basted seamline. Pin in place.

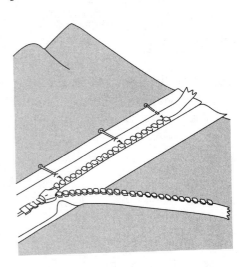

3 Starting from the top edge of the garment, and $\frac{3}{8}$-inch away from the zipper teeth, stitch just beyond the bottom of the zipper.

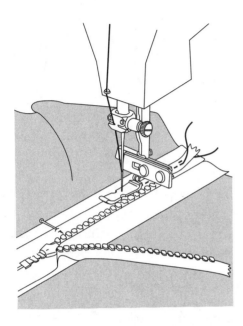

4 With the needle down, lift the presser foot and pivot the garment so that the bottom of the zipper can be sewn. Close the zipper at this time.

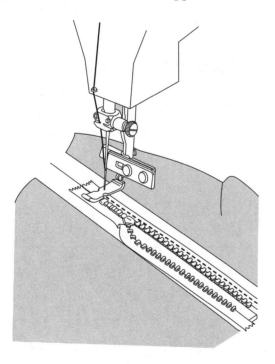

5 Lower the presser foot against the zipper, and stitch across the bottom

6 Once again, with the needle down, lift the presser foot and pivot the garment. Stitch along the other side of the zipper, $\frac{3}{8}$-inch away from the zipper teeth, to the top edge of the garment.

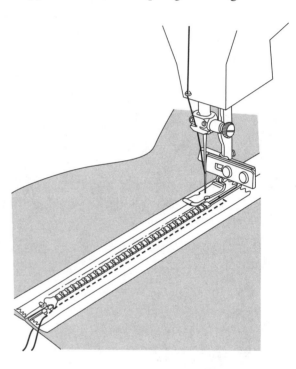

7 Carefully remove the basting stitches and press the completed zipper area.

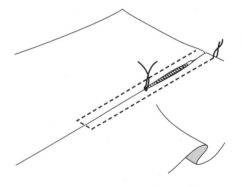

LAPPED ZIPPER APPLICATION

The lapped zipper application conceals the zipper with a fold of the fabric. Only one row of stitching is visible on the correct side of the garment. The lapped zipper application method is especially suitable for neckline zippers on dresses and back openings on skirts and pants.

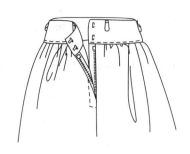

1 Machine stitch the seam, up to the zipper opening.

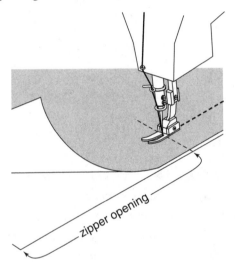

zipper opening

2 Press open the seam allowance needed for the zipper.

Note: *Home sewing patterns usually allow $\frac{5}{8}$-inch seam allowance for zippers. Industry patterns allow a $\frac{3}{4}$-inch to 1-inch seam allowance.*

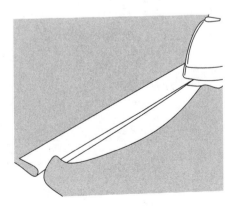

3 Working on the left seam allowance, slide out and pin this seam allowance $\frac{1}{8}$ to $\frac{1}{4}$-inch beyond the pressed seamline.

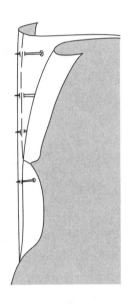

4 With the zipper closed and the correct side of the zipper and fabric area facing up, position one edge of the zipper teeth next to the folded extended seam allowance. Pin in place.

Note: *The zipper tape extends into the seam allowance on the upper edge of the garment.*

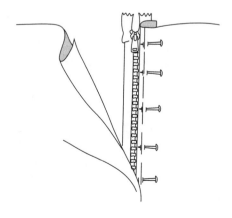

5 Using a zipper foot and starting from the bottom of the zipper, stitch close to the folded edge of the seam allowance for the entire length of the zipper.

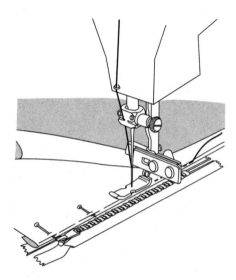

6 With the correct side of the garment facing up, pin the other seam allowance over the closed zipper so that it conceals the zipper and the other stitching.

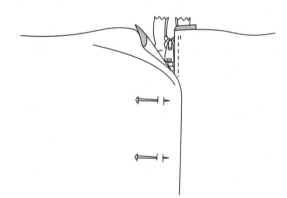

7 Machine-stitch ½-inch away from and parallel to the seam fold, through all layers of fabric and the zipper tape, and across the bottom of the zipper.

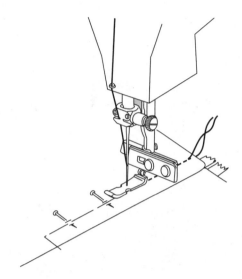

Note: *A variation for the final stitch is to open the zipper and, using a marking on the throat plate as a guide, machine stitch from the top of the zipper to within 1 inch of the bottom. With the needle down, lift the presser foot and close the zipper. Lower the presser foot and stitch to the end of the zipper and across the bottom.*

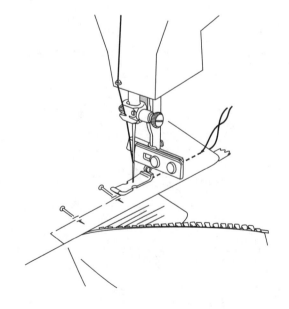

MOCK FLY-FRONT ZIPPER APPLICATION

The mock fly-front zipper application is most often used as a front closing for pants and some skirts. This is the less complicated method of inserting a fly-front zipper.

The pattern pieces will have an extended shaped seam allowance ($1\frac{1}{2}$-inch fly extension) where the zipper goes.

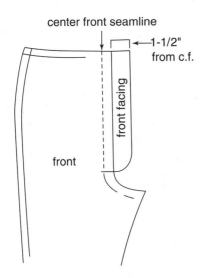

center front seamline

←1-1/2" from c.f.

front facing

front

1 Stitch the crotch seam to the zipper opening (the bottom of the fly extension). Clip at the bottom of the fly extension.

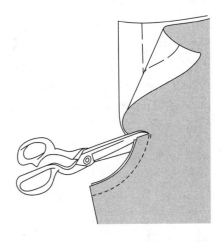

2 Press open the fly extension along the center-front line.

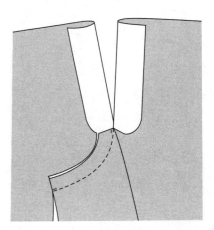

3 Slide out and pin the left fly extension $\frac{1}{8}$ to $\frac{1}{4}$-inch beyond the pressed center-front line.

Note: *This additional $\frac{1}{8}$ to $\frac{1}{4}$-inch must extend the entire length of the zipper opening.*

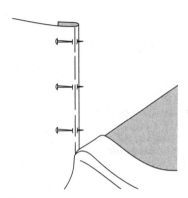

4 With the zipper closed and the correct side of the zipper and fabric facing up, position one edge of the zipper teeth next to the folded extended side. Pin in place.

Note: *The zipper tape extends into the seam allowance on the upper edge of the garment.*

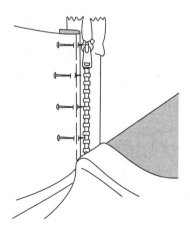

5 Using a zipper foot and starting from the bottom of the zipper, stitch close to the folded edge of the seam allowance, the entire length of the zipper.

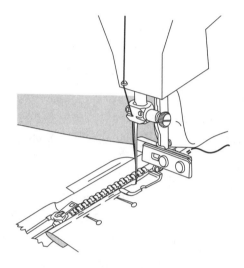

6 With the correct side of the garment facing up, pin the other folded fly-extension seam allowance over the closed zipper so that it conceals the zipper and the other stitching.

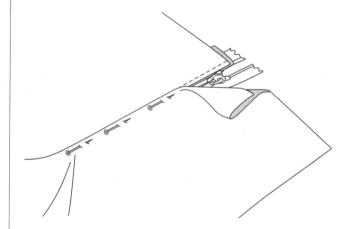

7 With the wrong side of the garment facing up, flip the garment back to expose the unsewn fly extension and zipper tape. Sew the zipper tape to the fly extension. Keep the garment free of this area so that this stitching will not go through the garment.

8 Turn the garment to the correct side. Machine stitch $\frac{3}{4}$-inch away from and parallel to the fly fold, through all the layers of fabric, curving to meet the bottom of the zipper.

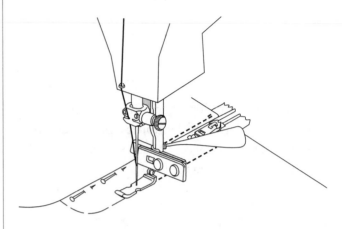

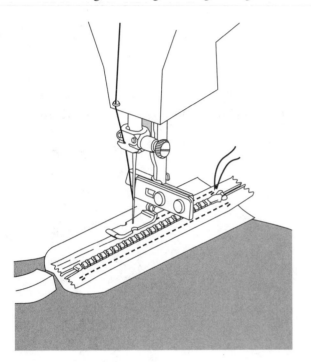

FLY-FRONT ZIPPER APPLICATION

The fly-front zipper application uses a more tailored detail and is used in both women's and men's fly-front-opening pants.

Prepare a separate zipper-facing piece (2 inches wide and the length of the zipper tape). Then prepare two fly-shield pieces (2 inches wide and the length of the zipper tape).

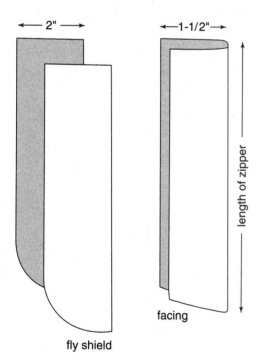

fly shield

facing

1 Stitch the crotch seam up to the zipper opening. Clip at the bottom of the fly extension.

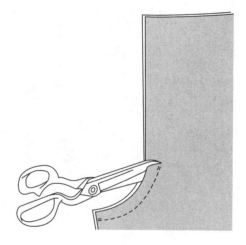

2 Fold the facing piece in half (correct side facing up) and place it to the correct side of the right crotch seam.

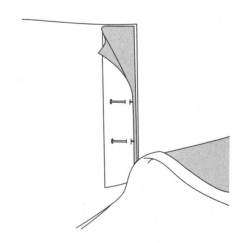

3 Stitch the facing piece to the crotch seam, using a $\frac{1}{4}$-inch seam allowance.

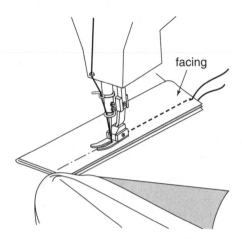

4 Flip the facing away from the pants and turn the seam allowance to the facing. Top stitch $\frac{1}{8}$-inch away from the seamline.

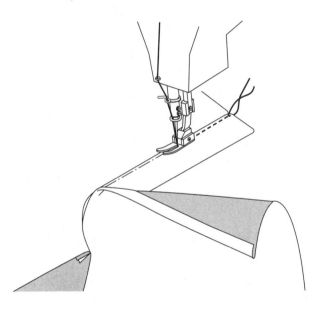

5 Prepare the fly-shield pieces by stitching the curved edges together, with a $\frac{1}{4}$-inch seam allowance.

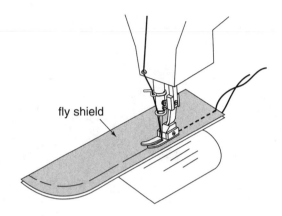

6 Turn the fly-shield pieces to the outside and press.

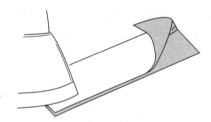

7 With the wrong side of the zipper facing up, place the zipper between the prepared fly shield and the correct side of the crotch seam. Pin in place.

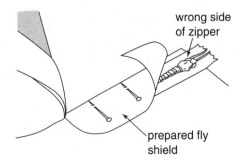

8 Using the zipper foot, stitch through all the layers of fabric and the zipper tape, the entire length of the fly shield.

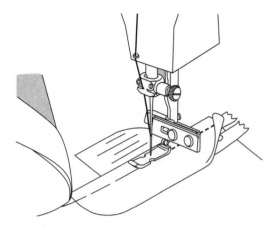

9 Lay the correct side of the pants facing up on the sewing table, with the zipper closed and the fly shield and zipper flipped away from the pants. To help reinforce and strengthen the zipper application, edge stitch the zipper seam.

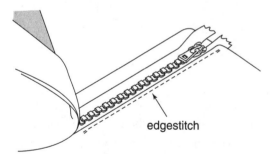

edgestitch

10 In this position, pin the other crotch seam (with the attached facing folded under) over the closed zipper so that the zipper is concealed.

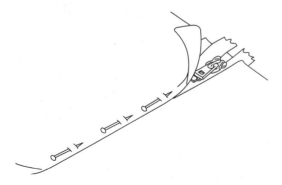

11 Turn the pants to the wrong side. Flip the garment back to expose the facing and the zipper. Sew the zipper tape to the facing. Keep the garment and the fly shield free of this area so that this stitching will not go through the garment.

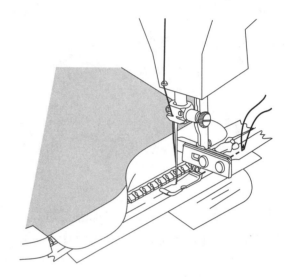

12 Turn the garment to the correct side. Hold the fly away from the zipper and keep the pinning in position. Machine stitch $\frac{3}{4}$-inch away from parallel to the seam, through all the layers of fabric, curving in at the bottom of the opening.

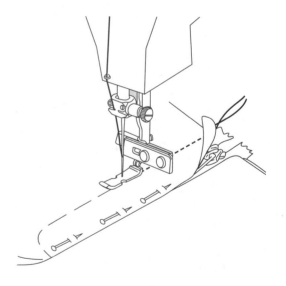

INVISIBLE ZIPPER APPLICATION

The invisible zipper is used instead of a conventional zipper if it is desirable to retain the look of a plain seam (for example, on an evening gown), where the zipper stitching would spoil the line of the garment.

Note: *A special zipper foot attachment is required to insert an invisible zipper. This special attachment may be purchased at most fabric stores.*

Note: *The invisible zipper is inserted before the two garment pieces are sewn together and before the top edge is faced or finished.*

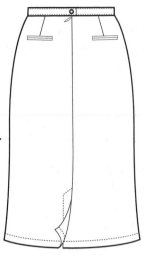

1 Press the zipper so that the coils stand away from the tape.

2 Open the invisible zipper and place it on the left garment piece, on the correct side of the fabric, with the wrong side of the zipper facing up. The zipper teeth should be placed along the stitchline and the zipper tape toward the outer edge of the seam allowance. Baste in place.

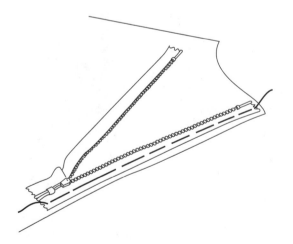

3 Place the lefthand groove of the zipper foot over the coils of the zipper. Roll the coil away from the zipper tape, and slowly stitch the zipper to the fabric until the foot touches the pull tab.

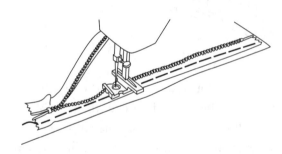

4 Close the zipper and place both the right and left garment pieces on top of each other, matching correct sides and zipper stitchlines. Baste in place.

Hint: *To help position the zipper correctly, use markings along the zipper tape and the seam allowance.*

Note: *The zipper teeth should be placed along the stitchline and the zipper tape toward the outer edge of the seam allowance.*

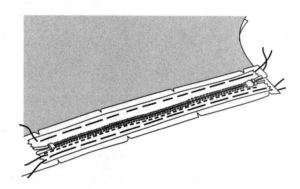

5 Open the zipper and position the righthand groove of the zipper foot over the coils of the zipper. Roll the coil away from the zipper tape and slowly stitch the second side in place, finishing at the pull tab.

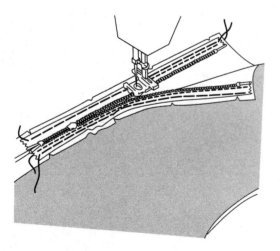

6 Close the zipper. Slide the special foot to the left so that the needle is in line with the edge of the foot. The conventional zipper foot can be placed on the machine at this time.

7 Place the end of the zipper out and away from the seam area. Stitch the garment seam closed along the seamline, from the bottom stitching of the zipper to the remainder of the garment seam.

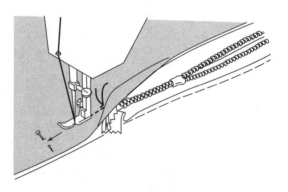

8 Press the seam allowance open and stitch the ends of the zipper tapes to the seam allowances.

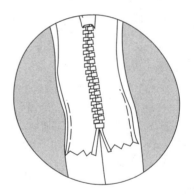

CHAPTER 13

Pockets

KEY TERMS AND CONCEPTS

A **pocket** is a shaped piece of fabric set either on the outside of a garment or into a garment seam or opening. Used as a decorative detail to carry small articles, such as handkerchiefs or coins.

Pockets are the most obvious details on men's and women's garments. Besides being functional, they add style to the design of the garment.

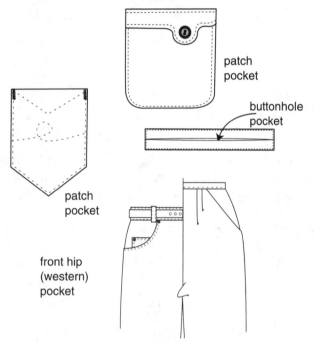

patch
pocket

buttonhole
pocket

patch
pocket

front hip
(western)
pocket

Pockets are designed in a variety of sizes and shapes and can be applied to the outside of the garment or sewn into the garment itself (for example, welt or buttonhole pocket). The special method of application required for each type of pocket is explained in this chapter.

There are four main types of pockets

- The **patch pocket** is stitched to the surface of the garment. It can have a rounded or square corners at the base. A patched flap for the pocket can be made in the same way. Patch pockets can be styled into skirts, pants, blouses, shirts, jackets, or coats.

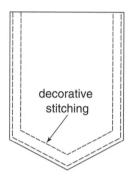

decorative
stitching

- The **in-seam pocket** is sewn neatly into the side seam or styled seam of a garment and is usually made from matching fabric. It cannot be seen when the garment is worn.

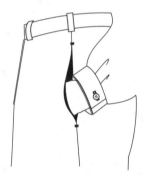

- The **front hip pocket** is an angled or curved pocket design on the front of pants and skirts. They are attached to the waist and side seam of the garment.

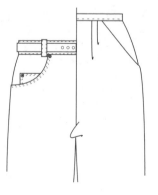

The **inside set-in pocket** is sewn into a slashed opening made with a single or double welt, with or without a pocket flap. These are usually referred to as "bound" pockets. They differ only in the style of the welts and/or flaps that are sewn into the slashed opening. The four most common bound pockets are

The welt bound pocket

The one-piece bound buttonhole pocket

The lined bound buttonhole pocket

The bound flap pocket

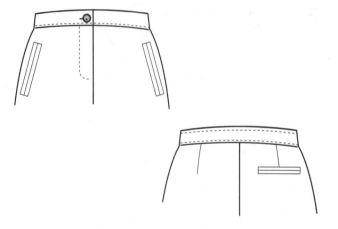

TRANSFERRING PATTERN MARKINGS

Transfer the exact markings indicating the location of the pocket from the pattern to the wrong side of the garment, with hand basting or pins. Pin and pencil mark the pocket markings to the correct side of the garment.

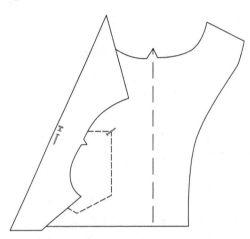

PATCH POCKET

Patch pockets are both decorative and useful and are most often part of the design for shirts, blouses, dresses, and jackets. They are made from a single layer of fabric that is hemmed and sewn to the outside of the garment with a finish suitable to the fabric. Patch pockets can be square, rectangular, pointed, or curved and can be decorated with braid or other trims.

Note: *Because patch pockets are attached to the outside of the garment, they must be made carefully and accurately to enhance and not detract from the garment's finished look.*

Note: *Refer to "Transferring Pattern Markings" on page 173 in this chapter.*

1 Cut the desired patch pocket shape and size needed for the garment design.

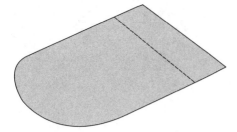

2 Fold over the top edge of the pocket $\frac{1}{4}$-inch and edge stitch.

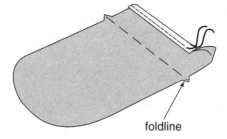

foldline

3 Turn the facing allowance along the foldline, correct sides together. Pin in place.

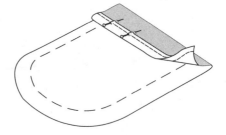

4 Stitch the pocket and the facing along the seamline, continuing around the pocket edge.

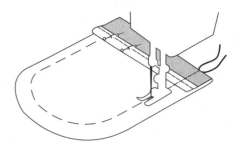

5 Trim the corners of the facing edge.

Note: *To create patch pockets with round edges, snip the curves to create a smoother surface. For square edges, miter the corners.*

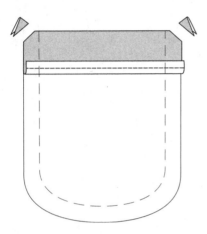

6 Turn the facing and the seam allowance to the inside, folding the seam allowance along the stitchline. Press in place.

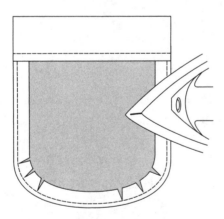

7 Lay the garment on a flat surface and carefully pin the pocket onto the garment at the desired pocket location.

8 Top stitch or edge stitch the pockets to the garment, using the edge of the presser foot as a seam guide.

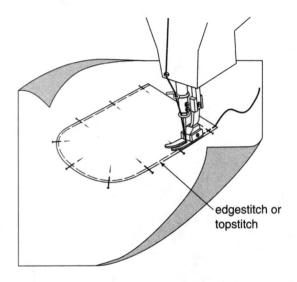

edgestitch or topstitch

9 Back stitch to reinforce the top corners of the pocket.

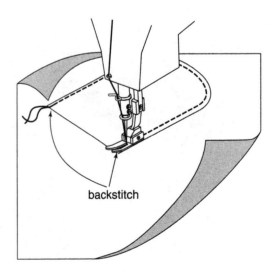

backstitch

LINED PATCH POCKET

A completely lined patch pocket provides a custom finish to a garment. The lining should be made of a traditional lining fabric and matched to the color of the garment fabric.

Note: *Refer to "Transferring Pattern Markings" on page 173 in this chapter.*

1 Cut the pocket and lining exactly the same size and shape.

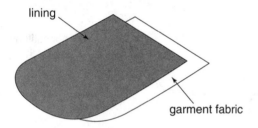

2 Pin together the correct sides of the pocket and the lining.

3 Stitch the lining to the pocket, following the seamline. Leave a small portion of the bottom edge unstitched.

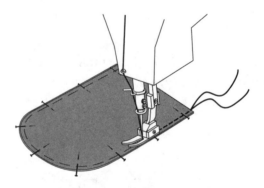

4 Trim the corners of the seam allowance, and, if necessary, trim the excess seam allowance.

5 Turn the pocket to the correct side, gently pushing the pocket through the open seam.

6 Carefully push out all the corners, using an awl or a pin. Roll the unsewn seam section at the bottom of the pocket to the inside so that the seam is not visible from the correct side of the pocket. Press the pocket flat.

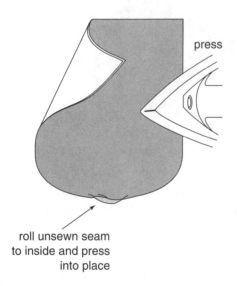

press

roll unsewn seam
to inside and press
into place

7 Lay the garment on a flat surface and carefully pin the pocket onto the garment at the desired pocket location.

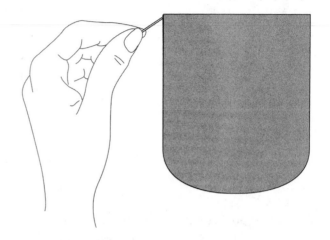

8 Top stitch or edge stitch the pocket to the garment, using the edge of the presser foot as a seam guide. Back stitch to reinforce the top corners of the pocket.

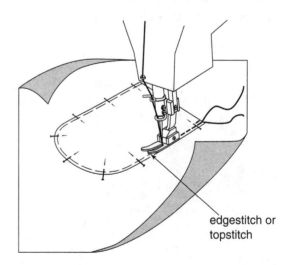

edgestitch or
topstitch

LINED PATCH POCKET WITH FACING

A lined patch pocket with an attached facing requires a partial lining and a facing on the inside of the pocket. This pocket functions the same as any other patch pocket; however, it provides a finish with more flair and adds style to the garment.

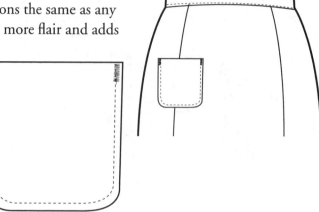

1 Cut two pocket pattern pieces, one from the garment fabric and the other from the lining fabric. The pocket lining should be measured while the pocket facing is folded. Measure from the bottom of the pocket up to the pocket facing stitch-line, with the pocket still folded, and then add a $\frac{1}{2}$-inch seam allowance. (This seam allowance is necessary to sew the lining to the facing area.)

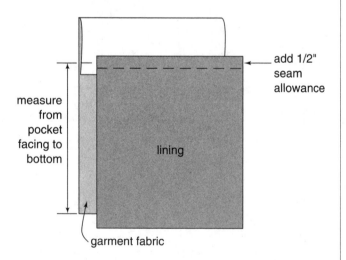

measure from pocket facing to bottom

add 1/2" seam allowance

lining

garment fabric

2 Pin the top edge of the lining to the top edge of the pocket (the extended facing portion), correct sides together.

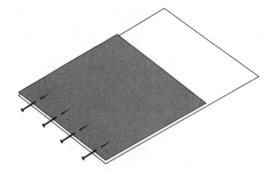

3 Stitch the lining and the pocket together, with a $\frac{1}{4}$-inch seam allowance along the top edge, using a permanent stitch. Leave a 1-inch opening at the center of the pocket. Press the seam open.

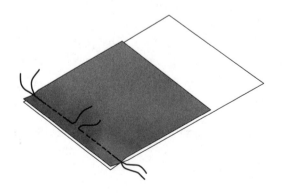

4 Pin the pocket and the lining together, matching all raw edges. The pocket pieces are still correct side to correct side.

Note: *The pocket facing area will automatically fold to the inside and create the facing area.*

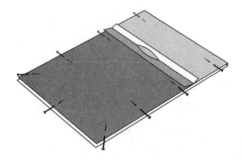

5 Stitch the lining to the pocket, following the seamline.

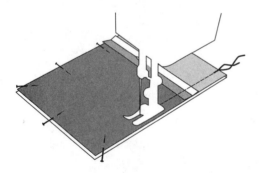

6 Trim the corners of the seam allowance, and, if necessary, trim the excess seam allowance.

7 Turn the pocket to the correct side through the opening in the seam. Carefully push out the corners with a pin. Press the pocket flat.

8 Slipstitch the opening closed.

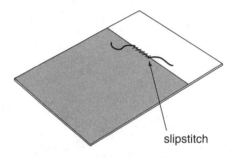

slipstitch

9 Lay the garment on a flat surface and carefully pin the pocket onto the garment at the desired pocket location.

10 Top stitch or edge stitch the pocket to the garment, using the edge of the presser foot as a seam guide. Back stitch to reinforce the top corners of the pocket.

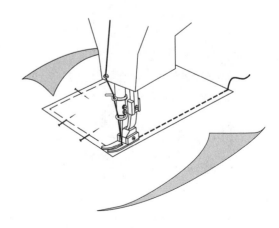

SELF-LINED PATCH POCKET

A self-lined patch pocket is a pocket cut double the size of the desired pocket and folded in the middle. This type of pocket is used in budget and easy-to-sew clothes.

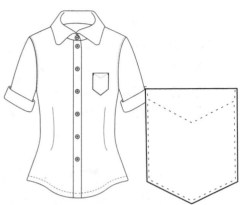

1 Double the size of the desired pocket and cut the piece.

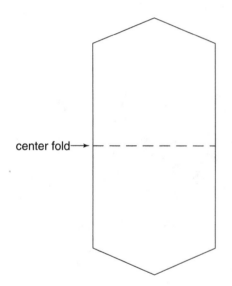

center fold→

2 Fold the pocket in half, with correct sides together. If necessary, pin in place.

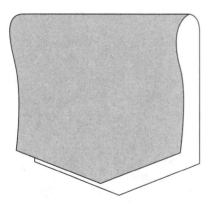

3 Stitch along the seamline.

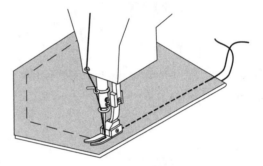

4 Slash one layer of the pocket near the bottom. If necessary, trim the corners and seam allowance.

slash one layer only

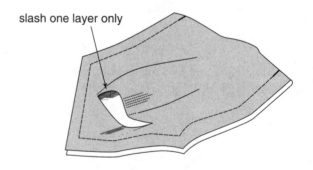

5 Turn the pocket correct side out, gently pushing it through the slash.

6 Push out all corners, rolling the seam to the inside (the slashed side) so that the seam is not visible from the correct side of the pocket. Press the pocket flat.

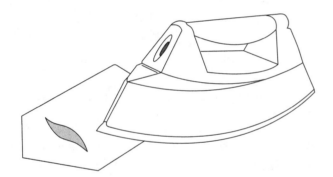

7 Lay the garment on a flat surface and carefully pin the pocket onto the garment at the desired pocket location.

Note: *The slash is hidden because it lays next to the correct side of the garment and remains unfinished.*

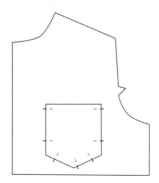

8 Top stitch or edge stitch the pocket to the garment, using the edge of the presser foot as a seam guide.

9 Back stitch to reinforce the top corners of the pocket.

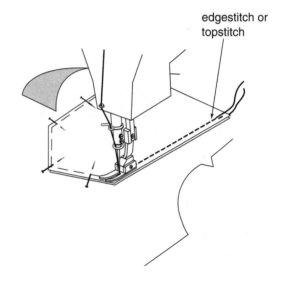

edgestitch or topstitch

FRONT HIP POCKET

A front hip pocket can have an opening in a variety of shapes, such as a square, diagonal, or slight curve. This shape is attached at the waistline and ends at the side seam of the garment. It is used in skirts and in both men's and women's pants.

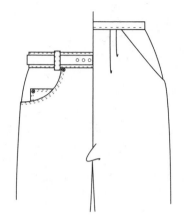

1 Cut a pocket facing and an under pocket. These pocket sections are usually cut out of the same fabric as the garment.

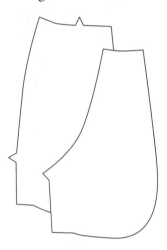

2 Place the pocket facing to the garment section, correct sides together, matching all raw edges.

3 Stitch the pocket facing to the garment.

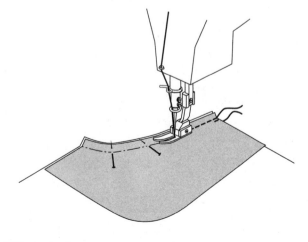

4 If the seam allowance is more than $\frac{1}{4}$-inch, trim it and clip any curves.

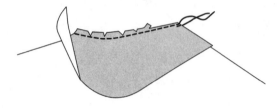

5 Understitch the seam allowance to the pocket facing.

Note: *Press the entire seam allowance to the pocket facing side and understitch the pocket facing $\frac{1}{8}$-inch from the seamline.*

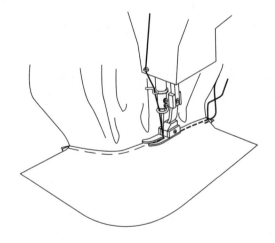

6 Turn the pocket to the wrong side of the garment and press.

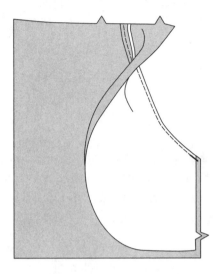

7 Pin the under pocket to the pocket facing along the pocket curved edges, matching correct sides.

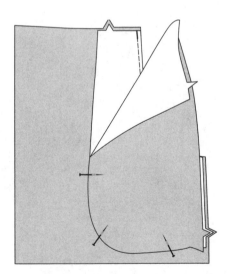

8 Stitch the pocket facing and the under pocket around the curved edges.

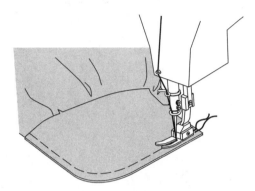

9 Finish pinning the pocket in place by matching the waistline of the pocket to the waistline of the garment and the side seam of the pocket to the side seam of the garment. If necessary, machine baste along these edges.

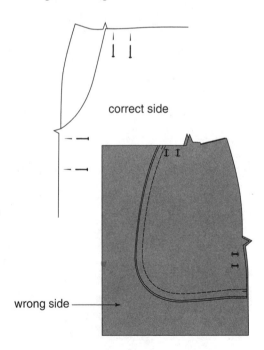

correct side

wrong side

IN-SEAM POCKET

An in-seam pocket is sewn into a seam and cannot be seen when the garment is worn. In-seam pockets are frequently placed in the side seams of dresses, skirts, and pants. This type of pocket is very popular because it is very useful.

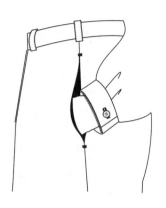

1 Cut two pocket pieces for each in-seam pocket.

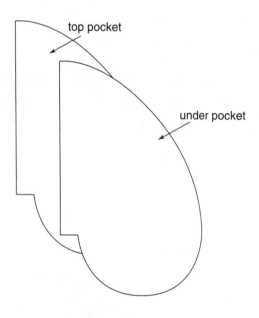

top pocket

under pocket

2 Pin the top pocket to the front seam of the garment and the under pocket to the back seam, correct sides together, matching the side seamline raw edges of the pocket extension.

3 Stitch the pocket pieces to the garment, following the length of the pocket opening at the seam.

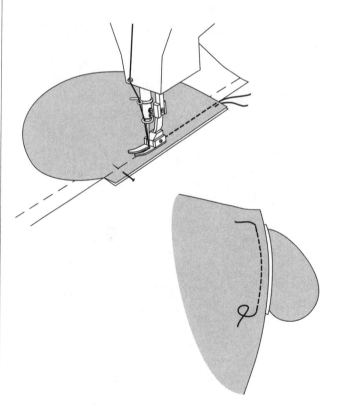

4 Press the seam allowance of each pocket open.

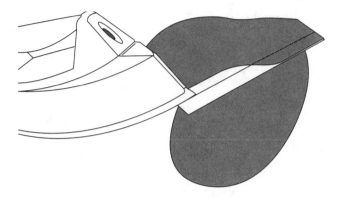

5 Place front and back garment pieces (with the attached pockets) correct sides together. Match the pocket shapes and the seams accurately.

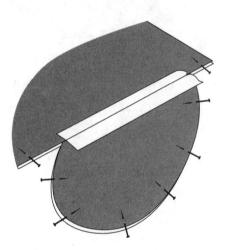

6 Sew the garment seam in one stitching process: Stitch from the top of the seam down to the end of the seam, following the markings and shape around the pocket area.

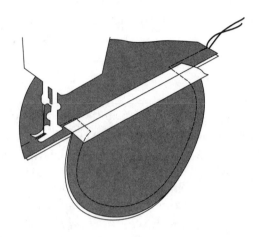

7 To press the pocket and side seams, turn the pocket toward the front of the garment. Clip the seam allowance at the top and bottom of the pocket. Press the seam allowances of the garment above and below the pocket open.

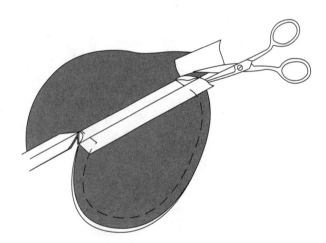

PATCH POCKET WITH FLAP OR DECORATIVE FLAP

A pocket flap is a free-hanging piece that covers the top of a patch pocket on a garment, such as a tailored shirt or vest for men or women. The separate flap of a patch pocket is stitched to the garment above the pocket opening, and then pressed down over the pocket and top stitched into the final position. Pocket flaps may be rounded or square at the lower corners. Sometimes flaps are sewn onto garments strictly as a decorative design detail.

1 Cut two identical pieces in the desired flap shape. If necessary, for lightweight fabrics, cut a third piece out of interfacing, and attach the interfacing to the outer flap piece.

Note: *The flap pieces are usually $\frac{1}{4}$-inch wider than the pocket pieces. The flap must extend beyond each side of the pocket. This ensures that the pocket edges are covered when the flap is down.*

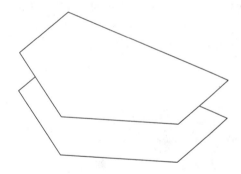

2 Pin the two flap pieces, correct sides together, matching all corners.

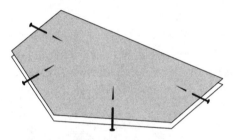

3 Stitch the two flap pieces together, following the stitchline around three edges. Leave the top portion of the flap open.

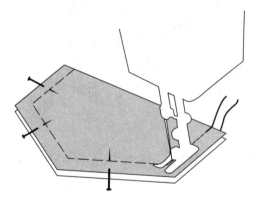

4 Clip the corners of the seam allowances. Trim the excess seam allowances.

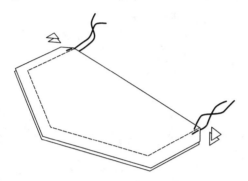

5 Turn the flap correct side out and carefully press flat.

6 If desired, top stitch or edge stitch the flap, using the edge of the presser foot as a seam guide.

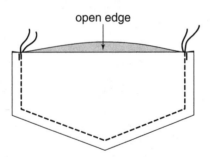

open edge

7 Place the flap above the desired patch pocket. (Follow the directions for any of the patch pockets discussed previously.) Remember that the flap must extend beyond each side of the pocket. (This ensures that the pocket edges are covered when the flap is down.) Pin in place.

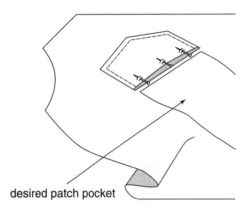

desired patch pocket

8 Stitch the flap to the garment along the stitch-line on the open edge. Industry garments usually use a $\frac{1}{4}$-inch seam allowance, and home sewing garments usually use a $\frac{5}{8}$-inch seam allowance.

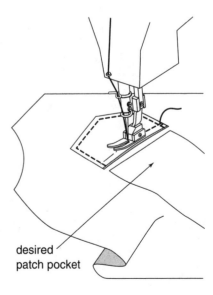

desired
patch pocket

9 Trim the seam allowance of this seam to $\frac{1}{8}$-inch to ensure that this seam is hidden under the top stitching you do in step 11.

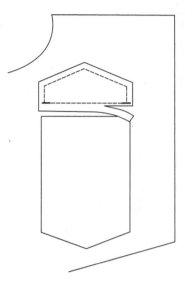

10 Fold and press the flap down in the finished position.

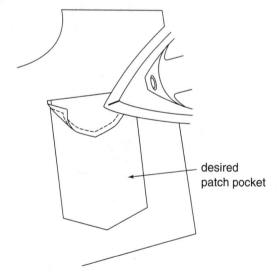

desired patch pocket

11 Top stitch the flap through all thicknesses, $\frac{1}{4}$-inch from the top folded edge. This stitch maintains the flap in position and completely encloses the seam allowance.

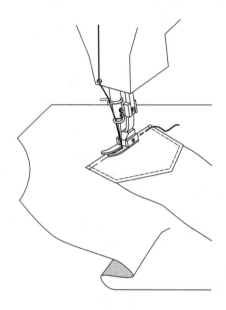

WELT BOUND POCKET

A welt bound pocket is a set-in pocket that is sewn into a special slashed opening, finished by an upstanding welt that may be from $\frac{1}{2}$-inch wide to 1-inch wide. Frequently used in designer coats and suit jackets as well as in pants, skirts, blouses, and shirts for women, men, and children. For different styling features, the fabric used for the welt may be different from the fabric used for the garment. Although the process for sewing welt pockets is simple, very precise construction steps are required.

1 Cut three pattern pieces: a top pocket lining, an under pocket, and the welt.

desired width +
seam allowance

welt | 2"

desired width +
seam allowance

1/2"

desired length

top pocket lining

3 Fold the welt piece in half, correct sides together.

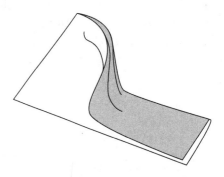

...d of the welt closed, usually with ... allowance. Trim the corners.

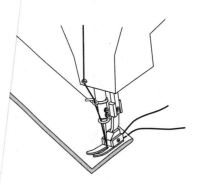

2 Mark the desired po... pocket on the corre... using a horizontal basti... amount needed for the... mines the length of th...

pocket position line

5 Turn the welt correct side out and press flat.

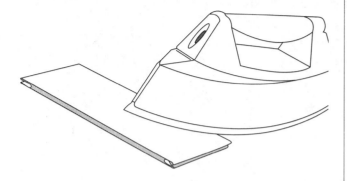

6 Place the garment on a sewing table, correct side up. Place the welt on the correct side of the garment, with the open edge along the pocket position line, as illustrated. Baste the welt in place.

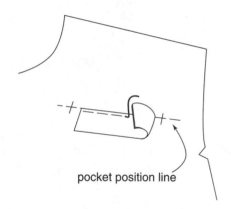

pocket position line

7 Place the under pocket piece (the longer piece) at the top of the pocket position, as illustrated. Place the top pocket lining (the shorter lining piece) over the welt and below the pocket position line, as illustrated, correct sides together. Baste the pieces in place.

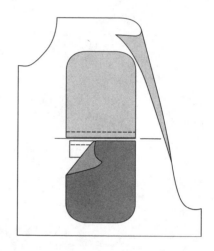

8 Stitch the welt and the two pocket pieces to the garment in a rectangle, $\frac{1}{4}$-inch from the pocket position line and $\frac{1}{2}$-inch from the pocket raw edges.

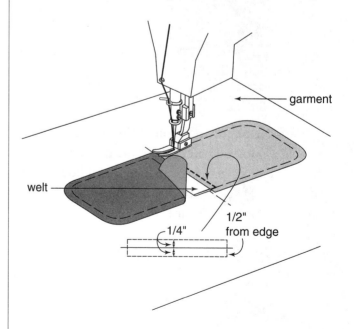

garment

welt

1/2"
from edge

1/4"

9 Cut through the garment along the pocket position line to $\frac{1}{2}$-inch from the ends and diagonally to the corners.

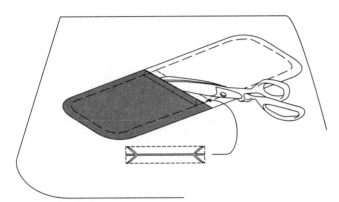

10 Turn the pocket pieces through the slit to the wrong side of the garment.

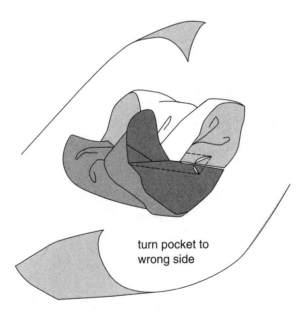

turn pocket to
wrong side

Note: *On the wrong side of the garment, the two pocket pieces will lay flat below the pocket opening, with correct sides together and edges matching. On the correct side of the garment, the welt will fill the pocket opening with the folded edge of the welt upward in position.*

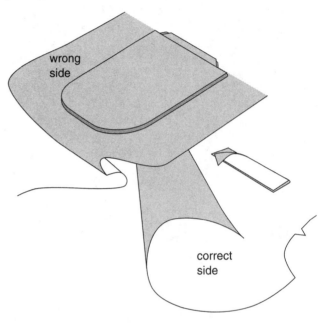

wrong
side

correct
side

11 Place the garment on a sewing table, correct side up. Fold the garment back, exposing the pocket pieces and the triangle created by the clipping. Stitch the pocket edges together, catching the triangle ends and following the stitchline around the pocket.

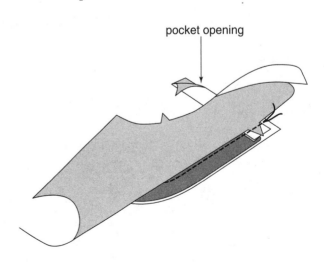

pocket opening

12 On the correct side of the garment, press the welt upward and pin into position.

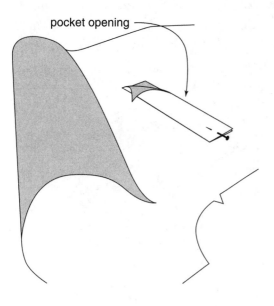

pocket opening

13 To complete the pocket, hand or machine stitch the welt piece to the garment along each edge.

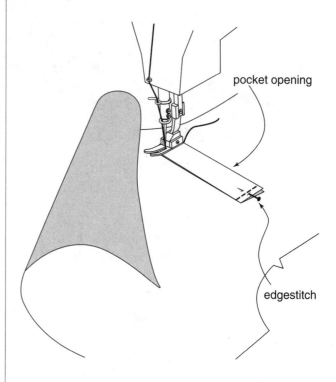

pocket opening

edgestitch

ONE-PIECE BOUND BUTTONHOLE POCKET

A one-piece bound buttonhole pocket is created by using a portion of the pocket section that is pleated into a sewn and slashed rectangular pocket opening, creating two small welts on both sides of the slashed opening. This gives the look of a bound buttonhole.

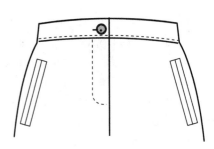

This type of pocket is usually made on garments made of lightweight fabric. (A heavier-weight fabric requires a lining and, consequently, a different sewing technique.) The one-piece buttonhole pocket is an easier and faster method than the lined buttonhole pocket. A one-piece buttonhole pocket is frequently used in designer coats and suit jackets, as well as in pants, vests, and shirts.

1 Double the size of the desired pocket, add 1-inch to the length, and cut the piece.

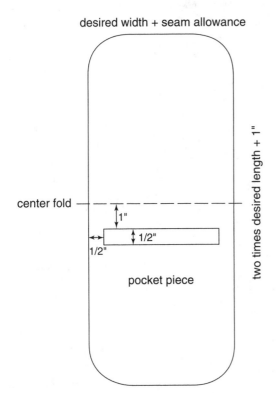

desired width + seam allowance

center fold

1"

1/2"

1/2"

pocket piece

two times desired length + 1"

2 Mark the desired pocket position on the correct side of the garment with a horizontal basting stitch or pencil line. The amount needed for the pocket hand opening determines the length of the line.

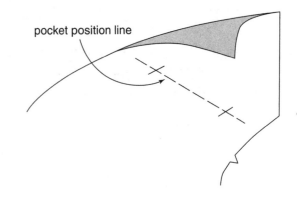

pocket position line

3 Place the garment on a sewing table, correct side up. Place the pocket piece on the garment, with the desired pocket opening along the pocket position line, correct sides together. Baste the pocket piece in place. The longer side of the pocket piece should be above the pocket placement line, toward the top of the garment.

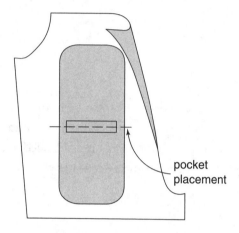

pocket placement

4 Stitch the pocket piece to the garment in a rectangle, $\frac{1}{4}$-inch from the pocket position line and $\frac{1}{2}$-inch from the pocket raw edges.

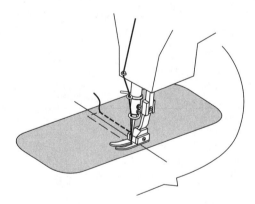

5 Cut through the garment and the pocket piece along the pocket position line to $\frac{1}{2}$-inch from the ends and diagonally to the corners.

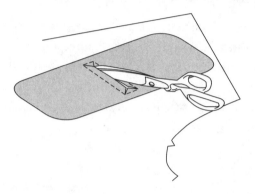

6 Turn the pocket piece through the slit to the wrong side of the garment, and fold the seams away from the opening.

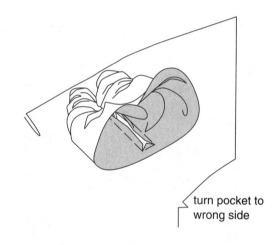

turn pocket to wrong side

7 After the pocket has been turned and before the welt pleats are made, the pocket piece will lay flat, with a rectangular-shaped $\frac{1}{2}$-inch pocket opening showing through the correct side of the garment. Press the pocket so that the opening looks like this.

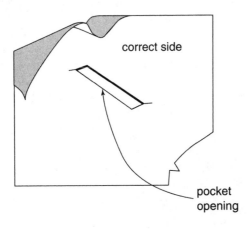

8 Working on the wrong side of the garment, make welts (pleats). Fold the pocket piece at the pocket opening into tiny, inverted pleats. Make sure the two folds meet in the center of the rectangular opening and are the same width. The illustration represents the welts (pleats) covering the rectangular shape from the wrong side of the garment.

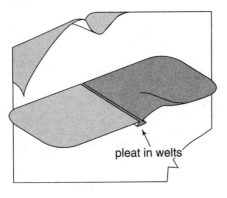

9 Press and baste the welt in place.

The illustration represents the welts (pleats) covering the rectangular shape from the correct side of the garment.

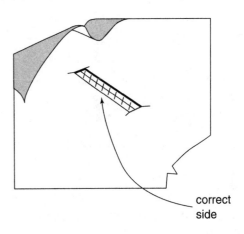

10 From the correct side of the garment, stitch each welt in the ditch formed by the seam.

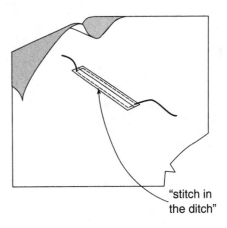

11 With the correct side of the garment still facing up, fold back the garment to expose the triangle created by the clipping. Stitch across the triangle and the welts (the tiny pleats).

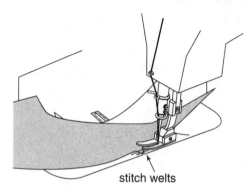

stitch welts

12 On the wrong side of the garment, fold the two halves of the pocket together, matching all edges. Pin in place.

Note: *The pocket piece will lay flat below the opening.*

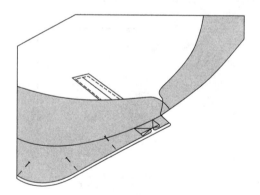

13 Place the garment on a sewing table, with the correct side up. Fold the garment back, exposing the pocket layers and the triangle created by the clipping.

Stitch the pocket edges together, catching the triangle ends and following the stitchline around the pocket.

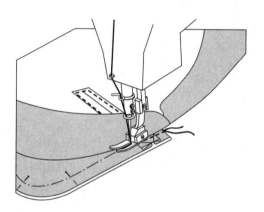

LINED BOUND BUTTONHOLE POCKET

A lined bound buttonhole pocket is made with two small welt pieces on both sides of a slashed opening in a garment, representing the look of a large bound buttonhole. The small welt pieces could be formed by using corded piping or with a zipper to add variety.

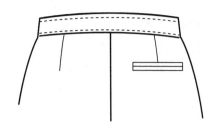

This type of pocket is usually made of a heavier-weight fabric, which requires a lining to prevent bulk with heavier fabrics or reduce costs in expensive fabrics. A lined bound buttonhole pocket is frequently used in designer coats and suit jackets, as well as in pants, vests, and shirts.

1 Cut five pattern pieces: two welts (lips), a top pocket lining with a facing, and an under pocket lining.

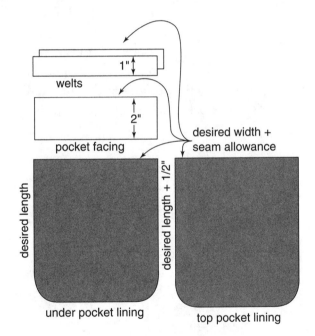

2 Mark the desired pocket position on the correct side of the garment with a horizontal basting stitch or pencil line. The amount needed for the pocket hand opening determines the length of this line.

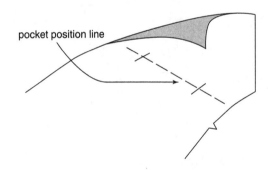

3 Fold both welt pieces in half, wrong sides together. Press.

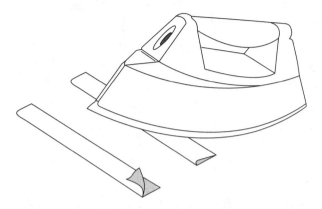

4 Place the garment on a sewing table, correct side up. Place the welt pieces on the correct side of the garment, with the raw edges along the pocket position line. Baste the welt pieces in place.

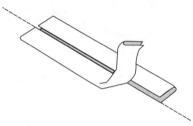

5 Stitch the facing piece and the under pocket piece together, with a $\frac{1}{4}$-inch seam allowance.

Press the seam allowance open and the pocket facing piece up.

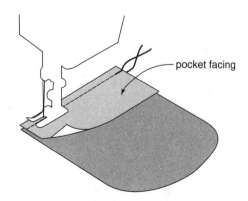

pocket facing

6 Place the under pocket piece (with the attached facing) over the welts, above the pocket position line, as illustrated, correct sides together.

Place the top pocket piece over the welt and along the pocket position line, as illustrated, correct sides together.

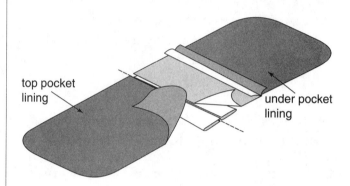

top pocket lining

under pocket lining

7 Stitch both welt pieces, along with the top and under pocket pieces, to the garment in a rectangle, $\frac{1}{4}$-inch from the pocket position line and $\frac{1}{2}$-inch from the pocket raw edges.

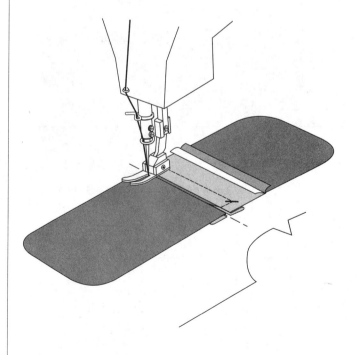

8 Cut through the garment along the pocket position line to $\frac{1}{2}$-inch from the ends and diagonally to the corners.

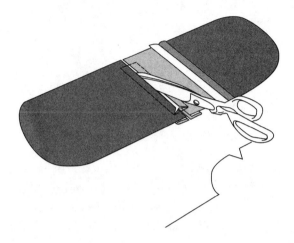

9 Turn the pocket pieces through the slit to the wrong side of the garment, and fold the seams away from the opening.

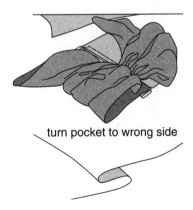

turn pocket to wrong side

10 On the wrong side of the garment, the two pocket pieces will lay flat below the pocket opening, with correct sides together and edges matching. On the correct side of the garment, the welts (lips) will fill the pocket opening with the folded edges in the center of the opening.

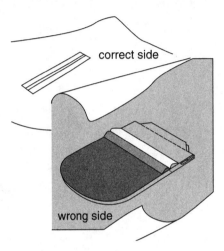

correct side

wrong side

11 Place the garment on a sewing table, correct side up, and fold the garment back, exposing the pocket pieces and the triangle created by the clipping. Stitch the pocket edges together, catching the triangle ends and following the stitch-line around the pocket.

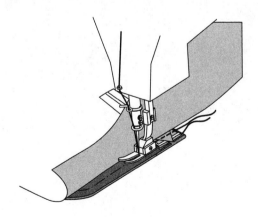

BOUND FLAP POCKET

A bound flap pocket is an inside pocket made with an inside welt and a styled flap sewn into a slashed opening in the garment. Although this pocket is similar to the other bound pockets, the outside pocket pieces are different. This style of bound pocket is frequently used in coats and suit jackets, as well as in tailored skirts and shirts. For a variety of styling features, the fabric used for the flap or flap lining may be different from the fabric used for the garment.

1 Cut six pattern pieces: a flap and a flap facing, an inside welt, a top pocket lining and a facing, and an under pocket lining.

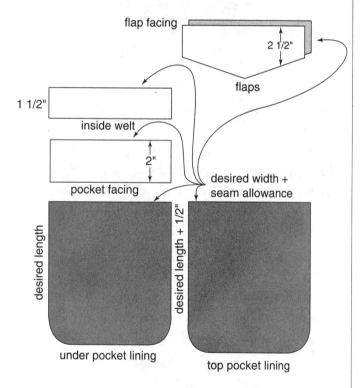

2 Mark the desired pocket position on the correct side of the garment with a horizontal basting stitch or pencil line. The amount needed for the pocket hand opening determines the length of this line.

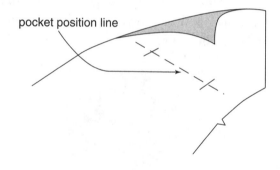

pocket position line

3 Pin the flap and the flap facing pieces, correct sides together, matching all corners.

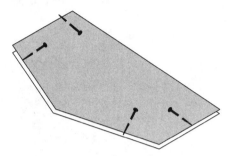

4 Stitch the two flap pieces together, following the stitchline (usually $\frac{1}{4}$-inch) around three edges. Leave the top portion of the flap open. Trim the corners.

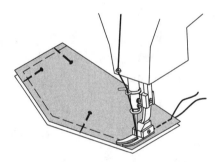

5 Turn the flap correct side out and carefully press flat.

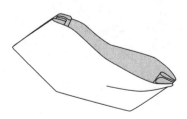

6 Place the garment on a sewing table, correct side up. Place the flap on the correct side of the garment, with the open edge just above the pocket position line. Baste the flap in place.

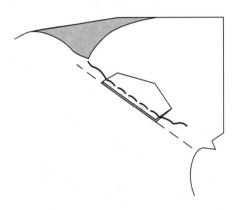

7 Fold the welt piece in half, wrong sides together, and press flat.

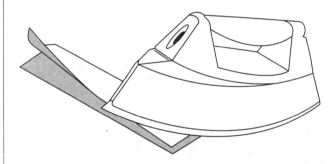

8 Baste the welt piece to the garment, with the open edge of the welt along the bottom of the pocket position line.

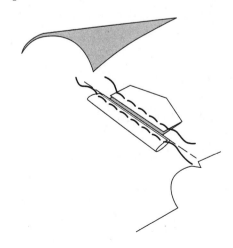

9 Stitch the facing piece and the under pocket lining piece together, with a $\frac{1}{4}$-inch seam allowance. Press the seam allowance open and the pocket facing piece up.

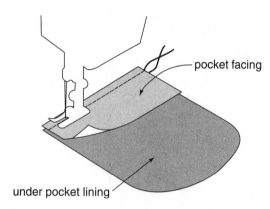

pocket facing

under pocket lining

10 Place the under pocket piece (with the attached facing) over the flap. Place the top pocket lining piece over the welt, as illustrated.

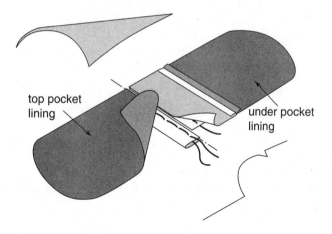

top pocket lining

under pocket lining

11 Stitch the flap and the pocket pieces to the garment in a rectangle, $\frac{1}{4}$-inch from the pocket position line and $\frac{1}{2}$-inch from the pocket raw edges.

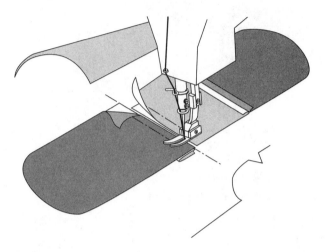

12 Cut through the garment along the pocket position line to $\frac{1}{2}$-inch from the ends and diagonally to the corners.

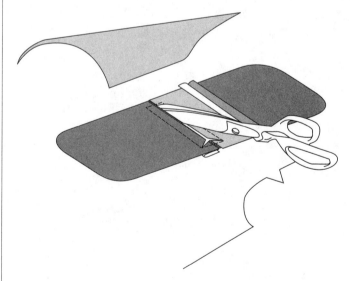

13 Turn the pocket pieces through the slit to the wrong side of the garment, and fold the seam away from the opening.

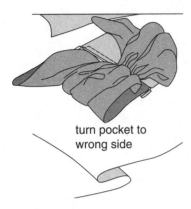

turn pocket to
wrong side

14 On the wrong side of the garment, the pocket pieces will lay flat below the opening, with correct sides together and edges matching. On the correct side of the garment, the flap will lay on top of the inside welt piece and fill the pocket lining.

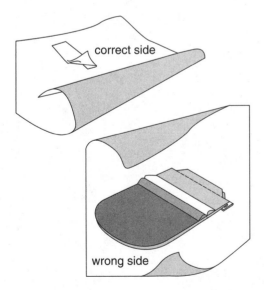

correct side

wrong side

15 Place the garment on a sewing table, correct side up. Fold the garment back, exposing the pocket pieces and the triangle created by the clipping. Stitch the pocket edges together, catching the triangle ends and following the stitchline around the pocket.

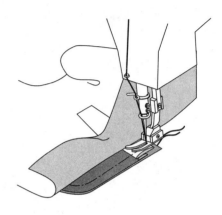

CHAPTER 14

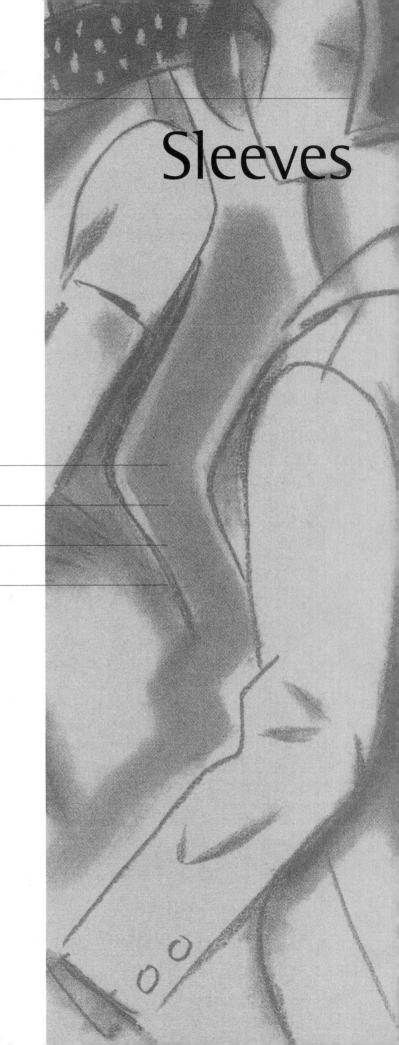

Sleeves

KEY TERMS AND CONCEPTS

A **sleeve** is the section of a garment that covers the arm. The sleeve usually joins the garment in a seam that encircles the arm over the shoulder.

A variety of sleeve designs are available, and each variation requires different sewing techniques. Sleeves generally are divided into four basic types:

- **Set-in sleeves**— The sleeve is completed before it is attached to the armhole. The garment armhole seam circles the arm near the shoulder because the side seams and shoulder seams of the garment are also previously sewn and the sleeve is set into the armhole.

set-in sleeve

- **Shirt sleeves**—The sleeve is stitched to the armhole while both the sleeve and garment seams remain open.

shirt sleeve

- **Raglan sleeves**—The sleeve is sewn into a front and back diagonal seam that extends from the armhole up to the neckline. It is sewn into an open seam while both the sleeve and garment seams remain open.

raglan sleeve

- **Kimono sleeves**—This sleeve styling does not require a traditional armhole. The sleeve is cut in one piece, with the front and back of the garment. The garment design has a shoulder seam and a side/underarm seam.

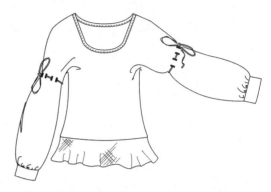

Sleeve lengths can be short, three-quarters, or long. **Sleeve widths** can be narrow or wide.

Sleeve openings serve a practical purpose, allowing one to get in and out of the sleeve. The most common sleeve openings are

- The continuous lap opening
- The rolled-hem placket opening
- The shirt sleeve placket opening

rolled hem placket

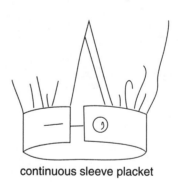

continuous sleeve placket

shirt sleeve placket

Sleeve plackets are applied to slashed or cut-out sleeve openings to reinforce the fabric and to finish the bottom of a sleeve before a cuff is attached. They are applied to the sleeve before the underarm seams are sewn, while the sleeve remains flat. The specific type of placket used depends on the style and shape of the sleeve.

A **cuff** is a finished detail attached to the lower edge of the sleeve of women's, men's, and children's garments. It includes a separate sewn or turned-back band. Usually cuffs are made of the same fabric used for the garment. However, they can enhance a garment's design by using contrasting colors, prints, or plaids.

There are two basic types of cuffs:

■ Detached cuff—This type of cuff is made from a separate piece of fabric attached to the lower edge of a sleeve. These cuffs control fullness by holding gathers or pleats on the lower edge of the sleeve.

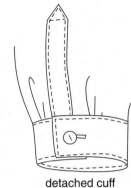

detached cuff

■ The fold-up cuff—This is an attached cuff formed just like a deep hem. The fabric is folded and held in position by being pressed into place.

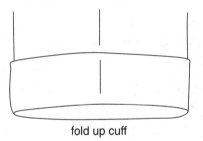

fold up cuff

SLEEVE DESIGNS

Set-in sleeve

A set-in sleeve is joined to a garment by an armhole seam that circles the arm; the shoulder seams and the side seams of the garment have been previously sewn. The sleeve is completed before it is attached to this armhole.

A set-in sleeve always measures more than the armhole of the bodice. The extra fullness in the sleeve is needed to create a "cap" to fit over the top curve of the arm. The sleeve cap may be styled from a minimum to moderate to a great deal of fullness and the sleeve can be finished with or without a cuff.

To prepare the garment for the sleeve, sew the underarm seam on the sleeve and the side seam of the garment.

Complete the cuff or hem finish.

Note: *The underarm sleeve or seams of the sleeve and the cuff or hem finish must be completed* before *the sleeve is set into the garment.*

1 From the front notch to the back notches, crimp or ease stitch the cap. Gather the cap for fuller sleeves. Refer to step 1 in "shirt sleeve," p 198.

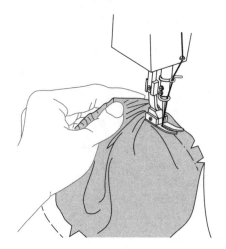

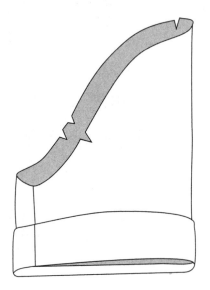

2 With the wrong side of the garment and sleeve facing up, place the sleeve through the armhole, correct sides together. Start to pin the sleeve cap to the garment armhole, matching the underarm seam of the sleeve to the side seam of the garment.

3 Continue to pin the sleeve cap to the garment armhole, matching

- The front notch of the cap to the front notch of the armhole

- The shoulder position notch (or marking) of the cap to the shoulder seam of the armhole

- The back notches of the cap to the back notches of the armhole

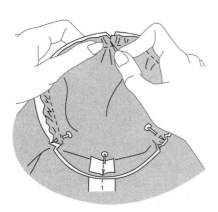

4 Continue to pin the sleeve cap to the garment armhole, making sure the raw edges match and that all fullness is distributed evenly between the notches.

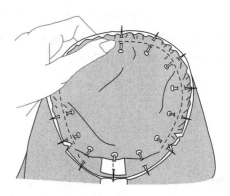

5 Stitch the sleeve cap to the armhole along the stitchline, with the sleeve side facing up. Be sure to control the fullness in the sleeve cap with your fingers. This helps to prevent tucks and puckers on the finished seamlines.

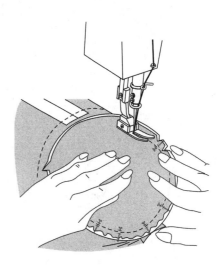

Shirt Sleeve

A shirt sleeve is sewn into a dropped shoulder armhole while both the sleeve and garment seams remain open. Therefore, there is very little curve in the sleeve cap and also very little ease stitching required in the sleeve cap when attaching the sleeve to the garment. This dropped shoulder sleeve styling is designed for women's, men's, and children's sportswear.

To prepare the garment for the sleeve, sew the shoulder and yoke seams of the garment. The underarm seams on the garment are not sewn until the sleeve is sewn into the garment. Complete the desired placket opening while the sleeve is still flat and before it is attached to the garment.

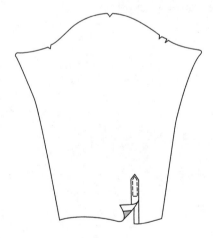

1 Crimp or ease stitch the cap from the front notch to the back notches of the sleeve. Refer to page 75 for detailed instructions for "Ease Stitches."

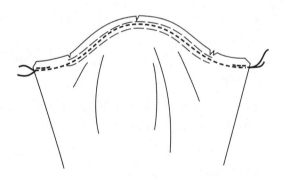

2 With the correct sides of the garment and the sleeve together, pin the sleeve to the armhole, matching

- The front notch of the cap to the front notch of the armhole
- The shoulder position notch (or marking) to the shoulder seam
- The back notches of the cap to the back notches of the armhole
- The underarm seams of the sleeve to the side seams of the garment

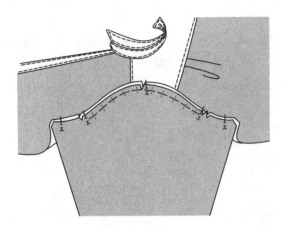

3 With the sleeve side up, stitch the sleeve to the armhole.

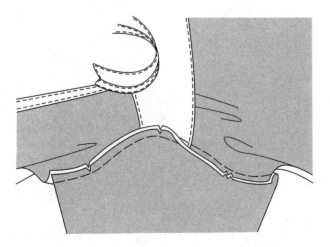

Hint: *A flat-felled seam can give a more tailored effect. Refer to "Flat-Felled Seam," page 92.*

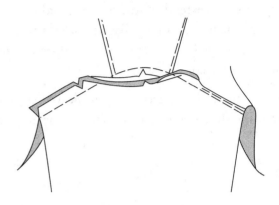

4 Complete the sleeve and the garment by matching and stitching the underarm seam of the sleeve and the side seam of the garment, using a regular machine stitch.

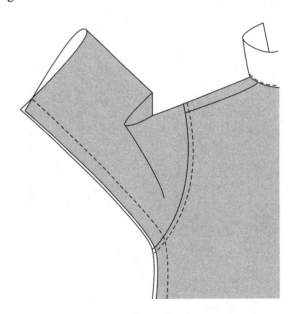

Raglan Sleeve

A raglan sleeve extends to the neckline and is attached to the back and front of the garment with a long diagonal seam running underneath the arm. The yoke area of the bodice is part of the upper area of the sleeve. A raglan sleeve is designed for comfort and ease.

Depending on the pattern, a raglan sleeve design may have a shoulder seam, a dart at the shoulder area, or no shoulder seam at all (usually only in knits).

You need to cut out all the pattern pieces. Illustrated here is a raglan blouse front, a raglan blouse back, and the raglan sleeves (front and back), with a shoulder seam.

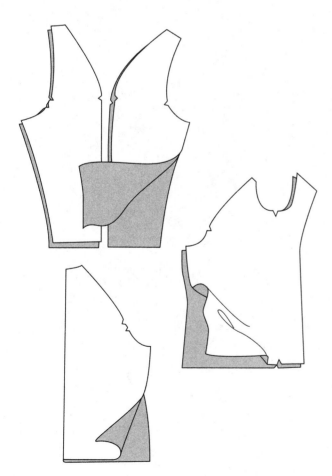

1 Place the shoulder seams of the sleeves together, correct sides together. Stitch the shoulder seams and press open.

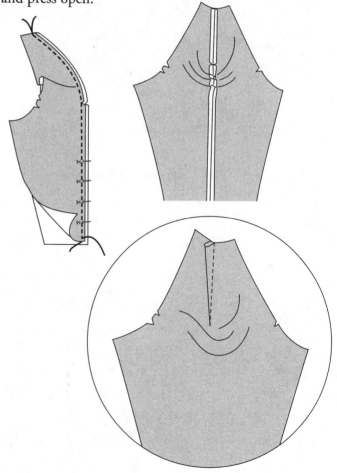

Note: *If the design includes a shoulder dart, sew the shoulder dart at this time.*

2 Pin the back raglan seam of the sleeve to the back raglan seam of the bodice. Match correct sides and all sewing notches. Stitch the raglan seams. Clip the seam allowances, and press the raglan seams open.

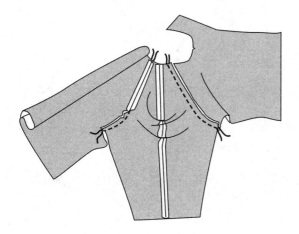

3 Pin baste the underarm seam of the sleeve and the front and back side seam to each other, correct sides together. Stitch and press.

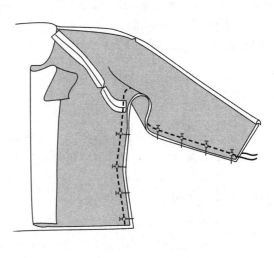

SLEEVE PLACKETS

Continuous Sleeve Placket

A continuous placket finishes the raw edges of the placket opening with a separate strip of fabric. This is the most commonly used placket opening, and is usually used in women's sleeved garments requiring a placket opening.

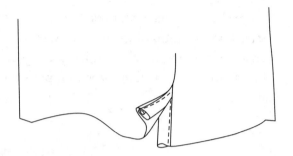

Cut the placket opening at the lower edge of the sleeve, where indicated on the pattern. Use a strip twice as long as the slashed opening (shown on the pattern), and at least 1½-inches wide.

Note: *To allow greater ease in sewing the placket in place, press all seam allowances and press the placket in half.*

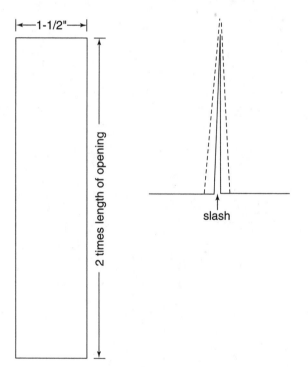

1 Place the sleeve on a sewing table, correct side up. Spread the sleeve slash open. Place the correct side of the placket to the wrong side of the sleeve opening. Pin in place.

Note: *The placket opening of the sleeve is placed in a V position to the edge of the placket piece.*

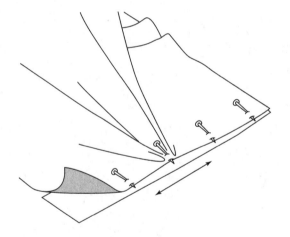

2 Stitch with a $\frac{1}{4}$-inch seam allowance along the entire placket opening.

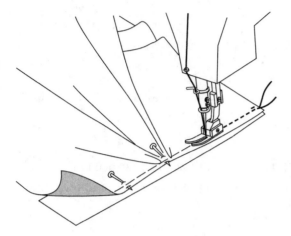

3 Press under the unsewn $\frac{1}{4}$-inch seam allowance.

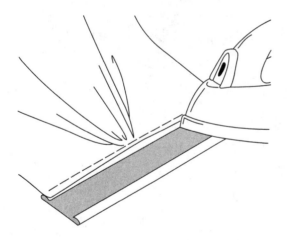

4 Fold over the placket to just past the original stitching. Top stitch the placket.

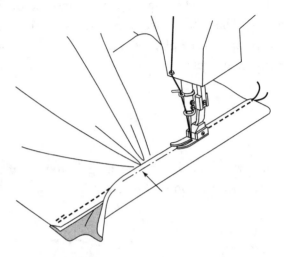

5 Press the placket away from the wrong side of the sleeve opening. Stitch the top of the placket at an angle.

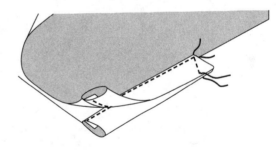

6 Place the placket in the final position to attach the cuff. The placket will fold under on the front section of the sleeve and extend over the back portion of the sleeve.

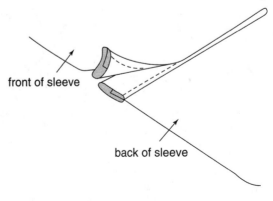

front of sleeve

back of sleeve

Rolled-Hem Sleeve Placket

A rolled-hem placket is a very simple method of creating a sleeve opening. The cuff is sewn from one end of the placket to the opposite end of the placket, and then the cuff is buttoned; the sleeve creates a pleat.

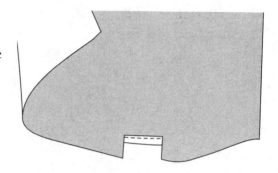

1 Snip the desired sleeve opening up to the stitch-line indicated on the pattern.

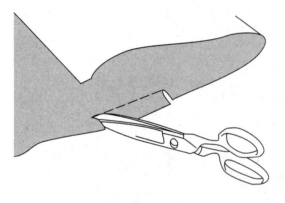

2 Fold the loose seam allowance twice (placket opening) to the wrong side, and machine stitch.

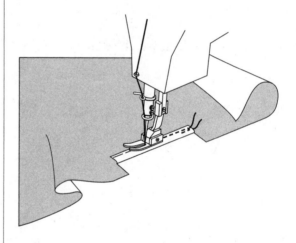

Shirt Sleeve Placket

A shirt sleeve placket is usually inserted into a women's or man's tailored shirt or jacket sleeve while the sleeve is still flat, before it is sewn into the garment. This placket opening has a top and an under piece, and it requires more sewing steps than a one-piece placket opening.

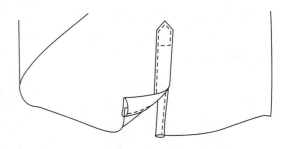

Cut an under placket piece and a top placket piece. Precut a sleeve opening the length of the desired opening, and note a $\frac{1}{4}$-inch stitchline.

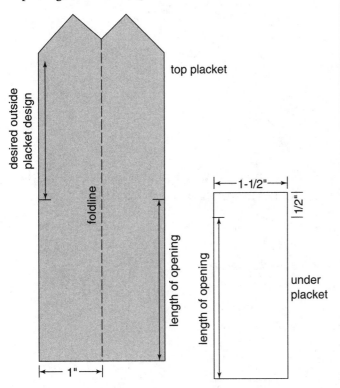

desired outside placket design

top placket

foldline

length of opening

1"

1-1/2"

1/2"

length of opening

under placket

Note: *To allow greater ease in sewing the placket in place, press all seam allowances and press the placket piece in half.*

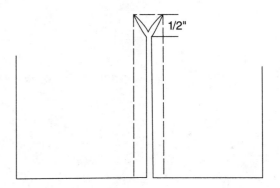

1/2"

1 Place the sleeve on the sewing table, wrong side up. Place the correct side of the under placket (the shorter piece) to the wrong side of the sleeve opening, as illustrated.

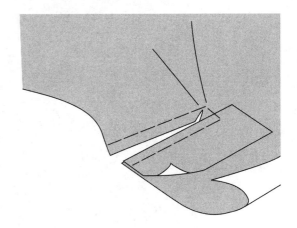

2 Stitch the placket and the sleeve, with a $\frac{1}{4}$-inch seam allowance. Begin stitching $\frac{1}{2}$-inch from the placket end.

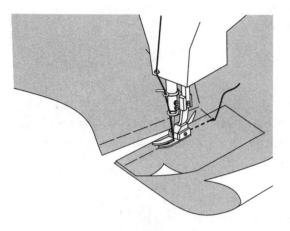

3 Press under the unsewn $\frac{1}{4}$-inch seam allowance.

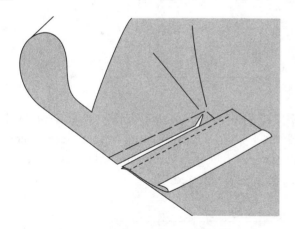

4 Flip the entire under placket to the correct side of the sleeve. Press the placket in half, just past the stitchline.

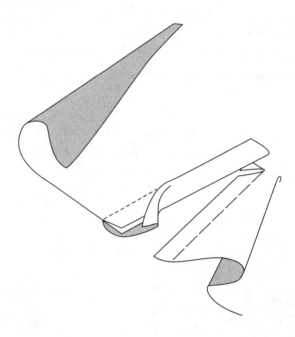

5 Top stitch the under placket in place along the folded-under seam allowance edge.

Note: *The placket piece is stitched to within $\frac{1}{2}$-inch of the top end of the placket. This is the entire length of the placket opening.*

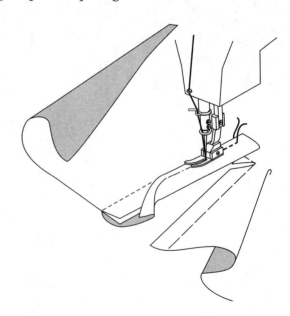

6 Flip the sleeve and the finished placket back to expose the $\frac{1}{2}$-inch placket tail and the clipped triangular piece. Stitch across the base of this area.

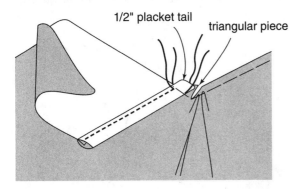

7 To prepare the top placket piece, first fold the top placket in half (correct sides together), and stitch closed the area above the desired placket opening. Next, turn the placket piece correct side out and pull out all corners. Press.

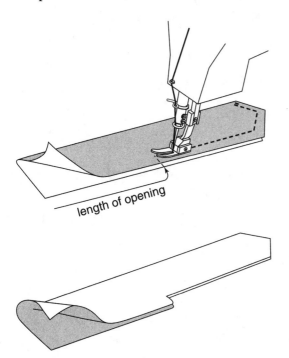

8 With the wrong side of the sleeve facing up, place one layer of the top placket to the sleeve opening as illustrated.

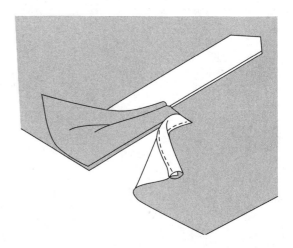

9 Stitch, with a $\frac{1}{4}$-inch seam allowance, along the placket opening edge to the end of this opening.

Note: *The top corner of this placket opening has already been clipped.*

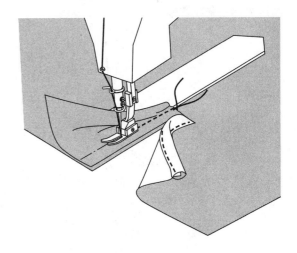

10 Turn the top placket to the correct side of the sleeve. Keep the under placket away from the top placket, and pin in place.

Note: *All seam allowances are turned under, and the ½-inch tail will be covered by the top placket piece.*

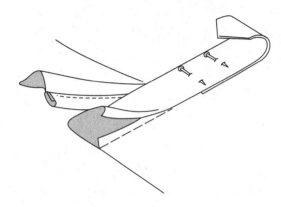

11 Top stitch the placket in place along all folded edges and seam edges.

Warning: *Keep the under placket away from the top placket to ensure that the stitching does not catch the under piece while sewing.*

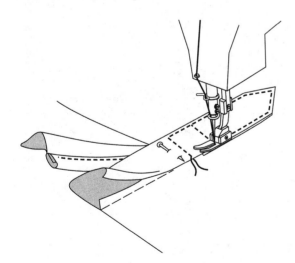

Note: *As a variation on the final stitch, you can top stitch the placket down to cover the ½-inch tail and leave the remaining amount of the placket loose. As shown here, a button and buttonhole can be added.*

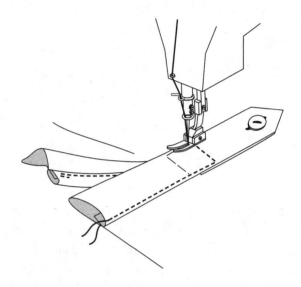

SLEEVE CUFFS

Buttoned Cuff

A buttoned cuff is a straight piece of fabric, that can be a variety of widths, sewn into the lower edge of the sleeve. Usually, it helps to control gathered fullness or pleats at the lower edge of the sleeve. It fits snugly around the wrist and fastens with a button or some other fastener. There must be some type of opening in the sleeve to allow the cuff to slide over the hand.

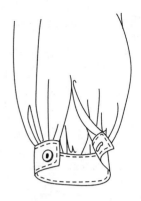

Outlined in this section are two sewing methods of attaching a buttoned cuff. You can use either method, depending on your preference:

- Standard sewing method—The cuff ends are sewn before the cuff is attached to the sleeve. The cuff is then turned correct side out and pressed in half, and the cuff is stitched to the sleeve.

- Shirt sewing method—One side of the cuff is sewn to the sleeve, the cuff is folded, and the ends are stitched.

To prepare the sleeve for either method, first sew the sleeve opening (placket) in place. Then sew the underarm seam. Complete any gathering or pleating at the lower edge of the sleeve before attaching the cuff. Refer to "Gathering," pages 76–77.

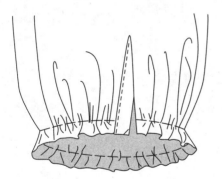

Attach the interfacing to the wrong side of the cuff. Refer to "Interfacing," pages 270–273.

Note: *The interfacing should extend $\frac{1}{2}$-inch past the center foldline of the cuff. This ensures that the foldline crease is soft and allows for more wear on the cuff.*

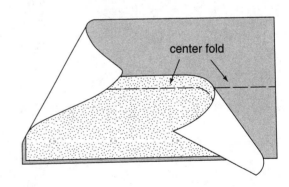

center fold

STANDARD SEWING METHOD

1 Fold the cuff in half lengthwise, correct sides together.

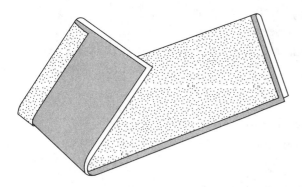

2 Stitch along the ends, from the foldline to the cut edges.

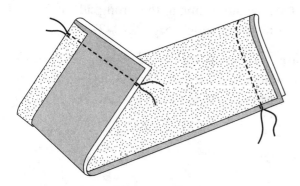

3 Trim the corners and edges if necessary.

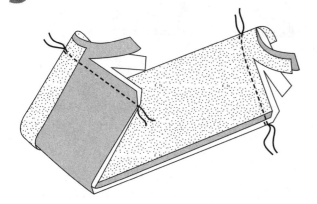

4 Turn the cuff correct side out and press.

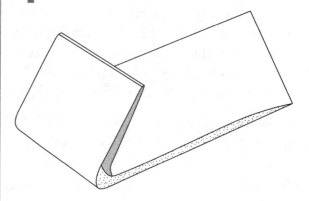

5 Pin the correct side of the cuff (one layer only) to the wrong side of the sleeve, matching the lower edge of the sleeve. The placket and the cuff ends should meet. Evenly distribute any gathers to fit the cuff, and pin with the pins on the sleeve side.

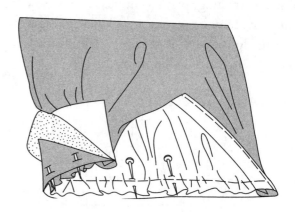

6 With the sleeve side facing up, stitch the cuff layer to the sleeve, following the stitchline.

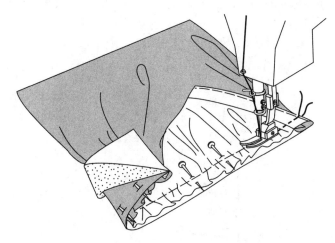

7 Turn the sleeve correct side out and pin the interfacing side of the cuff (with the seam allowance folded under) over the stitchline.

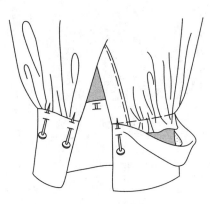

8 Edgestitch along the folded-under seam allowance through all thicknesses the entire length of the cuff.

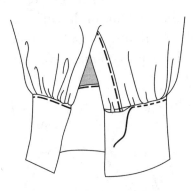

SHIRT SEWING METHOD

1 Pin the interfacing side of the cuff to the lower edge of the sleeve, correct sides together. The placket and the stitchline of the cuff ends should meet. Evenly distribute any gathers to fit the cuff, and pin, with the pins on the sleeve side.

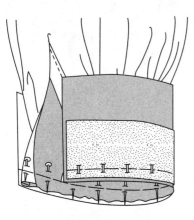

2 With the sleeve side facing up, stitch the cuff layers to the sleeve, following the stitchline.

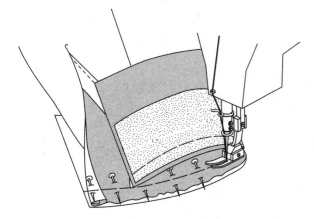

3 Fold and pin the cuff in half, correct sides together, matching all stitchlines. Press the seam allowances toward the cuff.

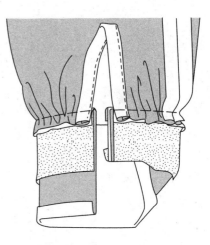

4 Stitch the cuff ends and trim the corners.

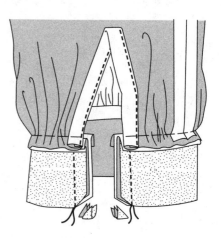

5 Turn the cuff to the correct side, pushing out the corners.

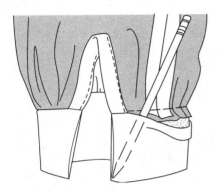

6 With the seam allowance of the under cuff turned to the inside, pin the folded seam allowance in place. Make sure the fold extends $\frac{1}{8}$-inch beyond the stitched seamline.

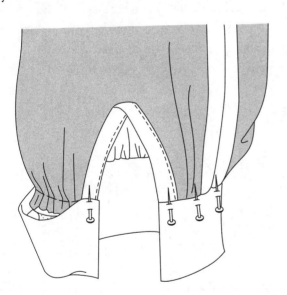

7 With the correct side of the sleeve facing up, stitch (in the ditch) the under cuff in place.

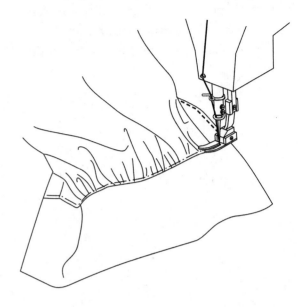

Barrel Cuff

A barrel cuff encircles the bottom of a sleeve and does not have a placket opening. Therefore, the cuff must be roomy enough to easily slip the hand and arm through the finished sleeve.

9" min.

Complete all gathering or pleating at the lower edge of the sleeve before attaching the cuff. Attach the interfacing to the wrong side of the cuff. Refer to "Interfacing," pages 270–273. Do not sew the underarm seams before attaching the cuff.

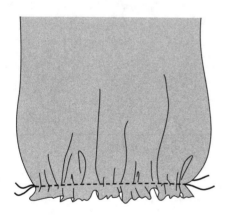

1 Pin the interfaced side of the cuff to the sleeve, correct sides together. The sleeve underarm seams and the ends of the cuff should match. Evenly distribute any gathers to fit the cuff.

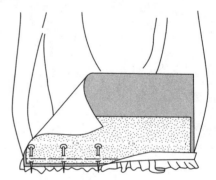

2 With the sleeve side facing up, stitch the cuff to the sleeve, following the stitchline.

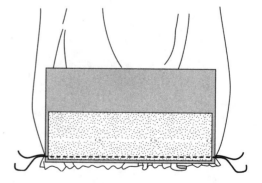

3 Press the unsewn lengthwise seam allowance toward the wrong side of the cuff. Press the seam allowance toward the cuff.

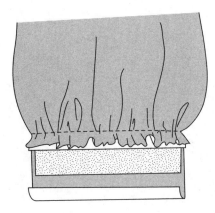

4 Match and pin the underarm sleeve seam and the cuff seam, correct sides together. Stitch in place.

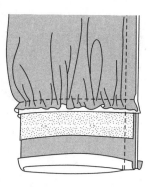

5 Fold the cuff along the center foldline, wrong side to wrong side and stitchline to stitchline. Pin in place.

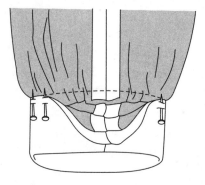

6 From the correct side of the sleeve, top stitch the cuff in place.

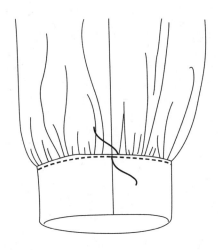

CHAPTER 15

Collars

KEY TERMS AND CONCEPTS

A **collar** is a separate piece of fabric attached to the neckline of a shirt, blouse, or dress. Collars can be made of matching or contrasting fabric and they can be trimmed in lace or embroidery. Collars enhance the neckline of a garment and contribute significantly to the total look of the garment. Some styles and shapes of collars require specific fabric and construction techniques, such as a purchased knit collar or collar made of a single layer of organza with a lettuce finish. All collars must be made and attached carefully for a professional appearance.

A **stand** is the height and portion of the collar that rises above the neckline to which it is attached. The stand extends from the neckline to the roll line.

The **roll line** is the line at which the collar is turned back onto itself at the top of the stand. The positioning of this line determines the height of the stand, and thus the fall of the collar.

A **collar style line** is the outside edge of the collar, as opposed to the neckline edge, which is sewn to the garment.

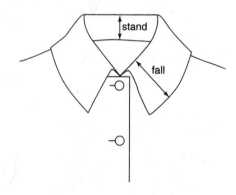

The basic difference among the various **collar types** is the way they encircle the neck edge. Collars fit into three basic categories:

- A **flat collar** (with a concave shape) lies against the garment, rising only slightly above the neck edge. The most common style is the Peter Pan.

- A **roll collar** (with a convex shape) stands up around the neckline in back, and then falls down against the garment in front. Rolled collars are used on dresses, blouses, coats, and men's sport shirts.

- A **stand-up collar** (with a straight line) stands up all around the neckline. It may be a narrow or wide single width, such as in a mandarin or tie collar. Or it may be a double-width band that folds back down onto itself, such as a turtleneck collar. A shirt collar with a stand is a variation of the standing collar.

For garments with buttons, a **buttonstand** (that is, a width of button) is added to the pattern from the center front. A facing (usually 2-inches wide) is then added to the buttonstand.

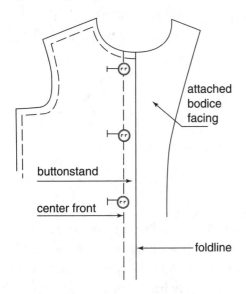

A **collar breakpoint** is the point where the lapel begins to fold back from the edge of the garment, usually relating to shawl collars, revere collars, or notched collars.

COLLAR CLASSIFICATIONS

There are three broad classifications of collars, which take different sewing applications:

■ Separate set collar, such as Peter Pan, convertible, or mandarin collars.

■ Collar designed as part of or with the bodice, such as a shawl or revere collar.

■ Two-piece notched collar, with a lapel and a separate collar.

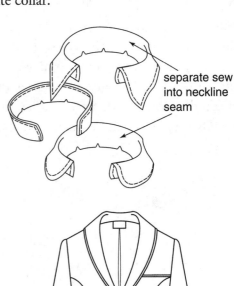

SEWING APPLICATIONS

There are three methods of sewing a collar into the garment neck edge, all of which are described in this chapter:

- The sandwiched method, with a full facing. Convertible, notched, and Peter Pan collars could be sewn using this method.

- The partially sandwiched method, with only a front facing. Convertible and Peter Pan collar could be sewn using this method.

- The edge stitched method, with no facing. The neckline is finished by turning the seam allowance up into the collar and finishing it with a machine stitch. Collars that would be sewn with this method are the mandarin collar, the shirt collar with a stand, the turtleneck collar, and the tie collar.

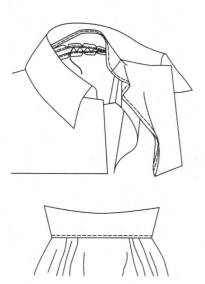

COLLAR DESIGNS

The **convertible collar** is a front-opening collar and can be worn either open or closed. This type of collar is considered a stand collar, and it falls flat and has pointed ends on the front. This style is suitable for almost any type of garment, from casual to dressy.

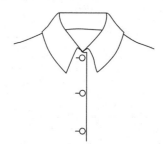

The **tailored shirt collar** usually has a stand around the neck that is placed between the collar and the shirt. This stand raises the collar so that its finished edge falls smoothly back over the neck edge.

The **Peter Pan collar** is usually rounded in shape and can be designed as one piece or as two pieces for front and back openings. The collar lays flat on the garment, with a slight roll over the neckline.

The **mandarin collar** is narrow and stands up from the neckline. It can be cut as a straight strip (usually on the bias) or with a slight curve. This type of collar is used on blouses, men's shirts, and dresses.

The **tie collar** is usually a straight collar with either attached or detached long, loose ends that can be tied into a knot or bow. This type of collar is used on blouses and dresses for a soft, draped look.

The **revere collar** is created when the facing of the lapel folds back to show the reverse side of the lapel. The revere collar is most often used on casual jackets.

The **notched collar** is a tailored collar with an indentation, or notch, cut out where the lapel joins the collar. Typically, the notch collar has a back neck stand that falls smoothly around to the front neckline. It can be used on dresses, vests, and jackets.

The **turtleneck collar** is usually a wide straight collar, cut on the bias, that stand up from the neckline and then rolls down back over the neckline. This type of collar is made out of knit or softly woven fabrics. This style is often used for casual or sporty garments.

The **sailor collar** lays flat on the garment, with a slightly curved stand at the neckline. Usually the back of the sailor collar hangs in a square shape, and the front tapers into a V neckline.

The **shawl collar** is a roll collar, which is designed and cut in one piece with the front of the garment, without separate lapels. The under collar is cut in one piece with the front facing sections. Typically, the collar and the under collar have a center back seam. The shawl collar is used on dresses, blouses, coats, and jackets.

FLAT, STAND, OR ROLL COLLAR

A flat, stand, or roll collar has two collar pieces: a top collar and an under collar (or collar facing). The outer collar shape can be pointed, rounded, or squared. Common flat or roll collars include the convertible, mandarin, Peter Pan, and sailor collars. When preparing these collars, accurate stitching, trimming, and turning are important.

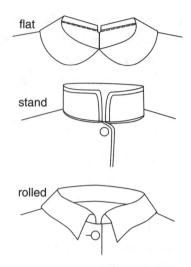

flat

stand

rolled

1 Cut a top collar piece, an under collar piece, and an interfacing piece. All three collar pieces should have center and shoulder notches.

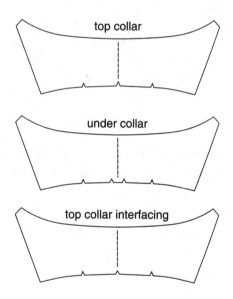

top collar

under collar

top collar interfacing

2 Attach the interfacing to the wrong side of the top collar. Refer to "Interfacing," pages 270–273. With correct sides together, pin the top collar and the under collar together, along the unnotched edges.

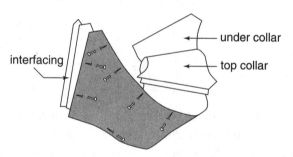

interfacing

under collar

top collar

3 Using the recommended seam allowances from the pattern pieces, stitch the under collar to the top collar, along the unnotched edges. Do not stitch the neck edge.

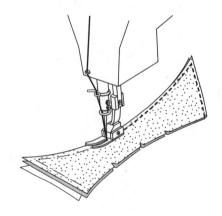

4 If necessary, trim the seam allowances to $\frac{1}{4}$-inch. Cut the corners diagonally and very close to the stitching.

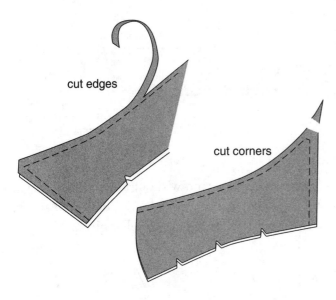

cut edges

cut corners

5 Turn the collar correct side out. Carefully pull out the corners with a pin or a point turner.

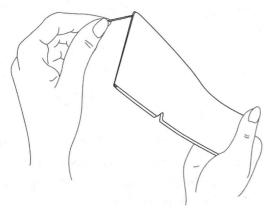

6 From the correct side of the collar, understitch the under collar to both seam allowances. Be sure to stitch as close to the corners as possible.

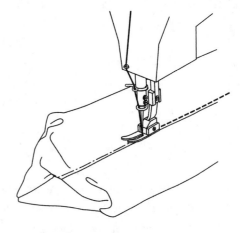

7 Top stitch, if desired, along the outer finished edges.

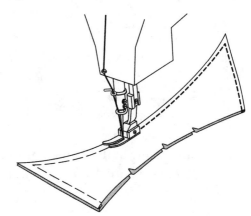

8 Press the collar flat, rolling the seam slightly to the under collar.

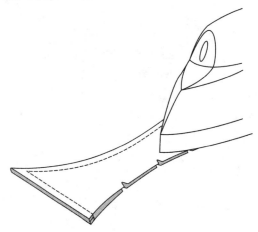

SHIRT COLLAR WITH SEPARATE STAND

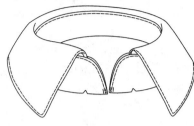

A shirt collar has a separate stand that is stitched to the collar before being applied to the neck edge of the garment. The stand raises the collar section so that its finished edge falls smoothly back over the neck edge.

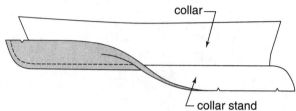

collar

collar stand

Note: *Before attaching the stand to the collar, you need to sew and press the collar pieces (follow "Flat, Stand, or Roll Collar" steps 1 through 8, pages 234–235). The collar section should be finished as illustrated.*

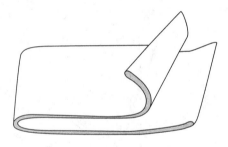

1 Attach the interfacing to the wrong side of the top collar stand section. Refer to "Interfacing," pages 270–273.

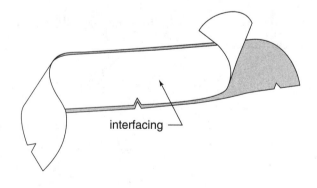

interfacing

2 Pin the collar stand without the interfacing to the collar, along the lower edge of the collar. Match the correct sides of the collar pieces.

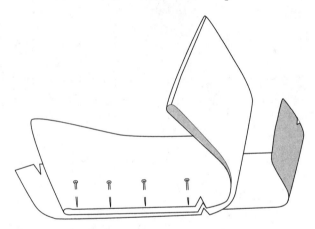

3 Pin the top collar stand with interfacing to the correct side of the top collar. Also, match the correct side of the pinned stand. Pin through all thicknesses, along the stitchline.

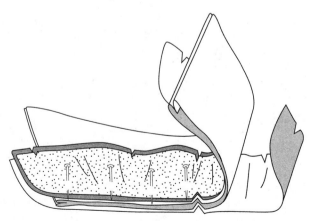

4 Stitch through all layers, from one end of the stand to the other.

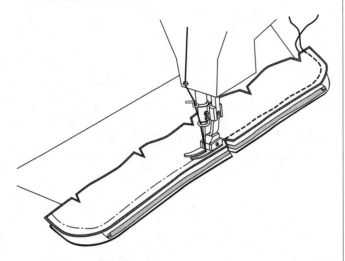

5 Turn the stand down, away from the collar. Press into position.

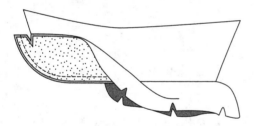

6 Top stitch, if desired, along the outer finished edges.

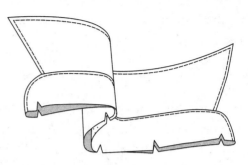

Note: *To attach this collar to a shirt neckline, refer to page 245 "Attaching a Collar Without Facings" or page 238 "Burrito/Sandwich Collar."*

BURRITO/SANDWICH COLLAR

The "Burrito" collar is a different technique for attaching a two-piece stand collar to a shirt neckline. These sewing steps lead to a "pull-through" procedure that creates a clean corner at the top of the placket/collar edge. It also finishes the front neckline seam on both sides of the collar stand, eliminating the need for handstitching.

1 Before attaching the shirt stand collar to the neckline, complete the sewing steps on page 236–237. Do not topstitch the collar until these sewing steps are completed.

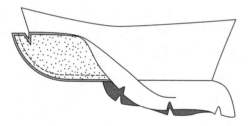

2 With the correct side of the shirt facing up, pin the outside layer of the collar stand to the neck edge, matching correct side to correct side. Match the following:

- The collar center back to the shirt center back.
- The shoulder position of the collar to the shoulder seam of the shirt.
- The collar center front to the shirt center front.
- The edge of the collar to the edge of the garment.

Note: *The top layer of the collar falls away from the garment.*

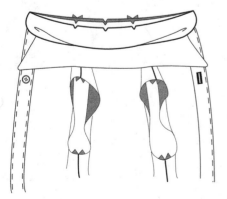

3 With the wrong side of the collar facing up, stitch the collar to the neck edge of the shirt. Keep the top layer of the collar away from the neck edge of the seam.

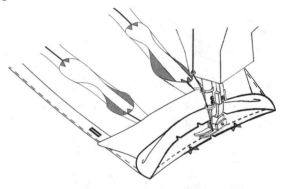

4 Enclose the right and left sides of the collar stand—one side at a time—using the following steps.

A. Fold the collar stand around collar matching correct side of the collar stands and aligning the neckline seams. This will encase the collar and part of the neckline/placket intersection, forming a "burrito sandwiching" of the collar/shirt.

B. Starting at the front intersection, sew along the neckline seam for two inches. Trim the corners.

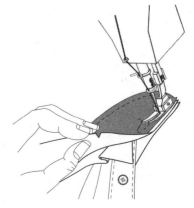

5 Turn the collar correct side out, pulling the collar out of the "burrito/sandwich" position.

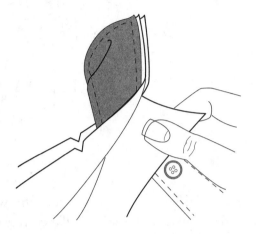

6 Complete the collar neck edge.

A. Fold under the unsewn seam allowance of the collar stand just past the original stitchline. Edgestitch the back collar stand through all layers from shoulder seam to shoulder seam.

B. Complete the collar by topstitching along the outer edges of the collar and collar stand. For a continuous line of sttching, leave the needle down in the fabric when turning the corners.

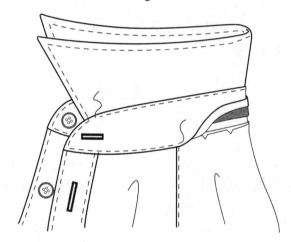

TIE COLLAR

A tie collar is similar to a straight band or mandarin collar. However, the collar pattern is longer on each end to create the ties.

1 Fold the collar strip in half, correct sides together.

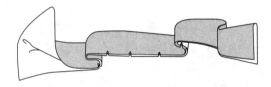

2 Stitch each tie end (the unnotched long pieces) with the desired seam allowance.

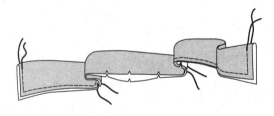

3 Turn each tie end to the correct side, this will automatically turn the entire collar correct side out. Press flat.

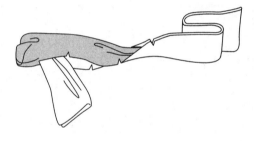

4 Stitch the neck edge, following the instructions in "Attaching a Collar Without Facings", pages 245–246.

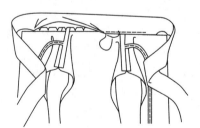

ATTACHING A COLLAR WITH FRONT AND BACK FACINGS

A collar with front and back facings is otherwise known as the *sandwich method*. This method means that a flat, stand, or roll collar can be sewn into the neckline at the same time the facings are sewn to the neckline.

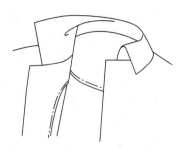

The collar is sewn to the center front of the garment—not to the garment edge. This sewing technique allows the collar to meet at center front when the garment is worn. At the same time, the button extension on the garment section extends past the collar. Collars that include a button extension (mandarin or shirt) are sewn to the garment edge. For these collars, follow the sewing directions in "Attaching a Collar Without Facings," page 245–246.

1 Sew and press the collar, (follow "Flat, Stand, or Roll Collar" steps 1 through 8, pages 234–235). The collar section should be finished as illustrated.

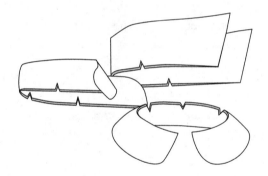

2 Sew the shoulder seams of the garment and the facing pieces together (refer to "Neckline and Armhole Facings," pages 274–275). Stay stitch or crimp the neck edge of the garment to prevent the neckline from stretching.

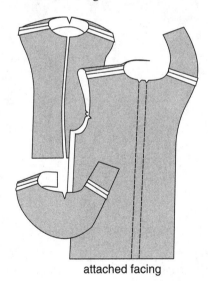

attached facing

3 With the correct side of the garment facing up, pin the notched edge of the collar (the open edge) to the neck edge of the garment. Match the following:

- The center back of the collar to the center back of the garment.

- The shoulder position of the collar to the shoulder seam of the garment.

- The center front of the collar to the center front of the garment.

Note: *The facings are placed away from the garment.*

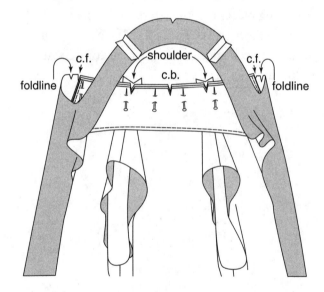

4 Place the correct side of the facing on top of the pinned collar, matching all raw edges carefully. Repin the neck edge so that the garment, collar, and facings are pinned together (repin the pins, one at a time).

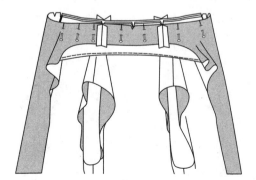

5 Stitch all layers together, starting from the folded facing neck edge. Continue to stitch the neck edge, until you reach the opposite folded facing neck edge.

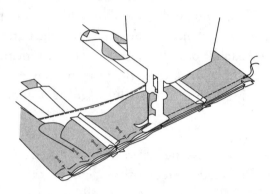

6 Turn the facings to the inside of the garment and press. Stitch the shoulder seam of the facing to the shoulder seam of the garment. If necessary, trim the seam allowance.

Note: *The collar has been sewn to the center front of the garment, not to the garment edge. This sewing technique allows the collar to meet at center front and create a button extension on the garment section.*

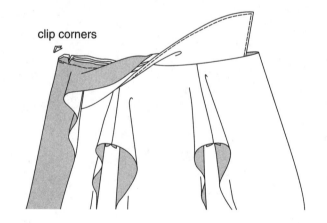

ATTACHING A COLLAR WITHOUT A BACK FACING

This section explains how to attach a flat, stand, or roll collar to a neckline without a back neck facing. The collar is applied with only a front facing instead of a complete neckline facing. The back of the collar is finished with top stitching. The collar is sewn to the center front of the garment—not to the garment edge. This sewing technique allows the collar to meet at center front when the garment is worn. Also, the button extension on the garment section extends past the collar.

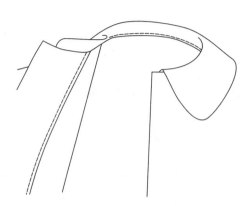

Collars that include a button extension (mandarin or shirt) are sewn to the garment edge. For these collars, follow the sewing directions in "Attaching a Collar Without Facings," page 245–246.

1 Sew and press the collar (following "Flat, Stand, or Roll Collar" steps 1 through 8, pages 234–235). The collar section should be finished as illustrated.

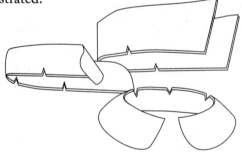

2 Sew the shoulder seams of the garment together. Stay stitch or crimp the neck edge of the garment to prevent the neckline from stretching.

Note: *This garment style has a button extension and an attached facing.*

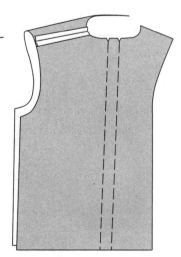

3 With the correct side of the garment facing up, pin the notched edge of the collar (the open edge) to the neck edge of the garment. Match the following:

- The center back of the collar to the center back of the garment.
- The shoulder position of the collar to the shoulder seam of the garment.
- The center front of the collar to the center front of the garment.

Note: *The facing is placed away from the garment.*

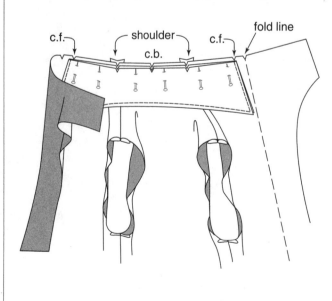

4 Fold back and position the correct side of the facing on top of the pinned collar, matching all raw edges carefully. Repin the neck edge so that the garment, collar, and facing are pinned together (repin the pins one at a time).

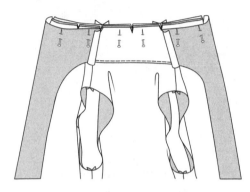

5 Clip the top layer of the collar at the shoulder seams. Repin the back neck area of the collar so that only one layer of the collar is pinned to the garment.

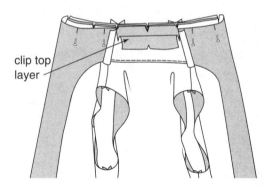

clip top layer

6 Stitch the collar and facing to the neck edge of the garment, keeping the top of the back collar area free and away from the neck seam. Stitch from neck edge to neck edge.

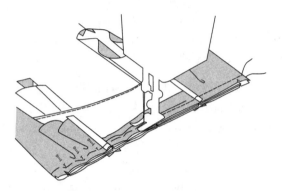

7 Turn the facing to the wrong side of the garment and press the collar up. Fold the unsewn seam allowance of the collar under, just past the original stitchline. Edge stitch the back neck area of the collar down. If necessary, stitch the shoulder seam of the facing to the shoulder seam of the garment.

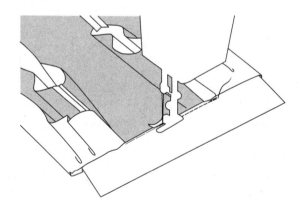

ATTACHING A COLLAR WITHOUT FACINGS

This section explains how to attach a stand collar (shirt or mandarin collar, with a button extension) into a neckline when the garment does not have any facings. Stand collars are usually applied to the neck edge without any facing. The collar is finished with top stitching.

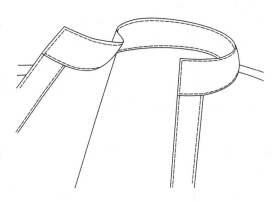

The front closure of the garment will have a placket instead of any facings; the placket should be completed before the collar is stitched.

1 To prepare the collar, sew and press the mandarin or shirt collar.

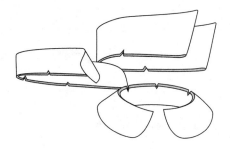

2 To prepare the shoulder seams, sew together the shoulder seams of the garment. Also, if the garment has a placket, stitch the placket before continuing to sew the collar. Stay stitch or crimp the neck edge of the garment to prevent the neckline from stretching.

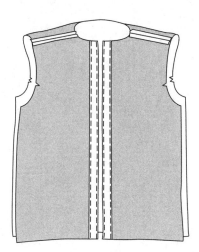

3 With the correct side of the garment facing up, pin one layer only of the collar (the open edge) to the garment. Be sure to keep the neck edges even. Match the following:

- The center back of the collar to the center back of the garment.
- The shoulder position of the collar to the shoulder seam of the garment.
- The center front of the collar to the center front of the garment.
- The edge of the collar to the edge of the garment.

Note: *The top layer of the collar falls away from the garment.*

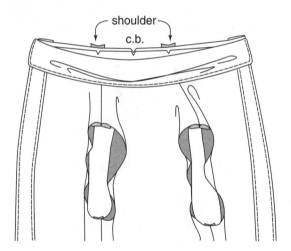

4 Stitch one layer of the collar to the neck edge of the garment. Keep the top layer of the collar away from the neck seam. Stitch from garment edge to garment edge.

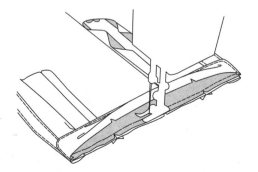

5 If necessary, trim the seam allowance of the neck edge. Press the seam allowance up toward the collar. Press the unsewn collar seam allowance up toward the collar.

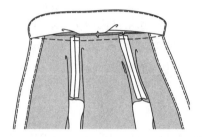

6 Place and pin the unsewn collar seam allowance just beyond the stitched neckline seam, and pin in place.

7 Edge stitch the collar to the garment, from collar edge to collar edge.

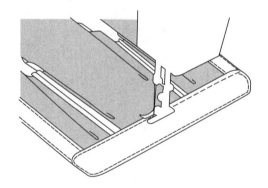

SHAWL COLLAR

A shawl collar is cut in one piece as part of the front of the garment and follows the front opening and has two separate lapels. The following instructions for the shawl collar are applied on a jacket, with no back neck facing.

1 Cut out all pattern pieces. (Illustrated here are a jacket front, a jacket back, a shawl collar facing, and a shawl collar interfacing.) Transfer all dart markings from the pattern to the fabric.

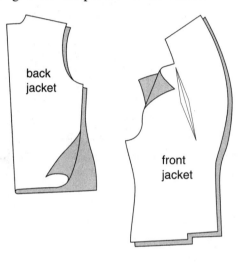

back jacket

front jacket

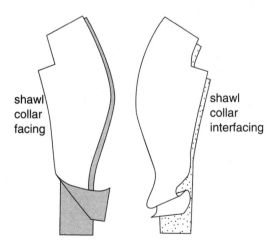

shawl collar facing

shawl collar interfacing

2 Sew the fisheye darts on the front jacket pieces. Press the darts toward the center front. Clip the widest part of the dart so that it lays as flat as possible.

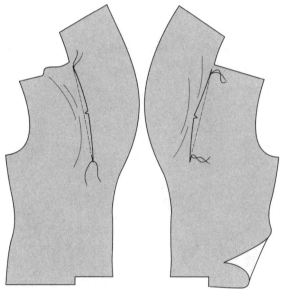

3 Attach the shawl collar interfacing pieces to the front jacket sections by edge stitching (or surging), and press. Refer to "Interfacing," pages 270–273.

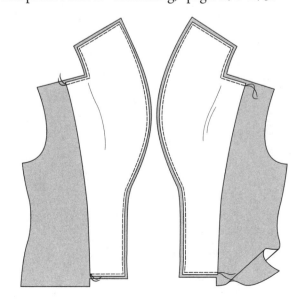

4 Pin and sew center-back collar seams of the shawl collar facing, correct sides together. Press seam open.

center back facing seam

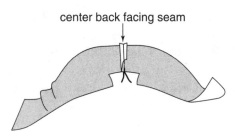

5 Pin and sew the center-back seam of the front jacket collar section, correct sides together. Press seam open.

shawl collar center back seam

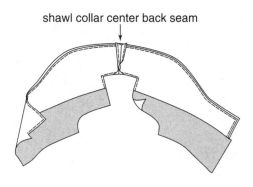

6 Sew the front and back jacket shoulder seams to each other, correct sides together. Press seams open.

7 Pin and sew the front jacket under collar neckline to the back jacket neckline, correct sides together.

pin and sew neckline

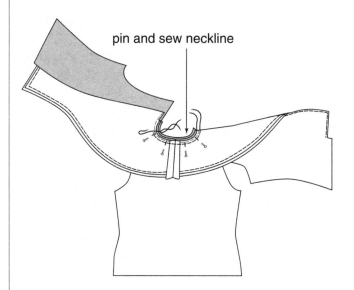

8 Pin the shawl collar facing outer edges to the jacket lapel outer edges. With correct sides together, match the following:

- The center-back collar seam to the center-back facing collar seam
- All shoulder positions

Sew the lapel and the collar outer edges.

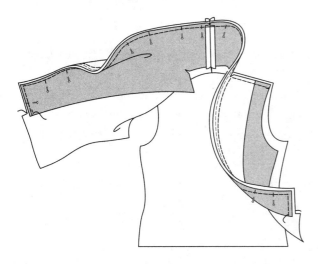

9 Turn the facing to the inside of the jacket. Match the shoulder seams of the facing and the jacket. Understitch the facing edge of the jacket up to the breakpoint of the jacket lapel. Understitch the jacket lapel edge of the jacket.

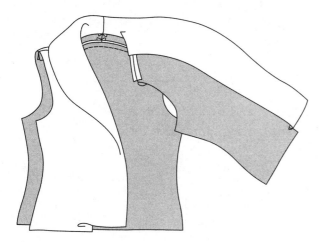

10 Tuck under the unsewn seam allowance of the back neck facing, toward the back neckline collar edge. Pin this seam allowance just past the stitchline of the back neckline seam of the jacket. Edgestitch the back neck area of the facing. Sew the shoulder seams of the facing to the shoulder seams of the garment.

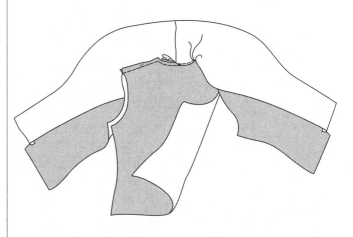

11 Finish sewing the remainder of the jacket.

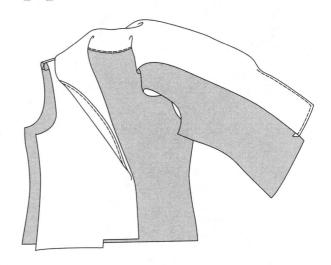

REVERE COLLAR

The revere collar is a collar in which the facing of the lapels folds back to show the reverse side of the lapel. (*Revere* is another name for *lapel*.)

1 After the pattern pieces are cut, sew the darts, style lines, and seams to complete the front and back jacket pieces. Press the darts and seams flat.

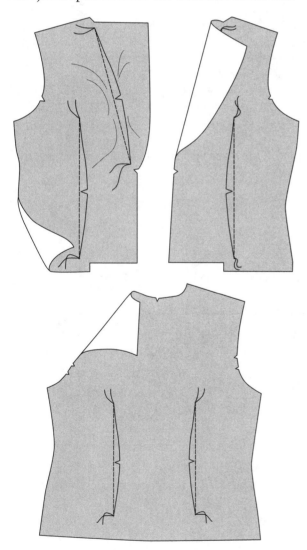

2 Attach the interfacing pieces to the front jacket section and the back neckline area by edge stitching or pressing. Refer to "Interfacing," pages 270–273. Placing the interfacing on the garment sections ensures that garment neck edges do not stretch out.

Note: *The interfacing is sometimes attached to the facing rather than to the garment pieces for easier sewing.*

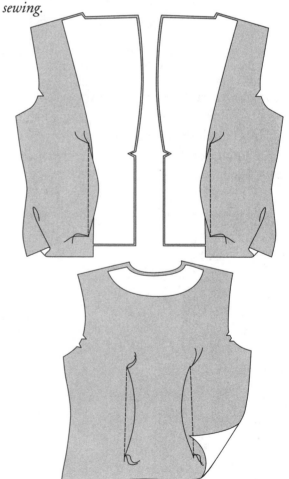

3 Sew the front and back shoulder seams to each other, correct sides together. Press seams open. Sew the front and back facing shoulder seams to each other, correct sides together. Press seams open.

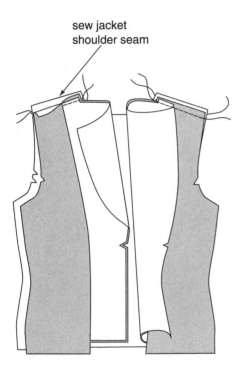

sew jacket
shoulder seam

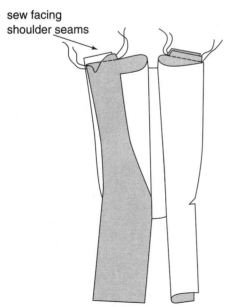

sew facing
shoulder seams

4 Pin the front and back jacket facings to the front and back jacket pieces. Match all lapel and neckline edges, with correct sides together. Also match center-back positions and shoulder seams. Sew the facing to the jacket, from the bottom of the facing up and around the neckline, and then down to the other facing edge.

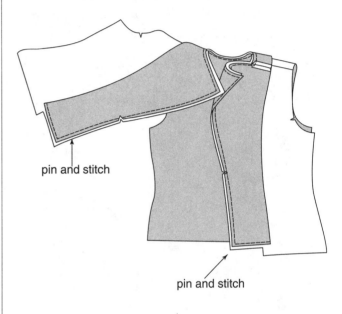

pin and stitch

pin and stitch

5 Turn the facing to the inside of the jacket. Understitch the facing edge of the jacket up to the breakpoint of the jacket lapel. Also, understitch the jacket lapel edge.

Note: *Understitching is achieved by folding all seam allowances to the facing side. From the right side of the facing, stitch through the facing and seam allowances, close to the seamline. This helps the facing seam to lay flat and minimizes bulk.*

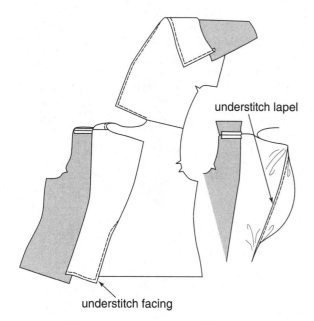

understitch lapel

understitch facing

6 Press the entire neckline and revere.

CHAPTER 16

Necklines

KEY TERMS AND CONCEPTS

A **neckline placket** is a visible overlapping strip of fabric sewn in a garment opening. It is used to reinforce and decorate the necklines of garments where an opening is desired.

A neckline placket uses two finished strips of equal width, applied to fill an oblong opening. The placket strips create a lapped closure, with the top placket visible on the face of the garment. A placket is used to

- Emphasize an opening in a garment
- Create design detail

Three types of placket styles are:

- The **shirt neckline placket** is sewn into a front neckline opening. The top and under plackets are different sizes and lengths, resulting in a clean finish on both the inside and outside of the garment.

- The **tailored shirt placket** is sewn along the entire front opening of a shirt.

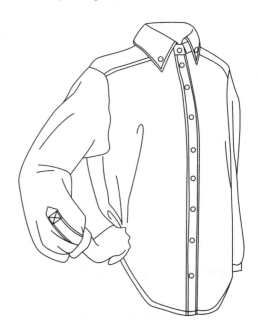

- The **budget shirt placket** is sewn into a front opening of a shirt. The top and under plackets are the same shape and length.

All plackets should be interfaced because buttons and buttonholes are usually sewn to them, and the interfacing provides the needed extra strength.

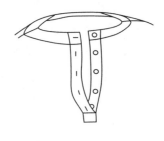

SHIRT NECKLINE PLACKET

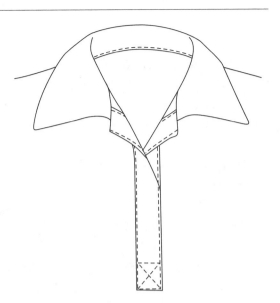

The shirt neckline placket is an ideal finish for neckline openings in women's, children's, and men's shirts. It is used to reinforce and add style to the necklines of garments where an opening is desired. The lower end of a placket can have a pointed, square, or rounded finish.

A neckline shirt placket is applied in a similar way as the shirt sleeve placket. However, in a neckline placket, the under plackets are often a different size from the top plackets, and the lower end of the placket is finished differently.

When the finished neckline placket is wider than 1 inch, the opening at the neckline is usually cut out. The amount that is cut out depends on the finished width of the placket pieces. Follow the pattern directions to determine this opening.

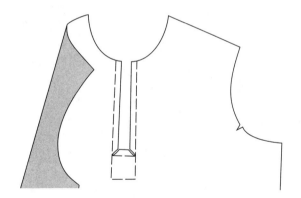

1 Cut two pattern pieces: an under placket and a top placket. The under placket should be slightly smaller in width than the placket.

2 Attach the interfacing to the wrong side of the fabric, on half of each placket piece along the foldlines.

Note: *To allow greater ease in sewing the placket in place, press all seam allowances and placket pieces in half along the foldline.*

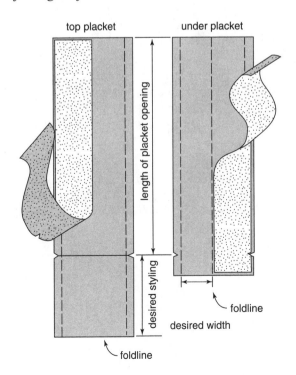

3 Place the garment on the sewing table, with the wrong side up. Place the correct side of the under placket (the shorter piece) to the wrong side of the garment opening, as illustrated.

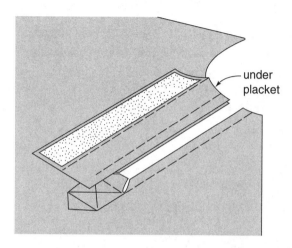

under placket

4 Stitch the placket to the garment with the recommended pattern seam allowance (usually $\frac{1}{4}$-inch for industry sewing and $\frac{5}{8}$-inch for home sewing). Start stitching at the neckline and stop $\frac{1}{2}$-inch from the end of the placket.

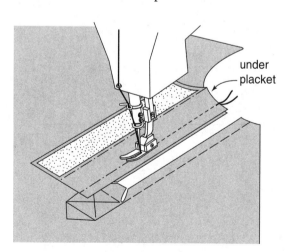

under placket

5 Press under the unsewn pattern seam allowance.

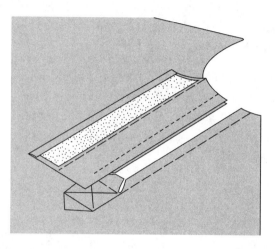

6 Turn the entire under placket to the correct side of the garment. Press the placket in half, just past the original stitchline.

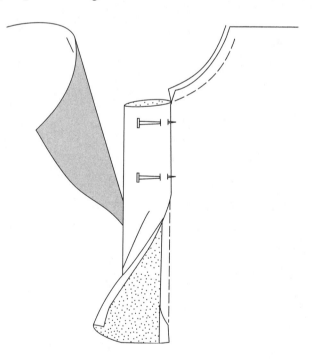

7 Top stitch the under placket in place along the folded seam allowance edge. Also, to balance the top stitching, edge stitch along the fold of the placket.

Note: *The placket piece is stitched to within $\frac{1}{2}$-inch of the end of the placket. However, this is the entire length of the placket opening.*

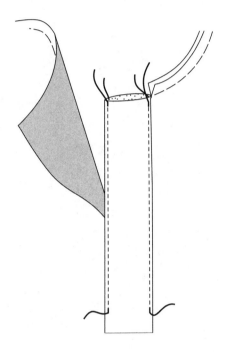

8 Flip the garment and the finished placket back to expose the $\frac{1}{2}$-inch placket tail and the clipped triangular garment piece. The tail will be exposed on the correct side of the fabric.

Note: *There is a clean seam on the under placket on the wrong side of the garment, and a $\frac{1}{2}$-inch tail on the correct side of the garment.*

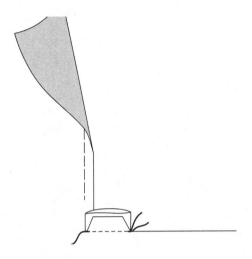

9 With the wrong side of the garment up, place one layer of the top placket (the longer piece), matching the correct side of the placket to the wrong side of the garment.

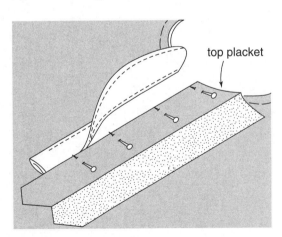

top placket

10 Stitch the top placket to the garment, with the recommended pattern seam allowance (usually $\frac{1}{4}$-inch for industry sewing and $\frac{5}{8}$-inch for home sewing). Start stitching at the neckline and stop stitching at the end of the neckline opening (the notch).

Note: *The corner of the placket opening has already been clipped.*

Press under the unsewn $\frac{1}{4}$-inch seam allowance.

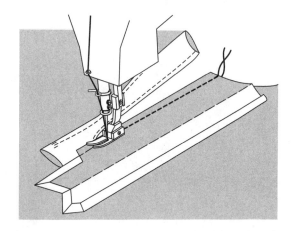

11 Press the entire top placket in half, turning it to the correct side of the garment.

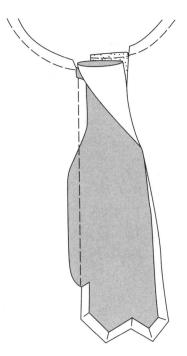

12 Keeping the under placket out and away from the top placket, top stitch the top placket in place. Stitch along the folded edge and the seam edges.

Note: *Stitch across the bottom of the placket and across the end of the placket opening, covering the $\frac{1}{2}$-inch tail of the under placket.*

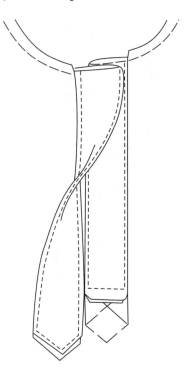

TAILORED SHIRT PLACKET

The tailored shirt placket method is the method most commonly used in the garment industry. It saves time and has a very clean, professional look.

The right and left front shirt placket pattern pieces are figured in the same manner as for the shirt neckline placket, however, the notches for the plackets are placed differently. The illustration shows the placket amounts and the notches transferred from the pattern.

1 Attach interfacing to the garment placket sections of the shirt.

Note: *Women's button opening is shown and described here, reverse the interfacing for the men's button opening.*

Place the interfacing on the left front shirt placket, $\frac{1}{2}$-inch from the outer edge of the garment piece, as illustrated. Place the interfacing on the right front shirt placket, along the outer edge of the garment piece, as illustrated.

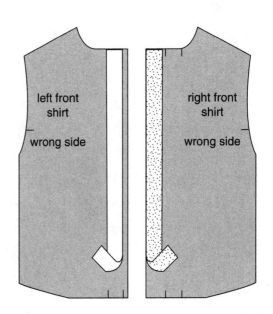

left front shirt

wrong side

right front shirt

wrong side

2 Sew the placket on the right side of the front garment. (Or on the left side for a men's shirt).

A. Fold and press the front shirt placket on the first foldline (the width of the finished placket).

B. Fold and press again on the second foldline.

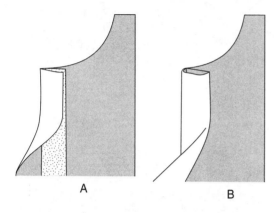

C. Stitch the placket $\frac{1}{4}$-inch away from the last foldline.

D. Press the placket out and away from the shirt.

Note: *This gives the right placket a clean-finished area on the inside of this placket.*

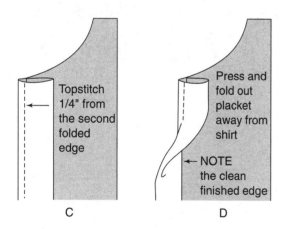

3 Sew the facing area on the left side of the front shirt placket area (or on the right side for a men's shirt).

A. Press the first edge of the left side of the shirt under $\frac{1}{2}$-inch (along the first edge of the interfacing).

B. Fold and press the foldine on the left side of the shirt (along the opposite edge of the interfacing).

C. Stitch the facing in place at the first foldline pressed edge. Top stitch the opposite edge for a placket finishing effect.

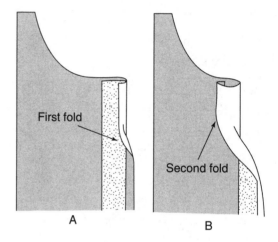

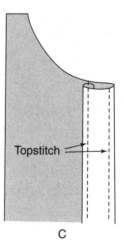

HIDDEN BUTTON PLACKET

The hidden button placket is another popular type of placket which is used for front opening areas of a bodice, shirt, dress or jacket. The hidden button placket is a method for clean-finishing the front opening, while at the same time hiding the buttons. This is a triple placket technique which eliminates the need for added facings.

On a woman's blouse with a hidden button placket, the right front blouse (side for the buttonholes) uses the hidden button placket; whereas the left blouse (the side for the buttons) uses only a facing. This is reversed on a man's shirt. This style of garment will require a collar design to clean-finish the top edge of the placket as well as to finish the neckline.

PREPARING PATTERN PIECES

The right and left front blouse placket pattern pieces are figured slightly different. The illustration below gives the placket amounts and the notches necessary for the pattern.

1 RIGHT SIDE OF THE BLOUSE:

A. Locate the center front line of the pattern.

B. Draw the actual placket $\frac{3}{4}$ inch on both sides of the existing center front line.

C. Add $1\frac{1}{2}$ inches (width of the placket) from the last line drawn parallel to center front.

D. Then add $1\frac{3}{8}$ inch (width of the under placket) two more times (from the last line drawn) parallel to center front.

E. Add $\frac{1}{4}$ inch seam allowance at the end of the last line drawn.

F. Place "foldline notches" on the FIRST PLACKET FOLDLINE from the edge and then again on the THIRD PLACKET FOLDLINE from the outer edge (second foldline notch).

2 LEFT SIDE OF THE BLOUSE:

A. Remove the last two placket widths from the outer edge.

B. Add a $\frac{1}{4}$ inch seam allowance at the outer edge of the remaining placket width.

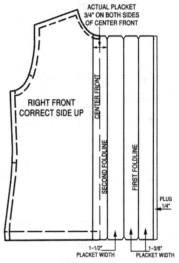

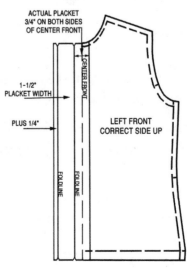

Sewing the Hidden Button Placket

1 Attach the interfacing to the wrong side of the blouse placket sections.

A. Align the interfacing on the RIGHT FRONT blouse placket between the first and second notch outer edge (as illustrated).

B. Place the interfacing on the LEFT FRONT blouse placket $\frac{1}{4}$ inch from the outer edge of the blouse (as illustrated).

2 Fold and stitch the RIGHT PLACKET:

A. Fold and press the RIGHT front blouse placket on the first foldline (width of the finished placket + the $\frac{1}{4}''$).

B. Fold and press again on the second foldline (refer to illustration).

C. From the correct side of the blouse, stitch the placket $1\frac{1}{2}''$ away from the last foldline.

Note: *The inside of the placket is automatically clean-finished.*

D. Press the placket on the stitchline until both folds meet. NOTE: Buttonholes can now be placed in the center of the underfold area.

3 Fold and stitch the LEFT PLACKET:

A. Press under $\frac{1}{4}$ inch on the first edge of the LEFT side of the blouse (along the edge of the interfacing).

B. Fold and press again on the foldline of the LEFT side of the shirt (along the opposite edge of the interfacing).

C. Stitch the facing in place at the first foldline pressed edge. Topstitch the opposite edge for a finished placket effect.

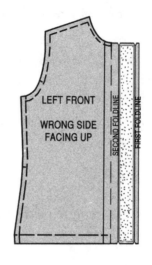
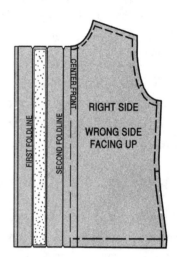

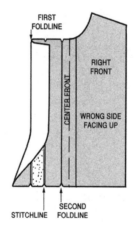
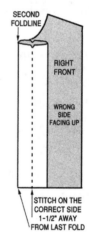
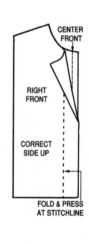

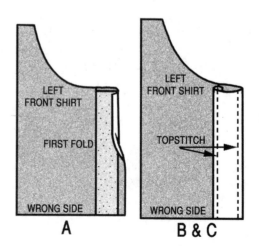

BUDGET SHIRT PLACKET

The budget placket method is a fast and fairly inexpensive way to sew a neckline placket. However, it gives the inside of the garment an unfinished look and should therefore be used only for budget garments.

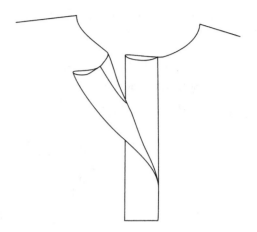

When the finished neckline placket is wider than 1 inch, the opening at the neckline is usually cut out. The amount that is cut out depends on the finished width of the placket pieces. Follow the pattern directions to determine this opening.

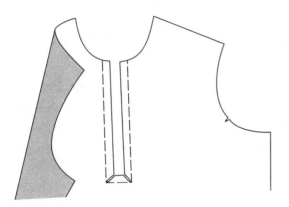

1 Cut two pattern pieces: an under placket and a top placket. The under placket should be slightly smaller in width than the top placket.

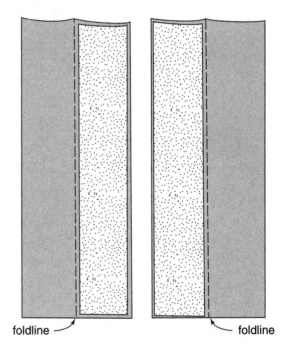

foldline — ↗   ↖ — foldline

2 If necessary, attach the interfacing to the wrong side of the fabric, on half of each placket piece.

3 Fold both placket pieces in half lengthwise, correct sides together. Stitch the neckline edges together, with a $\frac{1}{4}$-inch seam allowance.

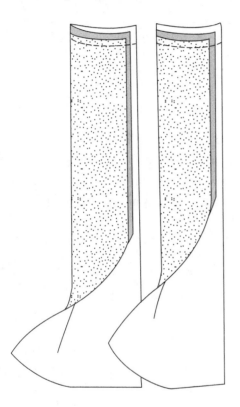

4 Turn each placket correct side out and press flat.

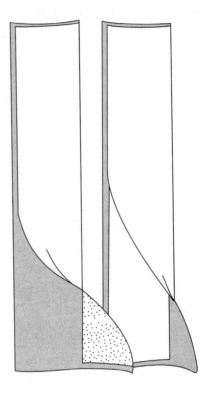

5 With the correct side of the garment facing up, pin both plackets to the garment. The interfaced side of the placket should be placed closest to the garment.

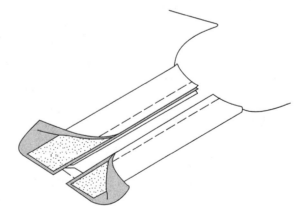

6 Stitch both seam allowances to the placket to the garment the entire length of the placket opening stitchline. Do not stitch across the bottom. Clip the corners.

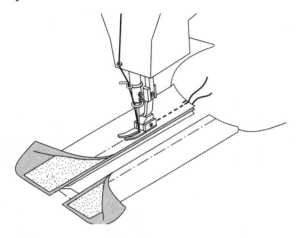

7 Flip the garment and both placket pieces back to expose the placket tails and the clipped triangular garment piece. The tail will be exposed on the wrong side of the fabric. (Plackets should lay right over left). Stitch across the base of this area.

Note: *This gives the right placket a clean-finished area on the inside of this placket.*

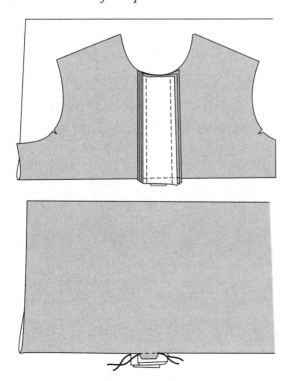

8 With the correct side of the garment up, press the placket into position.

Note: *For a variation on the final stitching, stitch one layer of the plackets to the correct side of the garment and hand stitch the plackets closed on the wrong side of the garment. Also, turn under the bottom of the top placket and hand stitch it into the finished position.*

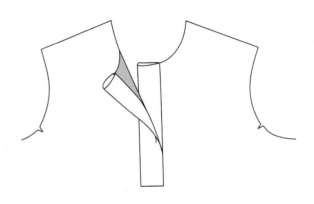

CHAPTER 17

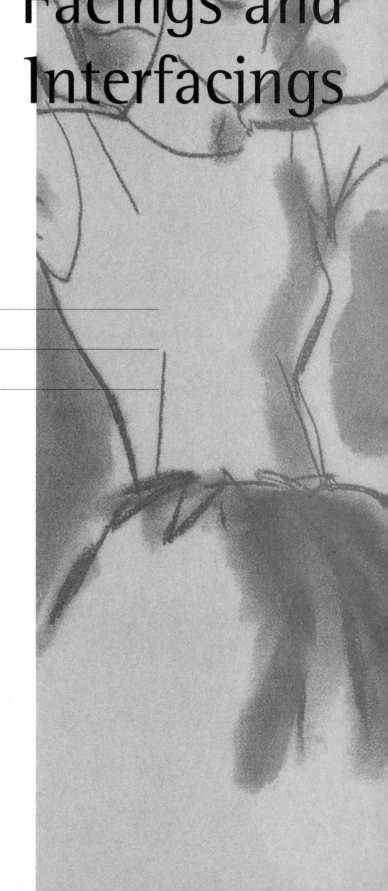

Facings and Interfacings

KEY TERMS AND CONCEPTS

A **facing** is a duplicate layer of fabric stitched to the raw edge of a garment for the purpose of clean finishing the seam. It is normally sewn, to the garment fabric, with the correct sides together, and turned to the inside of the garment and lays flat. However, it may be folded to the outside for decorative purposes.

Usually a facing follows the shape of the piece to which it is being attached, except if bias strips are used in place of the traditional facing.

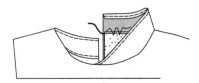

There are several types of facings, each requiring slightly different methods of construction. In some cases the type of facing needed is indicated by a separate pattern piece and in others the facing pattern piece is included with the garment section and cut along with the garment section. Some of the types of facings are

- **Bias facing**—A narrow bias strip of fabric, commercially or self-prepared, stitched to the garment and turned to the inside. It is a substitute for shaped and fitted facings of garments and is used to save fabric.

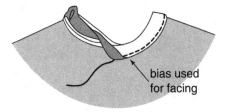

bias used for facing

- **All-in-one facing**—A facing area cut and shaped with a neckline and armhole combination. It is commonly used in vests, halters, and boleros.

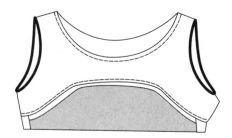

- **Shaped facing**—Facing cut in the same shape and grain as the area it will clean finish. It is stitched, and then turned to the inside of the garment. It is used on bodice necklines, bodice armholes, and waistlines of skirts or pants.

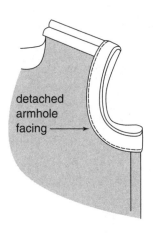

detached armhole facing →

- **Extended facing**—A facing unit cut in one piece with the garment and folded to the inside. It is used on a front or back opening to avoid the seamline produced by a joining separate facing. It reduces bulk when making garments of heavy fabrics.

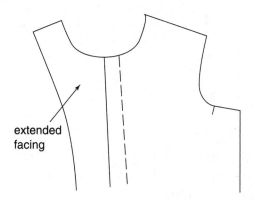

extended facing

- **Outside facing**—A shaped narrow piece or bias tape planned to be visible on the outside of the garment. This type of facing is a decorative finish that also conceals raw edges.

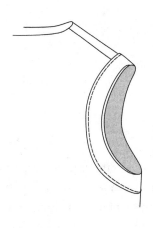

INTERFACING

Attaching Fusible Interfacings

Fusible interfacing is applied through the process of bonding. For additional information on interfacing, refer to pages 13–15, Chapter 1.

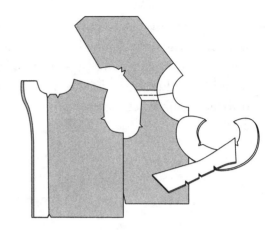

Most irons have a temperature range from cool to hot. If an iron is too hot, it can distort, melt, or scorch the garment fabric. If it is too cool, it may not be able to fuse the interfacing. Test the iron temperature with a small swatch of the garment fabric and interfacing.

1 Cut the interfacing. Place the coated side of the interfacing piece to the wrong side of the garment area to be interfaced.

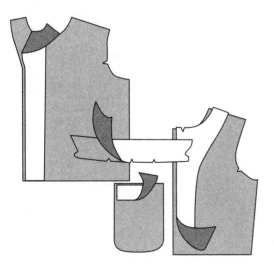

2 Using a steam iron, press the interfacing to the fabric by lifting the iron and steaming a section at a time. If the interfacing does not adhere to the fabric, use a damp pressing cloth between the iron and the interfacing to create more steam. Continue to use the steam setting on the iron and add pressure.

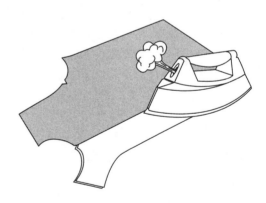

Note: *Using a pressing cloth can help create extra steam and make it easier to fuse interfacing to fabric. Dampen a lightweight towel. Place the damp pressing cloth between the iron and the garment. Continue to use the steam setting on the iron, and apply a bit of pressure as you press.*

3 Clean finish the outer edge of the facing piece, if desired, by folding the edge of the garment detail over the interfacing. Use a small hand hemming stitch or machine, surge, or zig-zag stitch to reduce bulk.

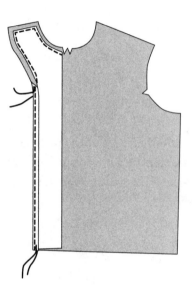

Attaching Nonfusible Interfacings

Nonfusible interfacing, or sew-in interfacing, is fabric without any glue that you attach by machine basting or surging it onto the garment.

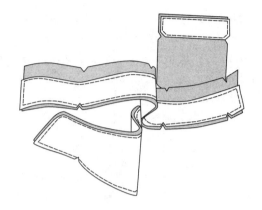

1 Cut the interfacing. Pin the interfacing to the wrong side of the garment or facing, placing the edge of the interfacing along the outer edge of the garment section.

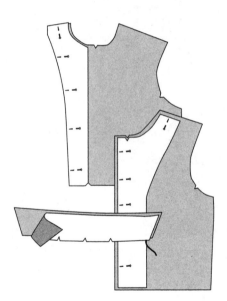

2 Machine stitch $\frac{1}{8}$-inch from the outer edge.

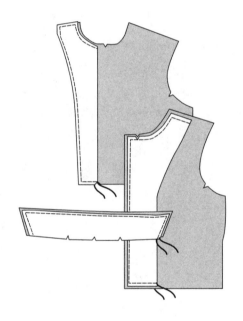

3 Machine or catch stitch the loose edge of the interfacing to the wrong side of the fabric if necessary.

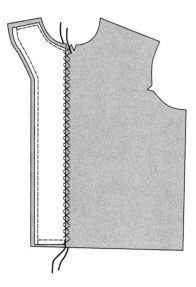

4 Clean finish the outer edge of the facing piece, if desired:

- First, fold the edge of the garment detail over the interfacing.

- Then, use a small hand hemming stitch or machine overlock or zig-zag stitch to reduce bulk.

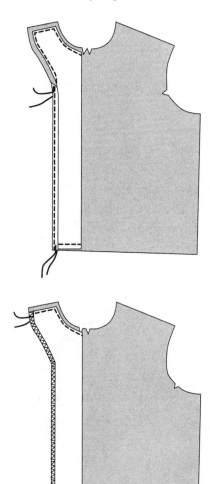

FACING

Facings are used to conceal raw edges of the garment, add support to the garment, and create smooth, flat edges at the neckline or armhole.

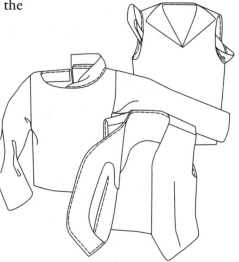

Most facing areas are interfaced. Before sewing the facing to the garment, attach interfacing to the garment side of the facing area. Refer to "Interfacings" in this chapter.

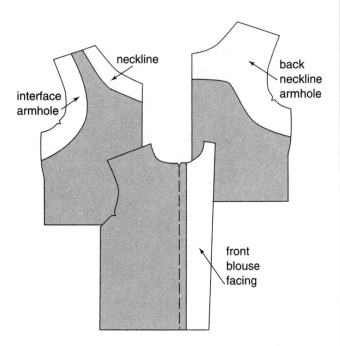

1 For neckline facings, sew the shoulder seams on the garment and all seams on the facing. For armhole facing, sew the side seams and shoulder seams.

Hint: *Stay stitch or crimp the neck edge of the garment to prevent the neckline from stretching.*

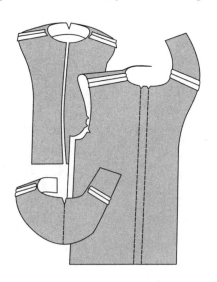

2 Pin the correct side of the facing to the correct side of the garment. Match all raw edges, notches, and seam positions.

3 Following the required seam allowances, stitch the facing to the garment.

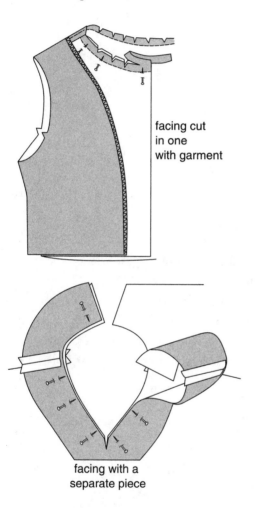

facing cut
in one
with garment

facing with a
separate piece

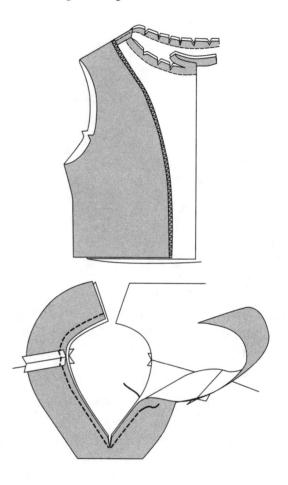

4 When sewing a V-shaped or square-shaped facing, clip into the corners or V position.

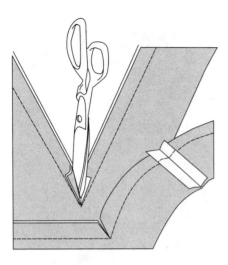

5 Understitch the facing seam. This is achieved by folding all seam allowances to the facing side. From the correct side of the facing, stitch through the facing and seam allowance close to the seamline.

Note: *Understitching helps to prevent the facing from showing on the correct side of the garment. This also allows the facing seam to lay flat and minimize bulk.*

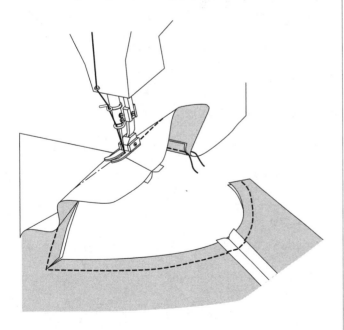

6 Turn the facing to the wrong side of the garment and press in place. If necessary, align the shoulder seamlines and stitch in place.

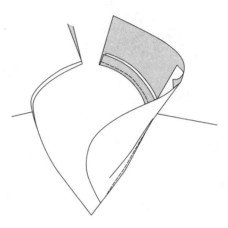

7 Finish the outer edges. Select a method to finish the outer edges of the facing that is suitable for the fabric. You can turn the fabric under $\frac{1}{8}$-inch and stitch close to the edge, or you can overlock or surge the edges. Regardless of the method used, the facing should have a flat finish.

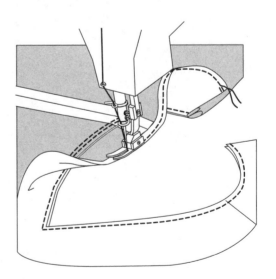

All-in-One Facing

All-in-one facing is usually used on a sleeveless garment with a fairly open neckline. There are several ways to attach an all-in-one facing; the method demonstrated here finishes the garment professionally.

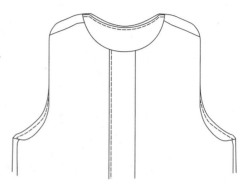

1 Attach interfacings to the wrong side of the garment, using the pressing or basting method.

2 Stitch all shoulder seams and side seams of both the garment and the one-piece facing, correct sides together. Press all seams open. Finish the outer edge of the facing either with an overlock stitch or with a machine stitch. Turn the edge under $\frac{1}{8}$-inch and stitch close to the edge.

3 Pin the facing to the garment, with the correct sides together. Match all notches and seams, and the center-front and center-back positions.

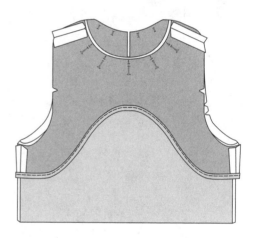

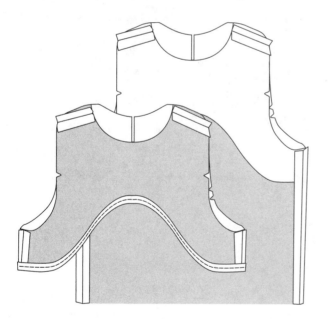

4 Keeping all raw edges even at the neck edge, stitch the neckline with the appropriate seam allowance. If necessary, trim seam allowance to $\frac{1}{4}$-inch.

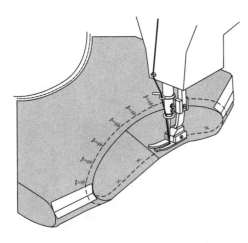

5 Understitch the neckline seam of the facing by folding the entire seam allowance toward the facing side and stitching on the correct side of the facing, close to the seam.

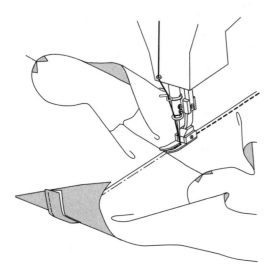

6 Turn the entire facing to the wrong side of the garment. Press the neckline seam.

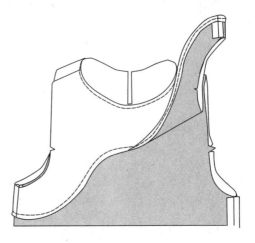

7 Lay the entire garment and facings flat, with the wrong side up, as illustrated, exposing the shoulder seams.

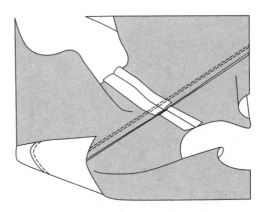

8 With the wrong side of the shoulder seams facing up, hold the armhole shoulder seam of the facing in one hand and the armhole shoulder seam of the garment in the other hand. Turn and match the garment to the facing, correct sides together. Pin or hand baste this area.

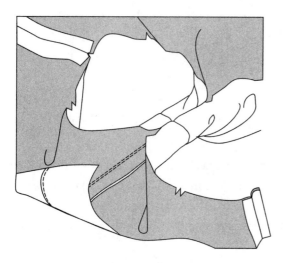

9 Working with the facing side up, continue to match the correct sides together at the raw edge of the armholes. Continue to pin or hand baste this area until the entire armhole has gone full circle. Repeat this turning process, and stitch the seam with the machine.

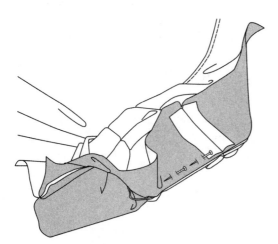

10 The facing will automatically turn to the correct side when the sewing process is completed. Press the neckline and armhole.

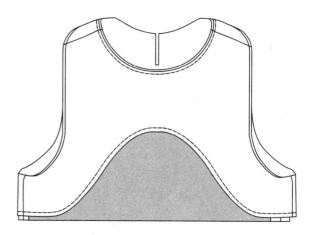

Bias Facing

Bias facing is a narrow bias strip of fabric stitched to the raw edge of the garment and then turned to the inside of the garment. It is a substitute for a shaped and fitted facing, and is also used as a facing on a collared neckline. The facing can then be either top stitched by machine or hand stitched.

Note that bias facing turns completely to the inside of the garment, whereas bias binding folds in half and leaves a bias finished edge showing on the outside and inside of the garment.

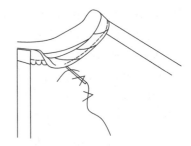

Use a 2-inch-wide strip of bias (usually in the same color as the garment or a contrasting color), or purchase a commercially prepared single-fold bias tape.

Refer to "Cutting Bias Strips" and "Joining Bias Strips," pages 130–131.

1 Pin the bias strip to the garment edge, correct sides together.

2 Stitch the seam, usually with a $\frac{1}{4}''$ seam allowance.

3 If a $\frac{5}{8}''$ seam was sewn, trim the seam to $\frac{1}{4}$-inch.

4 Fold the bias strip to the inside of the garment in the same manner in which a facing would be turned to the inside. The bias strip will not be showing on the outside. If desired, understitch the neckline seam.

5 Slipstitch or machine top stitch the bias strip in place.

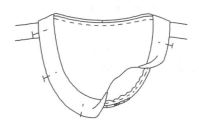

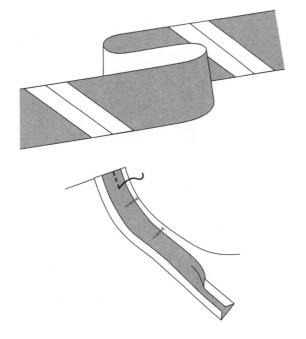

CHAPTER 18

Linings

KEY TERMS AND CONCEPTS

Lining is a duplicate of the garment, used to finish the inside of a garment and assembled in the same manner as the garment. The lining should be compatible with the fabric used for the garment. In most cases, except when desiring to add warmth, lining fabric should be relatively lightweight and have a slick finish. Lining is used to

- Provide a clean inside finish to a garment
- Provide a finished appearance in a garment
- Help maintain the shape of the outer layer, and prevent the garment from stretching or sagging
- Add warmth, if it is an insulated lining

There are three types of linings:

- **Construction linings**

    —The two layers—lining and garment fabric—are treated as one.

    —Each garment piece is lined, one at a time, and the lining influences the drape of the garment.

    —The garment pieces and lining are cut in the same shape.

    —Each lining piece is sewn or surged (overlocked) to the garment piece. After all the pieces requiring lining are prepared, the garment is constructed, following the regular sewing process.

- **Slip linings/free-hanging linings**

    —The layers are handled separately and are simplified by eliminating all facings, stylelines, extra pleat fullness, and pockets (however, darts are created in the facing).

    —The lining and the outer garment are sewn separately, until they are attached at the waistline or neckline, from which the lining hangs freely (hence the name).

    —The lining is about 1 inch shorter than the outer garment and is not sewn to the outer garment at the bottom edges.

—This type of lining is used in skirts, pants, and dresses.

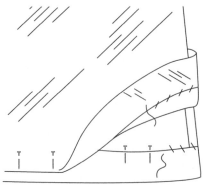

Lining hemmed separately

- **Clean linings**

    —The layers are handled separately, with or without facings.

    —A clean lining gives a completely finished look on the inside of vests, bustier bodices, and tailored jackets and coats.

    —The lining and the outer garment are sewn separately, until they are attached at all the outer edges and turned correct side out, giving a clean, finished look on both sides.

    —Sometimes these linings are used in addition to the facings, such as on tailored jackets. However, on garments such as vests, many times the lining replaces the need for facings and completely finishes the inside of the vest.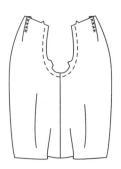

Some garments, such as jackets, have individual lining pattern pieces with built-in additional ease allowance for more comfortable body movement.

Linings for dresses, skirts, vests, or pants are usually cut the same as the outer pieces, but without stylelines or pockets.

Each lining type needs specific construction details so that the lining will not make the garment bulge or pull.

FREE-HANGING SKIRT LINING

The skirt lining is sewn separately from the outer garment, until the pieces are attached at the waistline. The lining is not sewn at the bottom of the skirt—it hangs freely.

The lining pattern is simplified by eliminating all stylelines, extra waistline pleat fullness (darts are used in place of pleats), and pockets. If there is a kick pleat, the pleat excess is eliminated. The pattern envelope should contain the separate lining pieces.

1 Cut out the lining pieces, following the same grainline as on the outer pieces.

2 Sew all the lining pieces except for the waist area because waistbands and waist facings are not sewn on the lining pieces. Also do not sew the zipper seam area or within 1-inch of it. Complete the hems at this time.

Note: *In linings, hems can be machine stitched (see page 328).*

3 Cut out and sew the outer garment pattern pieces, including all pockets, pleats, and stylelines. Attach the zippers and sew the hems. Do not sew the waistline finish.

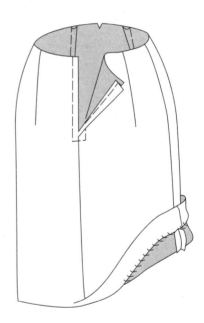

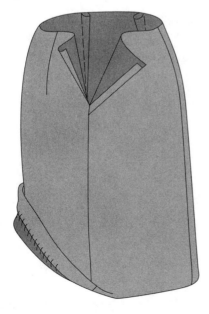

4 Pin baste the waistline area of the lining to the waistline area of the outer garment, wrong sides together and side seams together. Turn under the seam allowances at the zipper location and pin baste the zipper opening of the lining to the zipper tape.

5 Hand stitch the lining to the zipper tape.

6 Sew the lining and the outer garment waist area as one garment, with a waistband or facing.

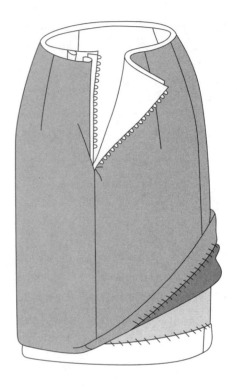

FREE-HANGING PANTS LINING

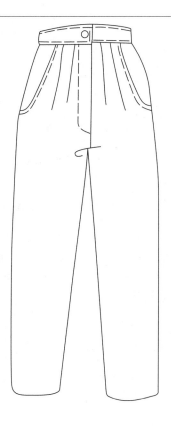

Pants lining is sewn separately from the outer garment, until the pieces are attached at the waistline. The lining is not sewn at the bottom of the pants—it hangs freely.

The lining pattern is simplified by eliminating all stylelines, extra pleat fullness (darts are used in place of pleats), and pockets. The pattern envelope should contain the separate lining pieces.

1 Cut out the lining pieces, following the same grainline as on the outer pieces.

2 Sew all the lining pieces except for the waist area because waistbands and waist facings are not sewn on the lining pieces. Also do not sew the zipper seam area or within 1 inch of it. Complete the hems at this time.

Note: *In linings, hems can be machine stitched (see page 328).*

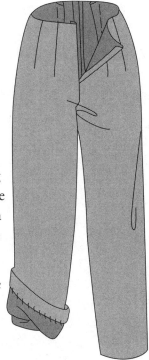

3 Cut out and sew the outer garment pattern pieces, including all pockets, pleats, and stylelines. Attach the zippers and sew the hems. Do not sew the waistline finish.

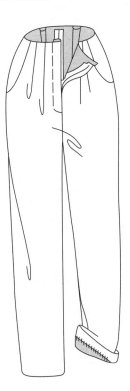

4 Pin baste the waistline area of the lining to the waistline area of the outer garment, wrong sides together and side seams together. Turn under the seam allowances at the zipper location and pin baste the zipper opening of the lining to the zipper tape.

5 Hand stitch the lining to the zipper tape.

6 Sew the lining and the outer garment waist area as one garment, with a waistband or facing.

VEST LINING

A vest is a sleeveless garment that extends to or below the waist. Vests are usually worn over blouses or shirts and sometimes under suit jackets. They are used as an accessory to complement or enhance an ensemble. A vest can be designed with or without a collar, and it can be fitted or loose.

The following instructions illustrate how to line a vest completely, give a finished look on the inside of the vest, and avoid the use of facings to clean finish the outside edges.

1 Using all the vest pattern pieces, cut out the vest.

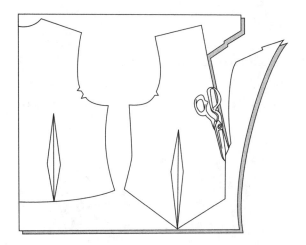

2 Cut $\frac{1}{8}$-inch from the outer edges of the lining pieces. This trimming step is necessary to ensure that the lining turns completely to the inside of the garment.

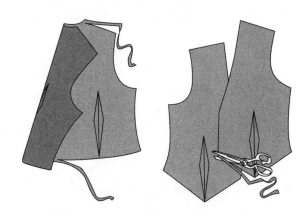

3 Sew the shoulder seams, darts, stylelines, and inside pockets on the vest and vest lining. Do not sew the side seams.

4 Pin baste the armholes, necklines, and front edges of the lining and the outer garment, with the correct sides together.

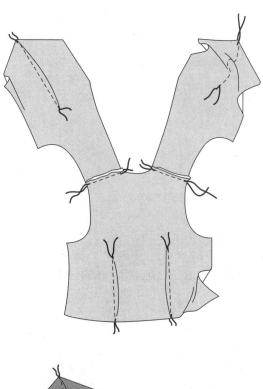

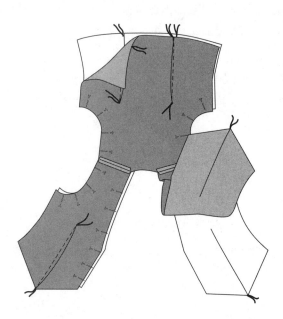

5 Machine stitch the outer garment and lining, leaving the side seams and the lower back edge unsewn. If necessary, trim all seam allowances to $\frac{1}{4}$-inch.

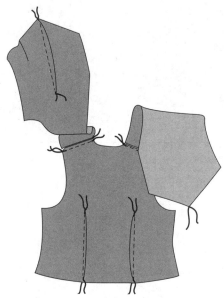

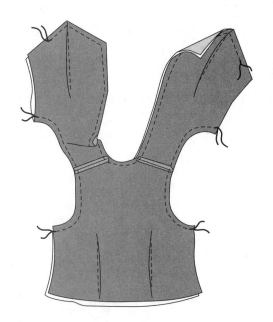

6 Reach into the vest and turn it inside out.

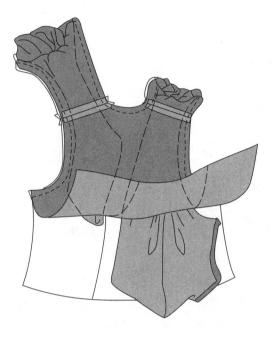

7 Carefully press the sewn seams flat before proceeding.

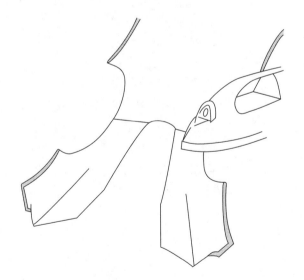

8 Match the side seams, with the correct sides together, and sew them together from the underarm armhole corner.

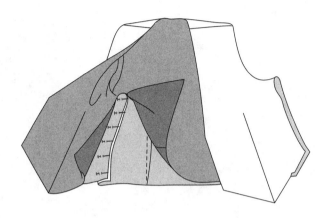

9 Press the side seams so that they lay flat.

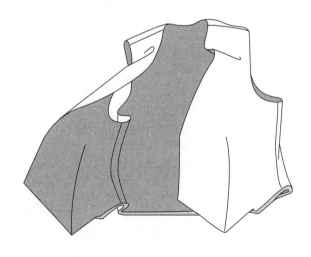

10 Turn the vest inside out. Pin together and stitch the lower edges of the vest, leaving the center-back area open several inches.

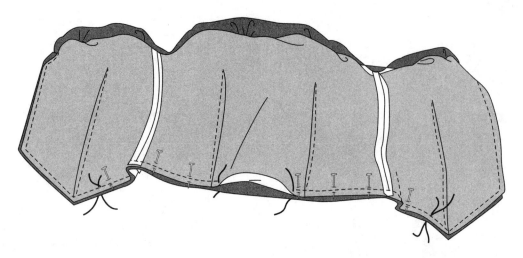

11 Turn the vest correct side out.

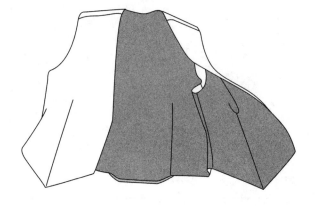

12 Blindstitch or machine stitch the center-back opening closed and press the vest.

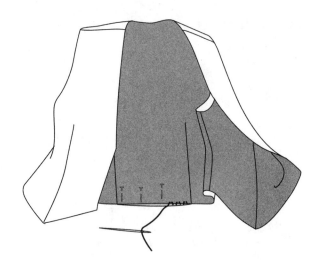

BUSTIER LINING

A bustier is a form-fitting strapless bodice that fits snugly around the rib cage. It is supported by boning and an extra tight fit under the bust and the side seams. The outside design can vary.

A bustier is lined and includes a foundation garment sewn between the lining and the outside fabric. The lining and the foundation garment always have princess seams in the front, side seams, and a one-piece back with a center-back zipper.

The foundation garment for the bustier is cut the same as the lining. The purposes of this foundation garment are to allow the boning to be stitched and to add extra body for maximum support. This foundation garment is cut out of a substantial woven fabric, the same shape as the lining pieces.

ATTACHING BONING TO THE BUSTIER FOUNDATION

1 Sew the entire bustier foundation in the desired fabric, leaving an opening at the center back. Press all the seam allowances open.

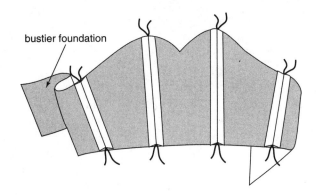

bustier foundation

2 Pin a strip of boning to each princess seam and side seam. The strips of boning should lay on the wrong side of the garment, covering the seam.

Note: *The boned end of each strip should be trimmed at each end (about $\frac{1}{2}$-inch), and the excess fabric at each end should be turned over the boned edges.*

Note: *Boning is a flexible narrow strip made of featherboning or stiff nylon, used to stiffen seams and edges of close-fitting garments to prevent them from slipping.*

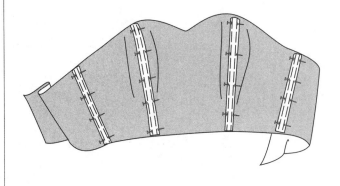

3 Using a zipper foot, stitch the boning to the princess seams and the side seams.

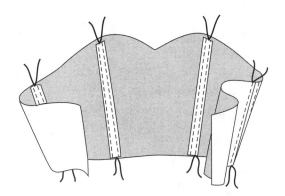

Note: *If more strength or support is needed, you can place extra boning in a variety of areas, such as across the side bust panel, from top to bottom.*

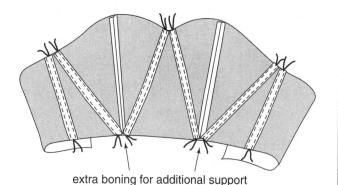

extra boning for additional support

PREPARING THE BUSTIER LINING AND THE BUSTIER

1 Using the same pattern as the bustier foundation, cut the lining from the desired lining fabric.

2 Sew all lining pieces together, leaving an opening at the center back. (this is usually for a zipper) Press all seam allowances open.

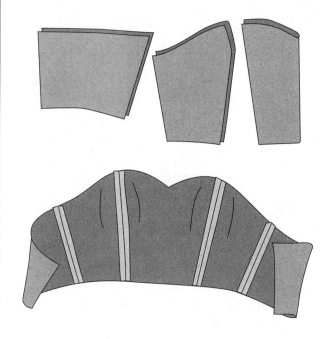

3 Sew the outside garment together, leaving an opening at the center back (this is usually for a zipper).

Note: *The outside design of the bustier can vary. When it is sewn together, however, the outside design has the same neckline as the lining and the foundation garment.*

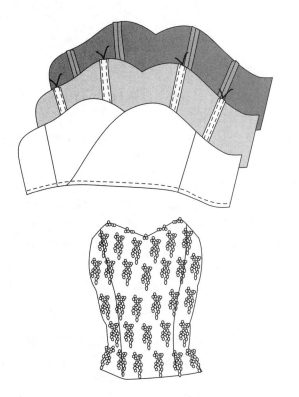

ATTACHING THE LINING TO THE BUSTIER

1 Pin the foundation garment to the wrong side of the lining. Stitch all outer edges together so that the lining and the foundation garment will serve as one piece.

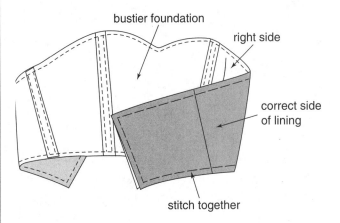

bustier foundation

right side

correct side of lining

stitch together

2 Place the lining, with the attached foundation garment, to the outside garment, correct sides together.

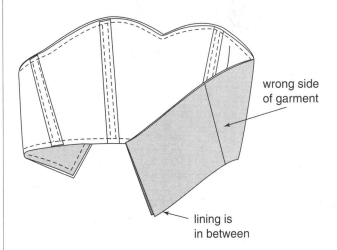

wrong side of garment

lining is in between

3 Using a $\frac{1}{4}$-inch seam allowance, stitch the bustline seams together.

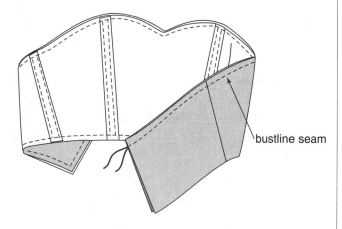

bustline seam

4 Exposing the bustline seam, place the lining, making sure the attached foundation garment and the outer garment are flat. Understitch all the layers of the seam allowance to the lining side.

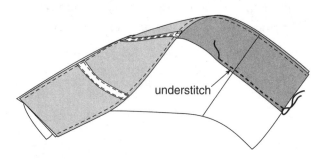

understitch

5 Turn the garment pieces so that the correct side of the lining and the outside garment are facing out.

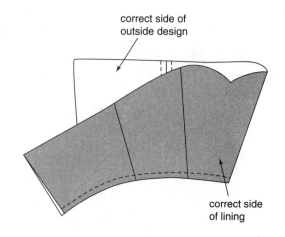

correct side of outside design

correct side of lining

6 The bustier is now ready to be attached to the skirt part of the garment. Sew the skirt and the bustier waist seams together. Pin and insert a zipper at the center-back seam. The zipper will extend at least 2 inches into the skirt.

CHAPTER 19

Tailoring

KEY TERMS AND CONCEPTS

Tailoring is a process of cutting, fitting, stitching, and finishing a garment to conform to the body by means of darts, linings, hems, and pressing techniques. Because tailored jackets and coats are typically worn over clothing, tailoring techniques support these garments during wearing and create a smoother outer garment shape.

Most jackets also have **lining fabric** attached inside to help the jacket slip over clothing more easily and hide the inside construction.

Note: *See pages 306–308 for sewing an unlined jacket.*

The **two-piece sleeve** is cut in two pieces—one for the underarm area, and one for the top arm area. The separate sections create more shaping in the elbow area and allow the arm to bend more freely.

Common terms used in tailoring include the following:

- **Lapel**—The front opening from the breakpoint of the garment to the turnback of the collar.

- **Revere**—The revere collar is a styled lapel without a separate collar.

- **Breakpoint**—The location on a line where a controlled turnback occurs, producing a roll, fold back, or flare point. This usually refers to lapels, shawl collars, revere collars, or notched collars.

- **Roll Line**—A designated line, usually in a collar or lapel, on which the collar or lapel turns back toward the neckline of the garment.

- **Interfacing** is always used to support and stabilize areas of a jacket that are frequently placed under stress.

- **Selecting interfacing for jackets and coats**—The correct interfacing adds additional support to the front jacket, around the neckline and shoulder/armhole areas, and in the lapel, collars, and hemlines. If interfacing pattern pieces are not available, you will need to create them from the existing jacket pattern pieces.

WEFT INTERFACING FOR WOOLENS AND MEDIUM TO HEAVY WEIGHT SUITING FABRICS

A weft interfacing is recommended for most tailored jackets. This product is a fusible polyester/rayon blend and ideally suited for women's wear front jacket applications. Weft interfacing is a lightweight, weft-inserted warp knit that creates a soft, lightly resilient, round hand when applied to fabric.

LIGHTWEIGHT INTERFACING FOR LINEN AND RAW SILK FABRICS

This product is a fusible polyester interfacing that creates a soft, stable hand without adding too much weight or body when applied to fabric. This is ideal for suits made of linen or raw silk fabrics.

SEWING SHORTCUT: BLOCK FUSING

When applying interfacing to entire outer jacket pieces, fuse interfacing to the fabric before cutting the outer jacket pieces. This time saving method is used in the garment industry. Additional support can be added later with smaller interfacing pieces, such as the neckline/armhole area pieces.

TAILORED JACKET WITH NOTCHED COLLAR

TAILORING METHODS

In the past, tailoring has been an intensive, more costly method. However, the following sewing steps illustrate the efficient process of tailoring that is used in the garment industry today. This method attaches interfacings and linings by machine; some people refer to this method as "bagging the lining."

Note: *When lining a shawl collar jacket or a revere collar jacket, the sewing steps for attaching the lining are the same as the notched collar.*

PREPARE THE PATTERN

Outer Jacket Pieces

- All outer jacket pattern pieces should have a $1\frac{1}{2}$ inch hem. Illustrated are the front jacket, back jacket, sleeve, topcollar, under collar and princess version of front jacket.

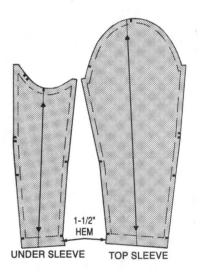

UNDER SLEEVE   TOP SLEEVE

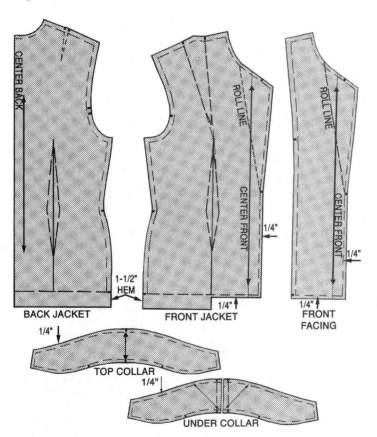

BACK JACKET   FRONT JACKET   FRONT FACING

TOP COLLAR

UNDER COLLAR

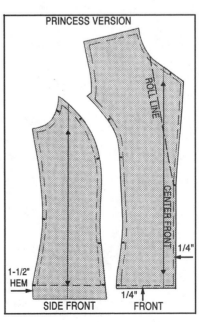

PRINCESS VERSION

SIDE FRONT   FRONT

Lining Pattern Pieces

- The lining jacket pattern pieces should have a $\frac{1}{2}$-inch hem ($\frac{5}{8}$-inch for home sewing). Illustrated are the front jacket lining, back jacket lining, and sleeve lining.

- A 1″ **pleat** should be included in the center back area of the jacket.

- The lining underarm and side seam corners should be extended up $\frac{1}{4}$-inch and out $\frac{1}{4}$-inch beyond the outer jacket pieces. Blend the new lines into the armhole notches and to 2 inches below the armhole on the side seam. (This adjustment creates more ease in the lining, preventing tears in the fragile fabric.)

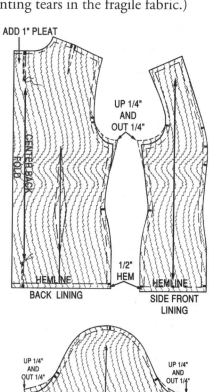

ADD 1" PLEAT

UP 1/4" AND OUT 1/4"

CENTER BACK FOLD

1/2" HEM

HEMLINE
BACK LINING

HEMLINE
SIDE FRONT LINING

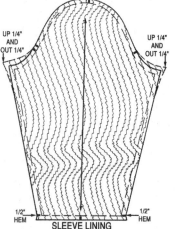

UP 1/4" AND OUT 1/4"

UP 1/4" AND OUT 1/4"

1/2" HEM

1/2" HEM

SLEEVE LINING

Interfacing Pattern Pieces

From the outer jacket patterns, make interfacing patterns featuring the following:

- **Front jacket**—Remove all seam allowances. (For princess styled jackets: Front Jacket and Side Front Jacket)

- **Front jacket lapel facing**—Remove all seam allowances.

- **Top collar**—Seam allowances are optional.

- **Back jacket neckline/armhole area**—(Similar to a back neck facing) Keep seam allowances.

- **Hem areas**—The hems of the front jacket, back jacket and sleeve should be interfaced with a $1\frac{1}{2}$ inch wide bias woven interfacing strip.

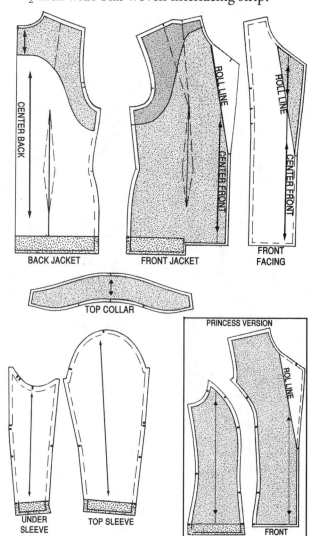

CENTER BACK

BACK JACKET

ROLL LINE

CENTER FRONT

FRONT JACKET

ROLL LINE

CENTER FRONT

FRONT FACING

TOP COLLAR

UNDER SLEEVE

TOP SLEEVE

PRINCESS VERSION

ROLL LINE

SIDE FRONT

FRONT

SEWING INSTRUCTIONS

1 Attach interfacing pieces to the following garment areas:

Refer to pages 270–271 for how to attach fusible interfacing. (Because fusible interfacings have greatly improved through modern technology, these interfacings are the best choice for tailoring.)

- Front jacket pieces (excluding the lapel area)
- Front jacket lapel facing
- Hem area of front jacket (bias interfacing)
- Hem area of back jacket (bias interfacing)
- Hem area of sleeves (bias interfacing)
- Top collar (some companies prefer to interface the under collar).
- Back neckline/armhole area of jacket. This piece helps reinforce the back jacket armhole and maintain its shape. (For princess seam styles, skip this piece until the princess seam has been sewn.)
- Front neckline/armhole area of jacket. This piece helps support the area and creates a more "tailored" finish. (For princess seam styles, skip this piece until the princess seam has been sewn.)

Note: *If using a lightweight fabric, you may want to interface the entire BACK pattern.*

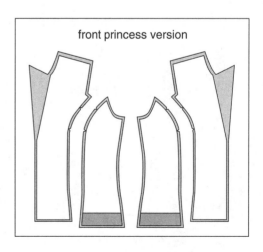

front princess version

2 **Sew all darts and/or stylelines (princess seams).** Clip the darts along the center folds and press open. Press all seams open.

Note: *After the princess seams have been sewn, attach the front and back armhole area interfacing pieces.*

Front princess seams:

A. Crimp or ease-stitch between the bustline notches on the side front panel.

B. Place the side front panel on top of the front panel, matching correct side to correct side, all raw edges, and all notches. Stitch the princess seams with the side panel on top. Press seams open.

Note: *Hem notches at the bottom of this panel will match, but the cut edges will not because the front panel has $\frac{1}{4}$-inch ($\frac{5}{8}$-inch for home sewing) seam allowances for the facing and the side panel hem amount is $1\frac{1}{2}$-inch.*

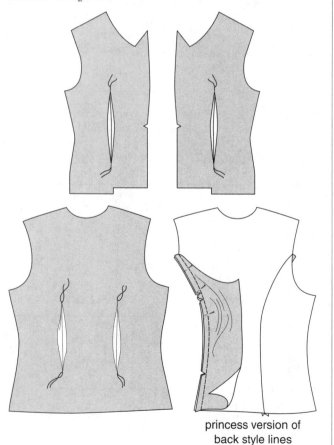

princess version of
back style lines

3 **Sew the pockets.** Most tailored jackets feature lined patch pockets, welt pockets, or bound pockets. Before starting, pencil mark the pocket placement location on the correct side of the garment.

The welt pocket, bound pocket, and lined patched pocket instructions are illustrated in Chapter 13.

4 Sew jacket seams.

- Sew all the jacket seams, including the shoulder seams and side seams, matching correct side to correct side. Press seams open.

- Pin and sew the jacket underarm sleeve seams, correct side to correct side. Press seams open. Crimp or ease-stitch the sleeve cap from the front notches to the back notches. Match and pin the correct side of the sleeve to the correct side of the jacket armhole. Match:
  —The front sleeve cap notch to the front armhole notch.
  —The sleeve shoulder position notch to the jacket shoulder seam.
  —The back sleeve cap notches to the back armhole notches.
  —The sleeve underarm seams to the jacket side seams.

Machine stitch the sleeves into the jacket armholes.

- Add shoulder pads. Turn the jacket wrong side out and whip stitch the edge of the pad to the edge of the armhole seam allowance. Tack the opposite edge to the shoulder seam allowance.

Note: *This is the method used in the garment industry, however, they use a special cylinder machine that stitches the shoulder pad into the seam allowance and automatically creates a sleeve head.*

5 Press the entire jacket.
To allow the lining to turn correctly and hang correctly (after it is sewn to the jacket), press the jacket and sleeve hems up $1\frac{1}{2}$-inches.

6 Sew the collar.
With the correct sides together, pin the top collar and the under collar together along the un-notched edges. Using the correct seam allowance, stitch the under collar to the top collar along the un-notched edges. (Do not stitch the neck edge.) Understitch the collar seam. Trim corners and turn correct side out. Carefully pull out the corners with a pin or a point turner. Press the collar.

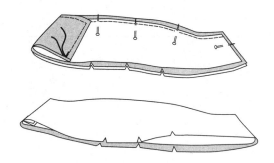

crimp cap of sleeve and sew in place   add shoulder pads

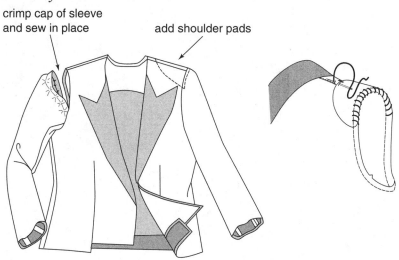

7 Pin and stitch the collar to the jacket. With the correct side of the jacket facing up, pin the notched edge of the collar (open edge) to the neck edge of the jacket. Match the following positions:

- Collar center back to jacket center back.
- Collar shoulder notch to the jacket shoulder seam.
- The edge of the collar to the jacket lapel notch.

Stitch all layers of the collar neck edge to the jacket, starting from the lapel notch. Continue to stitch the neck edge until you reach the opposite lapel notch.

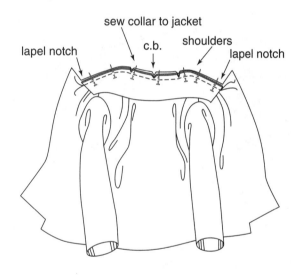

sew collar to jacket

lapel notch   c.b.   shoulders   lapel notch

8 Sew the jacket lining.

- **Front lining**—Stitch the jacket facing to the side front lining, matching correct side to correct side, all raw edges, and all notches. Leave 2″ unsewn at the bottom hem area. Press seams open.
- **Back jacket lining**—Sew the center back pleat at the neckline and the hemline. Stitch 1″ in from center (follow the notches) and 3″ long. Press pleat to one side for the full length of the back.
- Sew the back fisheye darts. Press darts toward center.
- **Shoulder seams**—Sew the shoulder seams and side seams. Press seams open.
- **Sleeve**—Crimp or ease-stitch the sleeve cap from the front notches to the back notches. Matching all notches, pin and stitch the correct side of the sleeve to the correct side of the jacket lining armhole. Steam and finger press the seam allowance toward the sleeve.
- **Inside Pockets**—If the design includes any inside breast pockets, sew them into the jacket. (Refer to "Pockets," pages 171–203.)

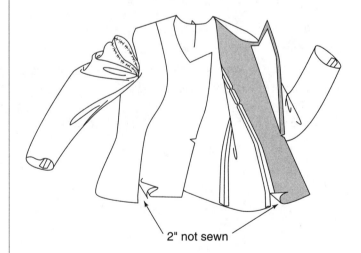

2″ not sewn

9 **Attach the lining to the jacket.** With the correct side of the jacket facing up, lay the correct side of the lining to the jacket so that the wrong side of the lining is facing up.

Match and stitch all outer edges, from the bottom of the facing up and around the neckline, and back down to the bottom of the opposite facing. Be sure, once again, to match the center back positions and the shoulder seams.

Note: *The collar should be flipped toward the jacket, sandwiched between the jacket and lining, so that the neckline areas are exposed.*

10 **Understitch the facing area.** Understitch the facing from the bottom hem up to the breakpoint of the jacket. To do this, fold all seam allowances to the facing side. From the correct side of the facing, stitch through the facing and the seam allowances close to the seam line.

Note: *Understitching helps the facing to lay flat and minimizes bulk.*

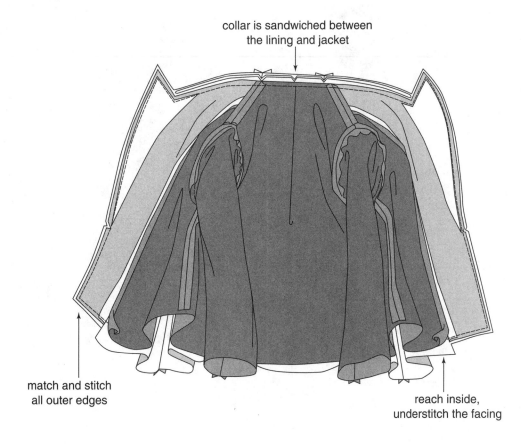

collar is sandwiched between
the lining and jacket

match and stitch
all outer edges

reach inside,
understitch the facing

11 **Sew lining hem to jacket hem.** Match the jacket hem edge and the lining hem edge, correct sides together. Stitch across the bottom of the jacket, starting from one facing across to the other facing.

Note: *A gapping effect occurs between the facing and the lining hem corner. Once the jacket is turned, this will create an automatic pleat between the jacket section and the lining.*

12 **Sew sleeve hems.** Turn both the lining sleeves and the jacket sleeves wrong side out, and position them over the shoulder area. Match and stitch the sleeve hem edges, correct sides together. (Turn the lining sleeves up like a cuff and slip them into the jacket sleeves to match the correct sides.) Match the back seams to avoid twisting.

13 Remove one of the stitched lining sleeve seams for about 12 inches.

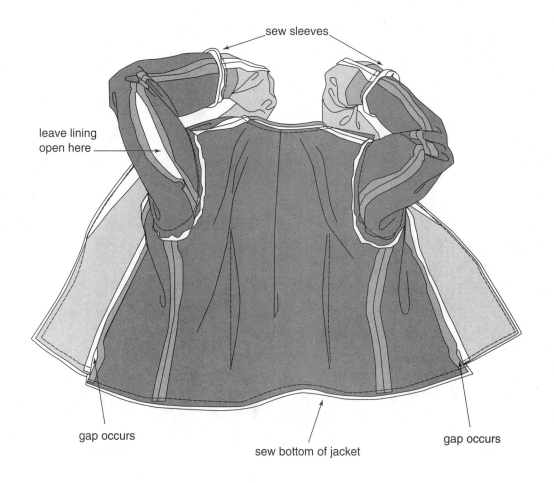

sew sleeves

leave lining open here

gap occurs

sew bottom of jacket

gap occurs

14 **Turn the jacket correct side out** through the opened sleeve seam in the lining. The pre-pressed hems will lay up into the appropriate position. A pleating effect is created at the lower lining hem edge where the jacket and the lining meet. This pleating effect is also created at the sleeve hems.

15 **Stitch the underarm seams together.** Reach inside the sleeve opening. Stitch or serge the underarm seam allowances of the sleeve lining to the underarm seam allowances of the jacket.

16 **Stitch lining sleeve seam closed.** Machine stitch the opening in the sleeve lining that was used for turning the jacket correct side out so that it is closed.

17 **Final pressing.** Give the entire jacket a final finish pressing.

18 **Sew buttons and buttonholes.** Space, mark, and machine stitch all buttonholes, starting at the breakpoint. Refer to the pattern for buttonhole placement. Attach all buttons.

NOTCHED COLLAR IN AN UNLINED JACKET

This section illustrates the sewing techniques needed to attach a notched collar with a large center-front/underarm facing to an unlined jacket. This facing stabilizes the front jacket and armhole areas so that no lining is needed. An unlined jacket with a notched collar provides a casual look and style. This style of notched collar should be constructed in a midweight to heavier-weight fabric. (Also refer to "Tailored Jacket with Notched Collar," pages 297–305.)

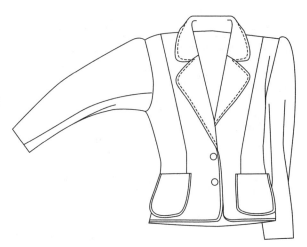

1 Cut out all the pattern pieces. Transfer all the pattern dart markings to the fabric.

2 Attach the interfacing pieces to the following garment areas:

- The front jacket facing (excluding the lapel area)—note the extended shape of the shoulder/armhole of the facing

- The front jacket lapel facing

- The top collar

- The hem area of the front and back jacket (bias interfacing)

- The hem area of the sleeves (bias interfacing)

Clean finish the outer edges of the facings.

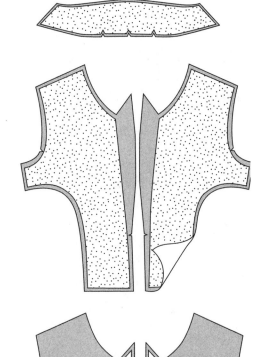

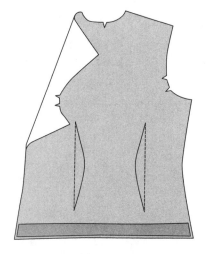

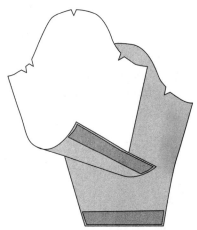

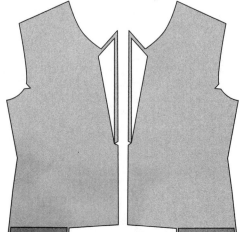

3 Sew all darts and/or style lines in all the jacket pieces. Sew the shoulder seams and the side seams. Press all seams open and all darts flat.

4 With the correct sides together, pin and sew the top collar and the under collar together, along the unnotched edges. Do not stitch the neck edge.

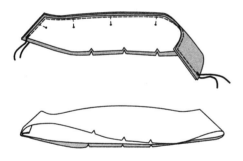

5 With the correct side of the jacket facing up, pin the notched edge of the collar (the open edge) to the neck edge of the jacket. Match the following:

- The center back of the collar to the center back of the jacket.
- The shoulder position of the collar to the shoulder seam of the jacket.
- The edge of the collar to the lapel notch of the jacket.

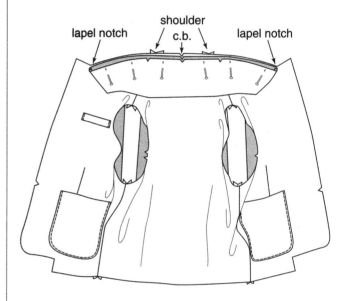

6 Place the correct side of the facing on top of the correct side of the jacket. Match all outer edges, shoulder seams, armholes, and underarm seams.

7 Clip the top layer of the collar at the shoulder seams. Repin the back neck area of the collar so that only one layer of the collar is pinned to the garment.

8 Sew all the outer edges, from the bottom of the facing up and around the neckline. Keep the top of the neck collar area free and away from the neck seams. Continue stitching down to the bottom of the outer facing edge.

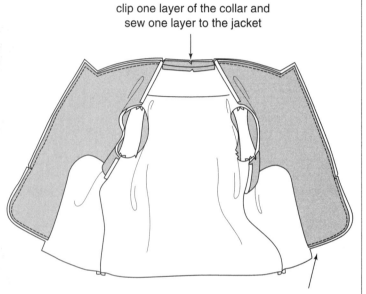

clip one layer of the collar and sew one layer to the jacket

stitch the facing to the jacket

9 Turn the facing to the inside of the garment and press the collar up. Fold the unsewn seam allowance of the collar under, just past the original stitchline. Edge stitch the back neck area of the collar down.

10 Under stitch the facing from the hem up to the lapel breakpoint. Refer to "Facing," pages 274–280. Serge or machine stitch the armholes together, with the wrong sides together and the side seam of the facing to the side seam of the jacket.

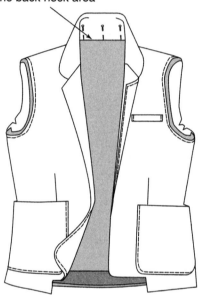

pin and edgestitch the back neck area

11 To finish the garment, carefully crimp the cap of the sleeves and machine stitch the sleeves into the jacket armhole. Hem stitch the jacket hem and the sleeve hems. Press the entire jacket. Hand stitch lined shoulder pads to the seam allowance of the sleeves and the shoulder seams.

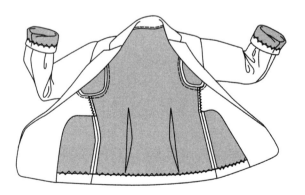

CHAPTER 20

Waistlines

KEY TERMS AND CONCEPTS

The waistline edge of a garment must be finished so that it lays smoothly and fits comfortably. Waistband and waistline finishes hold garments in the proper position on the body. Waistline edges can be finished with one of the following:

- **Straight Waistband**—A straight waistband is made with a straight, folded-over band. The band rests above the natural waistline on the body and is attached to a skirt or pants after all other construction details are completed. It should fit snugly and have about 1 inch of ease to keep it from being too tight.

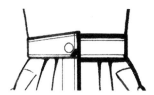

- **Contoured waistband**—A contoured waistband is designed to fit below the natural waistline. Therefore, the waistband pattern pieces are shaped (or contoured) to fit the body's curve, accommodating differences in measurement between the waist and hip. After the waistband pieces are sewn together, the contoured waistband is sewn to the garment in the same manner as a straight waistband.

- **Faced waistline**—A faced waistline uses a separate facing, usually $2\frac{1}{2}$-inches wide. This facing piece is stitched to the raw edge of any skirt waistline for the purpose of finishing the waistline edge. It allows the finished edge of a garment to rest at the natural waistline.

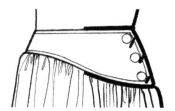

- **Elastic or drawstring casing**—Elastic or drawstring casing waistlines can be finished with an attached waistline folded edge. They can also have a separate waistband, cut the same length of the garment waist seam. Whether this piece is attached to or separate from the waistline, the casing area is sewn and elastic or a drawstring is inserted. The elastic or drawstring will allow the garment to be pulled over the hip and fit into the contour of the waist by pulling in the fullness.

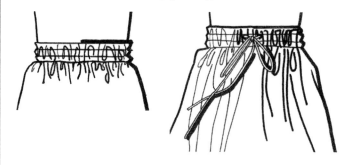

Waistline seams are sewn after the bodice and skirt are completely sewn, but before the zipper is attached. The placement of the seam for joining a bodice to a skirt may vary, depending on the design of the garment, the position can be

- Empire style, or at or just below the bust
- At the natural waistline
- At the high hip or torso level

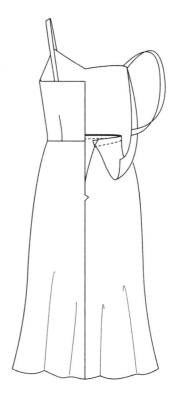

TRADITIONAL STRAIGHT WAISTBAND

Traditional straight waistbands are made with a folded-over band, cut on the lengthwise grain for the least amount of stretch. Always interface the waistband to ensure a smooth look and correct fit.

This waistband style rests above the natural waistline on the body; it should fit snugly and have about 1 inch of ease to keep it from being too tight.

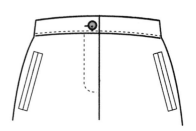

1 Attach the interfacing to the wrong side of the waistband.

2 Fold the waistband in half lengthwise, correct sides together.

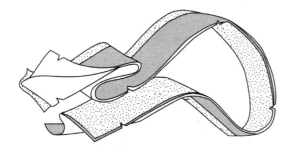

3 Stitch one end of the waistband closed, with the appropriate seam allowance. Stitch the extension end closed, with the appropriate seam allowance. Trim the corners and edges.

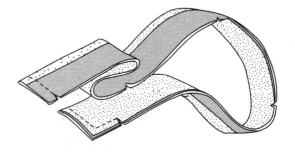

4 Turn the waistband correct side out and press.

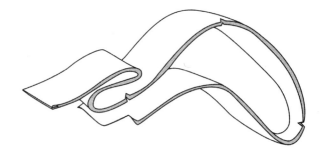

5 With the correct side of the garment up, pin the interfaced side of the waistband (one layer only) to the correct side of the garment, matching the following:

- The center front of the waistband to the center front of the garment
- The side seams of the waistband to the side seams of the garment
- The center back of the waistband to the center back of the garment

After the positions are matched correctly, distribute any fullness and pin at frequent intervals.

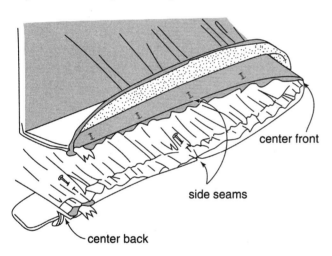

center front

side seams

center back

6 With the correct side of the garment up, machine stitch the pinned garment to the waistband, with the required seam allowance.

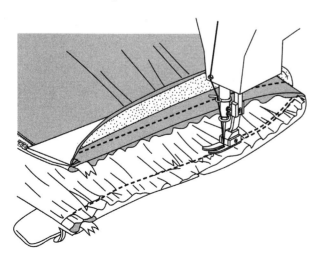

7 Turn the waistband to the correct side of the garment. Pin the interfaced side of the waistband (with the folded-under seam allowance) over the stitchline.

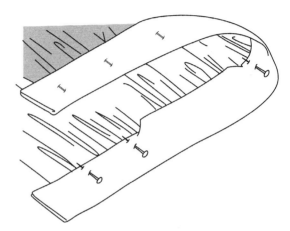

8 From the outside of the garment, edge stitch the waistband, along the folded-under seam allowance. Stitch through all thicknesses, the entire length of the waistband.

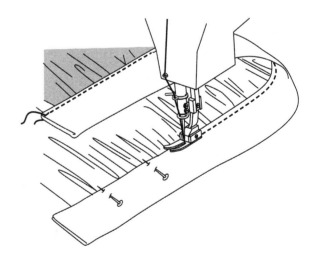

TAILORED STRAIGHT WAISTBAND

The following instructions are for preparing a straight waistband when using fairly heavy or bulk fabric. The waistband will lay flat and smooth and have a tailored look. A narrow bias strip of fabric is attached to conceal the raw edge of the inside waistband seam, known as a *Hong Kong finish*.

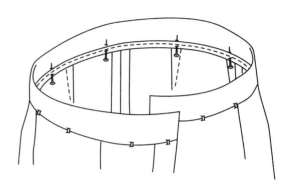

1 Attach the interfacing to the wrong side of the waistband.

2 Machine stitch a thin strip (about $\frac{1}{4}$-inch finished) of sateen fabric along the side of the waistband without the interfacing.

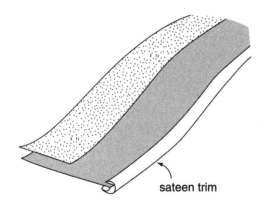

sateen trim

Hint: *You can purchase a sateen trim from the trim section of the fabric store.*

3 Fold the waistband in half lengthwise, correct sides together.

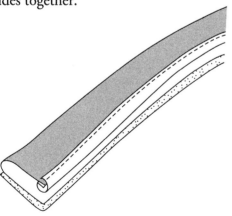

4 Stitch both ends, with the appropriate seam allowance. Trim the corners and ends, if necessary.

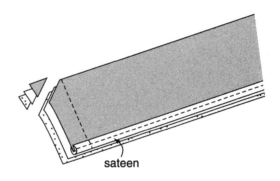

sateen

5 Turn the waistband correct side out and press.

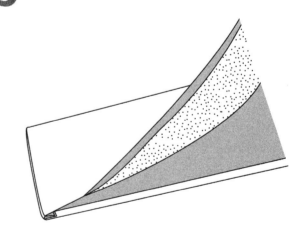

6 With the correct side of the garment up, pin the interfaced side of the waistband (one layer only) to the correct side of the garment, matching the following:

- The edge of the waistband to the front garment opening
- The side seams of the waistband to the side seams of the garment
- The center back of the waistband to the center back of the garment.
- The extension of the garment opening to the opposite end of the waistband

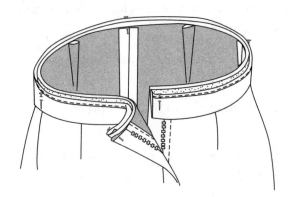

7 With the correct side of the garment facing up, machine-stitch the pinned garment to the waistband with the appropriate seam allowance.

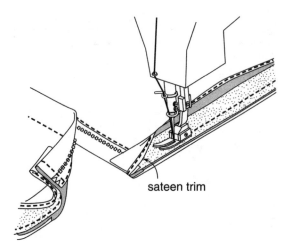

sateen trim

8 Turn the waistband to the inside of the garment, being sure the waistband is folded in half and not twisted. Pin the waistband flat.

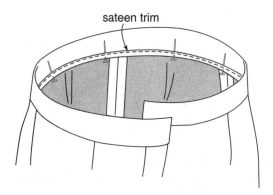

sateen trim

9 From the correct side of the garment, edge stitch the waistband, catching the inside layer of the waistband.

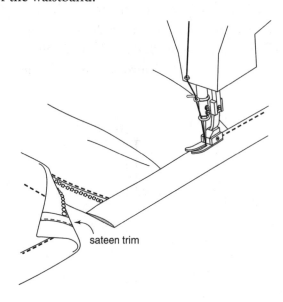

sateen trim

BELT CARRIERS

Belt carriers are narrow strips of fabric stitched to the waistband to hold a belt in place.

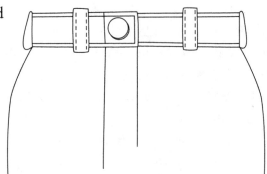

Loop belt carriers are cut and sewn as one long strip, and then sewn and cut into the individual carrier lengths. First, cut the length of the loop strip on the straight of the grain. Cut the strip long enough that you will be able to cut it into as many belt carriers as necessary, including 1 inch for attaching each. Then cut the width of the strip, which should be twice the desired width, plus $\frac{1}{2}$-inch for the seam allowance (at least $1\frac{1}{2}$-inches wide).

1 Press under $\frac{3}{8}$-inch on the long edge of the belt carriers. Fold the carrier in half lengthwise, with wrong sides together. Stitch close to both long edges, as shown.

2 Top stitch each edge of the carrier strip.

3 Cut each carrier to the appropriate length.

Note: *Each carrier should be the width of the waistband plus 1 inch for ease and seam allowance.*

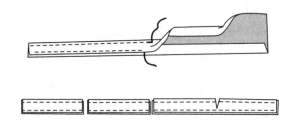

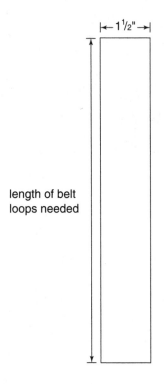

length of belt loops needed

← 1½" →

4 Pin the belt carriers, seam side up, to the raw edges of the waistline of the garment before attaching the waistband.

5 Space each belt carrier evenly on the front and back garment sections.

6 Stitch each belt carrier to the garment. Position and stitch the waistband to the garment waistline. (See "Traditional Straight Waistband," pages 312–313, and "Tailored Straight Waistband," pages 314–315).

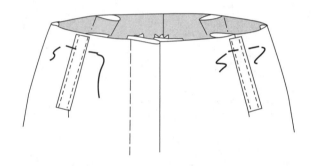

7 Complete the waistband construction. Press the belt carriers upward onto the waistband, turning under $\frac{3}{8}$-inch on raw edges. Each belt carrier should stand up from the waistband enough for a belt to fit under it. Top stitch each belt carrier.

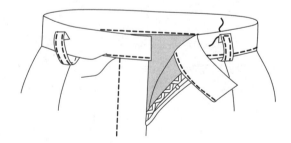

Note: *It is easy to vary the look of a garment by using different style of belt carriers. One popular style is a wide-tab belt carrier that is secured in place with a button.*

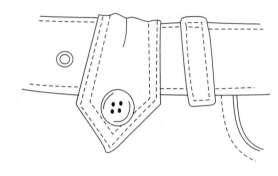

ELASTIC WAISTBAND

The elastic waistband is created from a piece of fabric that is double the width of the waistband. This piece is attached to the waistline area of pant's or a skirt and allows for them to be pulled on over the hips.

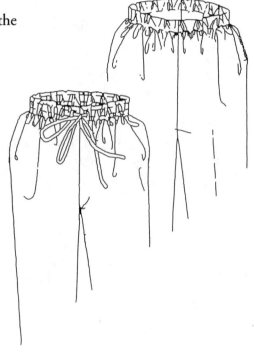

An elastic waist is sometimes used on skirt and pants waistlines instead of a straight waistband. Follow these instructions to prepare an elastic waistline in which the elastic does not roll or twist. Use $\frac{3}{4}$-inch-wide elastic for the best results.

1 Measure the elastic so that it is the length of the desired waistline, minus 1 inch. Overlap the ends and stitch securely. Fold the elastic in half and pencil mark this position. Fold each halved area in half and pencil mark.

2 Position the elastic on the waistband extension of the garment, $\frac{1}{4}$-inch from the upper edge. Pin the elastic to the upper edge of the garment waistband extension area, matching the pencil markings to the center front, the center back, and the side seams.

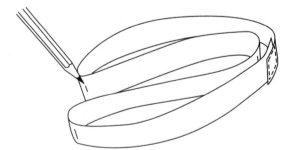

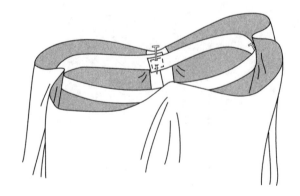

3 Stretch the elastic and sew it to the waistband area using a zig-zag stitch. Refer to, "Stretching and Sewing Elastic," page 78.

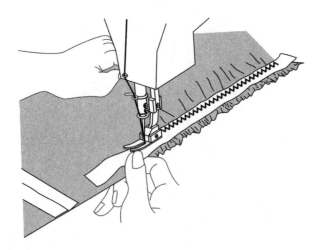

4 Turn the waistband extension area to the inside of the garment along the foldline.

5 Turn under the edge of the casing area $\frac{1}{4}$-inch. Stretch and sew the casing area.

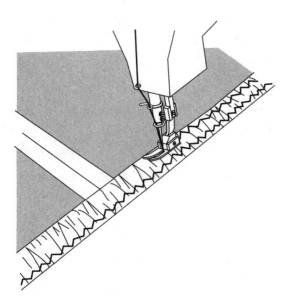

As a variation for the final stitching, you can turn under and stitch the waistband along the extension area. Sew along the foldline, leaving about 1 inch of the seam unsewn. Measure the elastic so that it is the length of the desired waistline, minus 1 inch. Attach a safety pin at one end of the elastic and tunnel the elastic through the garment. At the unsewn stitchline, pull the elastic out. Overlay and stitch the ends. Adjust the elastic within the waistband area and stitch the area closed.

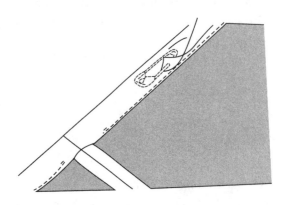

DRAWSTRING WAISTBAND

When sewing a drawstring waistband, you make a double row of stitching in the center of the waist casing. You also create an eyelet buttonhole on the face of the garment, in which cording or ribbon is inserted between the double row of stitching.

1 Cut a length of cording or ribbon twice the waistline measurement to tunnel into the casing.

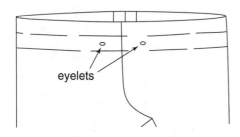

2 Make eyelets either by using a small machine buttonhole or by inserting plastic or metal eyelets. The eyelets should be placed 1 inch from either side of the center front, in the middle of the waistband casing.

3 Edgestitch, overlock, or press the upper edge of the waist area.

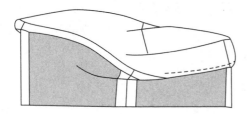

4 Fold the casing at the foldline notches. Stitch the waistband casing down at the original waistline.

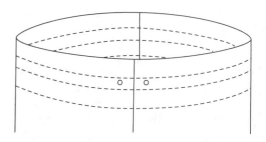

5 Top stitch the waistband casing. Make a double row of top stitching $\frac{3}{8}$-inch wide in the middle of the waistband casing area.

6 Insert a drawstring. Tunnel the drawstring through the double row of topstitching, starting at one of the eyelet buttonholes. Finish tunneling the drawstring at the other eyelet buttonhole.

7 Evenly space the waistline fullness.

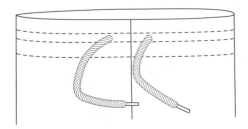

FACED WAISTLINE

A faced waistline is created using separate facing pieces cut in the same shape as the waistline and the width of a facing. The facing is turned to the inside of the garment and lays flat. These pieces are stitched to the raw edge of a skirt or pants waistline to finish the waistline edge. This sewing technique creates a finished waistline edge and produces a flat finish that does not extend beyond the waistline edge.

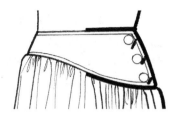

1 Attach any needed interfacing to the facing pieces.

2 Sew the side seams of the front and back waist facing to each other.

3 Finish the lower edge by turning under $\frac{1}{4}$-inch or by serging.

4 Pin and sew the waistline of the facing to the correct side of the waist seam.

5 Understitch the waist seam edge.

6 Turn the facing to the inside of the garment. Press flat.

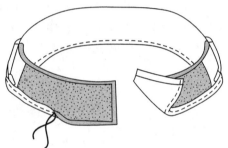

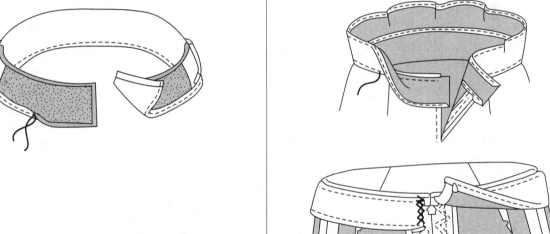

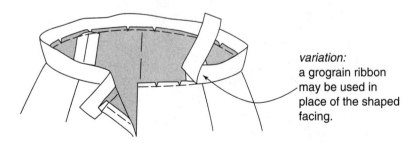

variation:
a grograin ribbon may be used in place of the shaped facing.

ATTACHING A BODICE TO A SKIRT

The placement of the seam for joining a bodice to a skirt can vary, depending on the style of the garment. A skirt can join a bodice at the bust, the waistline, or the hip. This waist seam of a dress is sewn after the bodice and skirt are sewn, but before the zipper is attached.

Note: *Check the fit of both the bodice and the skirt before joining these pieces. Make any necessary fitting changes at this time.*

1 With the correct side of the bodice facing up, pin the correct side of the skirt to the correct side of the bodice. Be sure to match the following:

- The center front of the bodice to the center front of the skirt
- The side seams of the bodice to the side seams of the skirt
- The center back of the bodice to the center back of the skirt

After matching the positions correctly, distribute any fullness evenly and pin at frequent intervals.

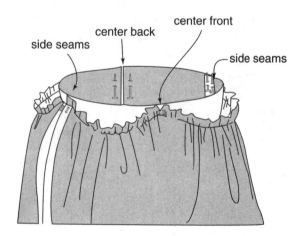

2 With the wrong side of the skirt facing up, machine stitch the bodice to the skirt, with the appropriate seam allowance. Keeping the raw edges even, stitch from the garment opening to the opposite opening.

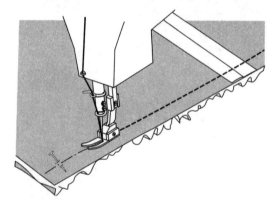

3 Carefully press the entire seam allowance toward the bodice.

THREAD LOOP FOR BUTTONHOLE OR BELT

A thread loop is created by using the same color of thread or buttonhole twist, and working a chain stitch. It is applied at the waistline of a dress. A thread loop can also make an almost invisible buttonhole at a neckline, above a back zipper or a slit opening.

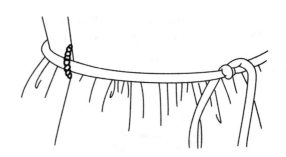

1 Cut a long piece of thread (about 72 inches), and fold it in half. Place the folded thread area into the eye of a needle. Bring the folded thread down to meet the ends. Four strands of thread now exist. Knot all four threads at the end.

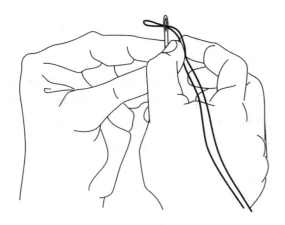

2 Bring the needle and thread through the garment, from the wrong side to the correct side, at the desired position for the belt loop.

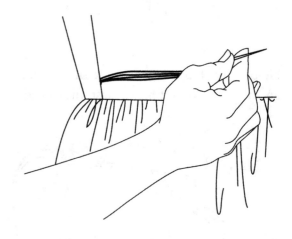

3 Slipstitch the needle and thread through the correct side of the garment at this position until a loop is formed.

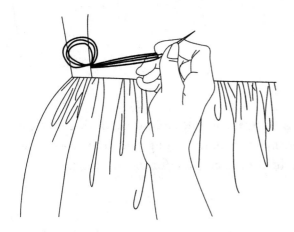

4 Holding the loop open with the thumb and one finger of the left hand, grasp the thread.

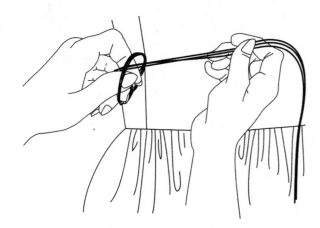

5 Draw the thread through the existing loop and pull it toward the garment until the first loop is closed and forms a chain stitch. Continue this looping process until the belt loop is the desired length.

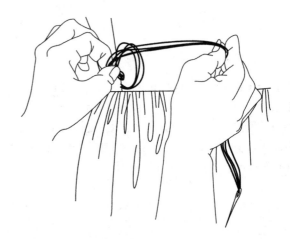

6 Slip the needle through the last loop to tie off the chain. Pass the needle and thread through the garment to the wrong side and slip knot it in place.

OUTSIDE CASING

An outside casing is created to insert a drawstring (such as a ribbon, a spaghetti belt, or elastic). This drawstring gathers a dress at the waist or a blouse or jacket at the lower edge.

The length of the casing is determined by the length needed for the casing on the finished garment. The width is usually $1\frac{1}{2}$ to 2 inches. Sometimes a prepackaged bias tape can be used.

1 Fold under all seam allowances (the length and the width of the casing), and press flat.

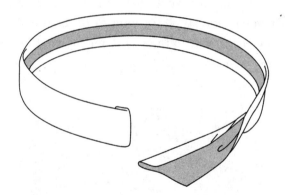

2 Pin the casing to the garment, matching the wrong side of casing to the correct side of the garment.

3 Edge stitch the casing to the garment on both edges of the casing.

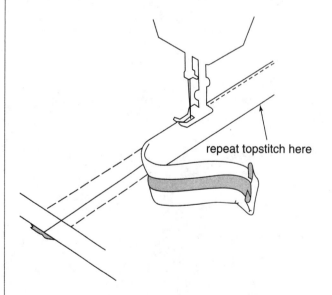

repeat topstitch here

ELASTIC ENCLOSED IN A WAISTLINE SEAM

You use the elastic enclosed in a waistline seam method to insert elastic in a dress or pantsuit waistline seam allowance. These sewing steps eliminate the need for a separate casing.

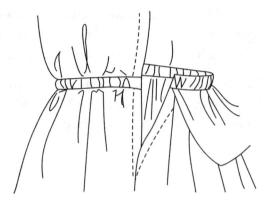

1 Measure and cut elastic the length of the waistline, minus 1-inch. Generally $\frac{1}{4}$-inch-wide elastic is used.

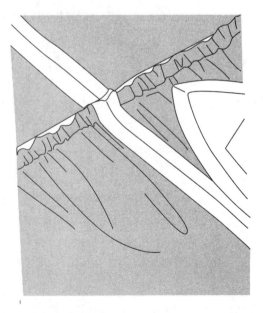

2 Sew the bodice and pants or skirt seam, and press up the seam allowances.

3 Stitch the top edge of the seam allowance, leaving about 1-inch of the seam unsewn.

4 Attach a safety pin at one end of the elastic and tunnel the elastic through the garment.

5 At the unsewn stitchline, pull the elastic out. Overlap and stitch the ends of the elastic. Adjust the elastic within the waistband area and stitch the area securely.

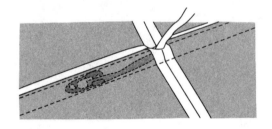

CHAPTER 21

Hems

KEY TERMS AND CONCEPTS

A **hem** is a finished lower edge of a garment that prevents raw edges from fraying or tearing. Hems can be

- Turned to the inside of the garment and finished with a hand stitch
- Turned to the outside of the garment as a decorative finish
- Left unturned and finished with a decorative stitch, such as a lettuce stitch
- Glued
- Faced
- Finished with bias binding
- Decorative

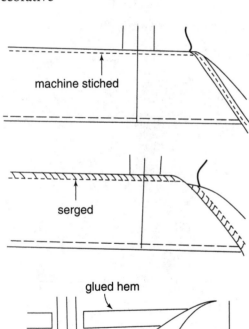

machine stiched

serged

glued hem

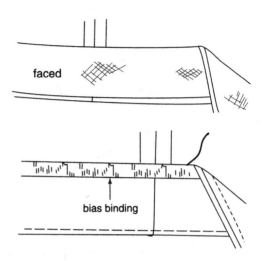

faced

bias binding

A **hemline** is the designated line along which the hem is to be folded, faced, or finished.

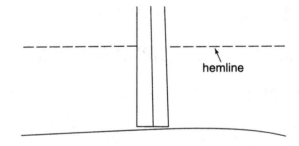

hemline

The **hem allowance** is the extension at the bottom of skirts, dresses, blouses, sleeves, and pants that is turned under and sewn with an appropriate hemming stitch.

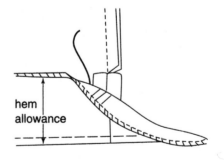

hem allowance

Hems can be finished by serging, using a hand or machine stitch, or using a bonding material. Special hemming devices are sometimes used to duplicate the stitch pattern and appearance of handwork.

The following are some examples of hemming finishes:

- Machine stitched hems can be made to show on the outside of the garment.

- Hand stitching (using a variety of different stitches) to secure the hem to the inside of the garment is not visible on the outside of the garment.

- Lettuce edging with a frilled, unturned finished edge can be created by stretching a knit or crinkled fabric as it feeds into a serging machine.

- A marrowed finish is produced by serging a very narrow finish on the outside edge of the hem.

- A decorative finish can be applied with lace, bias binding, seam tape, or netting.

- A wired hem can be produced by incorporating a slender piece of plastic (such as fishing line) into a narrow, folded hem.

- An interfaced hem may be needed for suit jackets, loosely woven fabrics, or knits.

- A rolled hem can be used on sheer and delicate fabrics. You roll the fabric between your fingers, and then sew it with tiny hand stitches.

MARKING AND TURNING A HEM

A hem is the finished raw edge at the bottom of a skirt, a dress, a blouse, a sleeve, or pants. It is held in place with either hand or machine stitching. The type of hem used depends on the fabric type and garment design.

1 The desired length of the garment depends on the fashion for the season, the style of the garment, and personal choice. Mark the hem evenly from the floor to the desired length, using a measuring device (such as a yardstick). If the garment was not carefully made or if you stand crookedly, the hemline will not measure evenly from the floor.

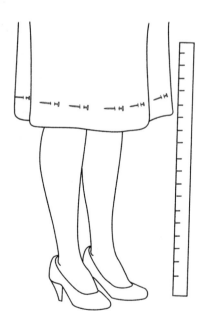

2 After measuring the length at which to hem the garment, measure the desired width of the hem, usually 1 to $1\frac{1}{2}$-inches. Cut off all excess fabric.

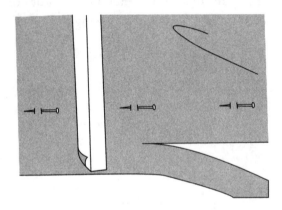

3 The outer edge of the hem should be finished so that it does not ravel. You can sew on bias tape, turn the edge under $\frac{1}{4}$-inch and stitch, or serge the outer edge or hand stitch.

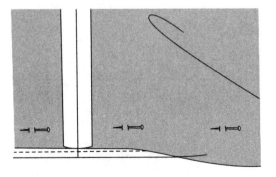

4 With the wrong side of the garment facing you, fold the hem up at the desired hem position. Pin in place.

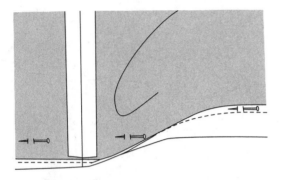

5 Select an appropriate hemming stitch and sew the hem in place. Refer to "*Hand Hemming Stitches*," pages 80–82.

Note: *If the garment is flared, it will be necessary to reduce hem bulk. Crimp the outer edge of the garment hem and then finish the outer edge.*

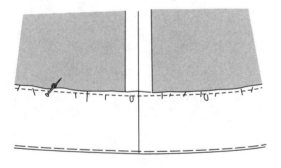

6 After completing the desired hemming stitch, press the hem in place. Be sure the hem is pressed clean and flat from the inside of the garment.

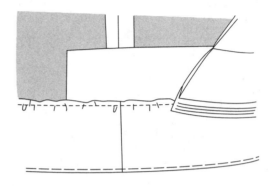

CORNER HEM

A corner hem is used to finish the place where a buttoned front facing and the bottom of a blouse, dress, jacket, or skirt meet. The hem of the garment will automatically be turned up into position using this technique.

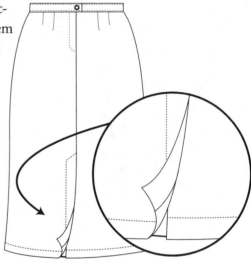

1 Turn back the facing onto the garment at the required foldline position, correct sides together.

2 Machine stitch the facing to the garment at the desired hemline position.

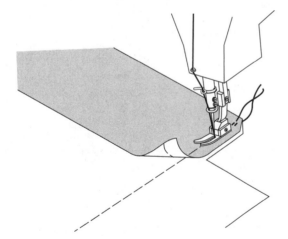

3 Trim the corner and turn the facing to the wrong side of the garment.

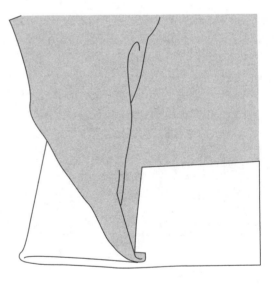

MITERED HEM

A mitered hem is used when a sharp square corner with a diagonal line from the corner is desired. Mitered hems can be used on items such as vests, tablecloths, and placemats.

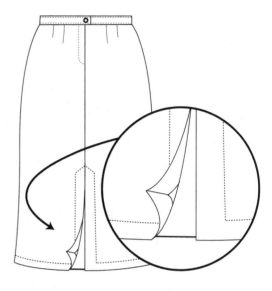

1 Turn back the width of the hem, matching the edges diagonally from the seam allowance (or hem allowance) to the corner. Make sure the correct sides are together.

2 Stitch diagonally from the corner.

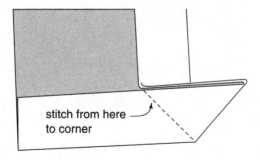

stitch from here to corner

3 Trim away surplus material, to $\frac{1}{4}$-inch of the stitchline. Press the seam open.

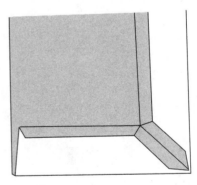

4 Turn the hem to the inside (the wrong side) of the garment. Finish the hem with a hand stitch.

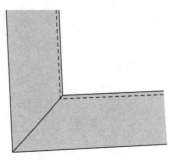

CHAPTER 22

Closures

KEY TERMS AND CONCEPTS

Closures are devices that are used to fasten garments securely. They are designed for a variety of holding purposes and can be decorative as well as functional. They can be the focal point in a garment design, to enhance the look of the garment. The type of closure selected depends on the design and use of the garment, and the care, weight, and type of fabric. Closures include the following:

- **Buttons** are three dimensional and available in a wide variety of natural or manufactured materials, including pearl, wood, bone, fiber, fabric, glass, jewels, plastic, steel, and other metals. Buttons can be covered with fabric or other materials to complement a garment. Buttons are available in a range of sizes and shapes. There are two types of buttons:

  - The **sew-through button** has two or four holes for attaching the button to the garment.

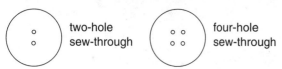

two-hole sew-through

four-hole sew-through

  - The **shank button** has a metal, fabric, plastic, or thread extension under the surface of the button for attaching the button to the garment.

metal shank   cloth shank   thread shank

- **Buckles** come in a variety of sizes and shapes, and are used to close tabs or belts.

- **Hooks and eyes** are available in various sizes and styles, and are designed as a closing device for garments.

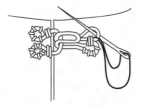

- A **velcro fastener** is two woven nylon strips, one with tiny hooks and one with a looped pile. The hook-and-loop intermesh when hooked together, available in a variety of sizes and shapes.

- **Snaps** are circular plates molded with a mating ball and a socket. They can be a variety of sizes and are used to fasten a garment area where a smooth, flat closure is desired.

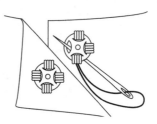

- A **metal eyelet** is a small, round metal tube, with an opening of approximately $\frac{1}{4}$-inch used to accommodate lacing and as a design detail.

- **Zippers** are devices for fastening a garment open or closed. A zipper is a device made of metal teeth or synthetic coils that make a complete closure by means of interlocking. (See Chapter 12 for a complete discussion of zippers.)

BUTTONS AND BUTTONHOLES

A buttonhole is a finished opening sized to accommodate a button. Buttonholes can be used on any edge that overlaps, such as a cuff, waistband, or blouse. There are three types of buttonholes:

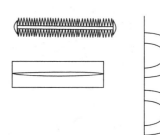

- Machine-worked buttonholes are made by using a machine attachment or with zig-zag stitching.

- Bound buttonholes are made of separate strips of fabric. They are constructed before facings are applied.

- Loops are made of bias tubing, thread, or cording. They are placed to extend beyond the edge of the garment in lieu of the extension of the garment.

Buttonholes are placed on the righthand side of the garment openings of women's or children's clothing, and on the lefthand side of men's and boy's clothing. Buttonholes are usually placed in a horizontal direction, except on shirt plackets, where they are usually placed vertically.

Some sewing machines have buttonhole attachments. It is important to refer to the manual provided with the sewing machine for directions on the correct use of the attachment. Buttonholes can also be made using the zig-zag stitch on the sewing machine.

A pattern suggests the position of buttonholes. The spacing can be adjusted to suit your adaptation of the garment design.

Mark the width of the button for a horizontal and vertical buttonhole on the center-front line with a chalk pencil.

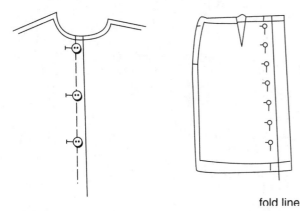

fold line

Horizontal buttonholes are placed $\frac{1}{8}$-inch beyond the center line of the garment and extend (the length of the button) into the garment (not into the extension area).

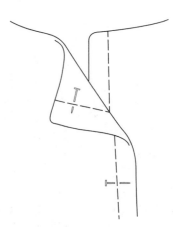

Vertical buttonholes are placed on the center line (not the edge) of the garment or placket. The vertical spacing is determined by the design of the garment.

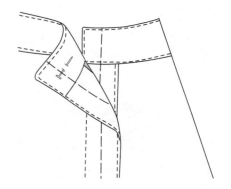

MACHINE-WORKED BUTTONHOLES

Machine-worked buttonholes can be made even if the sewing machine does not have a buttonhole attachment, but does have a zig-zag feature. Attach the zig-zag throat plate and zig-zag presser foot to the sewing machine. Adjust the stitch length to its smallest setting, and adjust the zig-zag width to the middle setting.

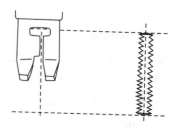

1 Working on the correct side of the garment, insert the machine needle into the fabric at one end of the buttonhole. Slowly zig-zag stitch the length of the desired buttonhole. Complete this stitch with the needle down and on the side of the buttonhole opening.

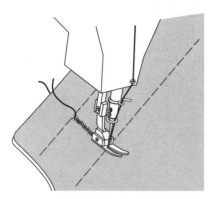

2 With the needle down, raise the presser foot and pivot the garment completely around.

3 Raise the needle position and adjust the zig-zag width to the widest setting. Stitch about five times at the end of the buttonhole; this is called a *bartack*.

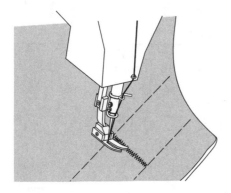

4 Again, raise the needle position and readjust the zig-zag width to the middle section. Stitch the other side of the buttonhole, the length of the buttonhole.

5 Again, raise the needle position and adjust the zig-zag width to the widest setting. Stitch this end about five times to create another bartack.

6 Open the buttonhole by cutting through the middle of the stitches using a seam ripper or sharp scissors.

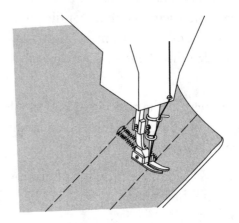

Buttonhole Loops

Bias tubing buttonhole loops are made of bias tubing. They extend beyond the edge of the garment instead of including an extension on the garment.

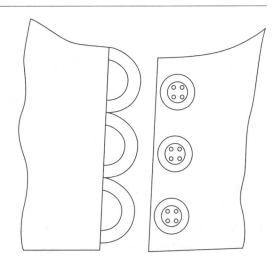

1 Make the bias tubing long enough so that it can be cut apart into as many loops as necessary. Each loop must be long enough to fit over the button and provide a seam allowance on each end. Refer to "Bias Tubing," page 126.

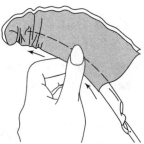

2 Loop the finished tubing around the desired button to figure the amount of loop needed for the button.

3 Make a copy of the facing out of shelf paper. Note the stitchline. Also, draw in a second line that shows the width of the loop needed. This ensures that each button loop will be exactly the same size.

4 Stitch the loops to the paper pattern. Start stitching at the top of the pattern. Form loops pointing away from the edge, matching the outer edge and the second line. Stitch the loops on the seamline, one at a time.

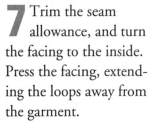

loop length line

paper strip

5 Pin the paper pattern, with the attached loops, on top of the correct side of the garment. Pin the facing over the paper pattern.

6 Stitch along the seamline. Trim the ends of the loops to reduce thickness. Tear away the paper pattern.

7 Trim the seam allowance, and turn the facing to the inside. Press the facing, extending the loops away from the garment.

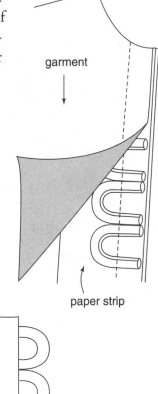

garment

paper strip

garment

Placing and Sewing Buttons

It is important that the size of the button fits the size of the buttonhole. An accurate button size will prevent the garment from twisting or pulling.

To mark the position of the buttons, start at the neck edge or top of the garment, and match the center of the garment along the center-front line. Pin the garment closed. Place a pin through the center position of the desired buttonhole. Mark the pinned position on the button side.

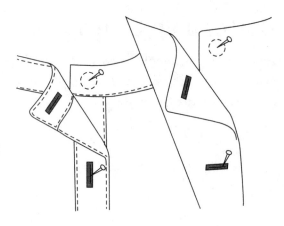

FLAT BUTTONS

A shank needs to be constructed while the button is being attached to prevent the garment from pulling at the buttonhole location.

1 Repeatedly draw the thread through one hole of the button (from the wrong side) and down through the opposite hole (from the correct side of the button) into the fabric.

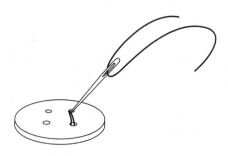

2 Slip a straight pin underneath the thread on the correct side of the button. Continue to follow the stitching process in step 1, repeating the stitches several times.

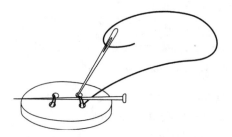

3 Remove the straight pin from the button and slightly pull the button away from the garment. This will leave a shank, created by the thread between the garment and the button. Wind the thread tightly around this thread shank to complete the process. Knot and cut the thread at the base of the shank.

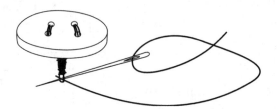

SHANK BUTTONS

Shank buttons are recommended as closures on heavyweight garments such as coats. An additional shank is sewn when attaching a shank button to the garment, similar to the procedure used to create a shank for a flat button.

1 Make a couple small stitches at the marking for the button on the garment.

2 Repeatedly bring the thread through the shank of the button and back into the fabric. While sewing the shank, hold the button away from the garment about a finger's width. Stitch using this method for about six stitches.

3 While holding the button away from the garment, wind the thread tightly around the shank created by the thread. Knot and cut the thread at the base of the shank.

Velcro

Velcro is a substitute for zippers, buttons, and adjustable waistlines on garments for men, women, and children. Velcro is available in many widths and colors. One layer of Velcro has a hook side and the other layer has a loop side. When these two layers are pressed together, they lock into place until pulled apart.

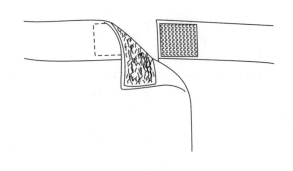

1 Position the hook layer of the Velcro on the bottom garment piece. Edge stitch around the entire piece.

2 Position the loop portion of the Velcro on the overlapping portion of the garment. Edge stitch around the entire piece.

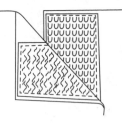

Hooks and Eyes

Hooks and eyes are available in a variety of sizes and types. The type and size of the hook and eye used is determined by the type of closure and the position on the garment, such as at the top of a zipper closure on waistbands or necklines.

The general-purpose hook with a straight eye or round eye is the most commonly used.

The special-purpose hook and eye is used primarily for waistbands.

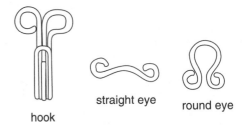

hook   straight eye   round eye

1 Position and stitch the hook first, using overhand stitches. Stitch around the hook and through the fabric, being careful not to allow the stitches to show on the other side of the garment. Then stitch across the end of the hook.

2 Close the garment and put a mark or pin where the hook meets the other garment section. Position the eye, and stitch around each end of the eye, again using overhand stitches.

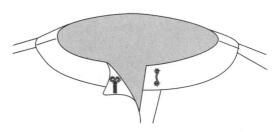

general purpose hook with straight eye

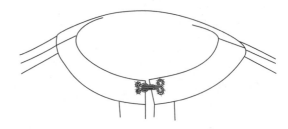

general purpose hook with round eye

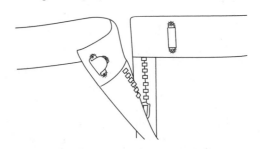

special purpose hook and eye

Glossary of Sewing Fabric Terms

Adjustment line: a double line printed on a pattern to indicate where alterations of lengthening or shortening may be made.

A-line: a silhouette shape of a simple dress or skirt, fitted at the top and flaring wider at the hemline, resembling the shape of an A.

Alter: changing a pattern or garment so that it fits the body and represents the body measurements and proportions.

Alternate clipping: several small straight cuts, clipping each layer of seam allowance separately to allow the seam allowances to lay flat.

Appliqué: a cut out decoration, design, or small motif to be sewn over the main fabric or garment.

Armhole/Armscye: the garment opening for the arm or for the insertion of the sleeve. Another name is armscye.

Backstitch: the reverse stitch on the machine to sew backward and forward in the same place reinforce the stitching at the beginning and ending of seams.

Bar tack: short zigzag cross stitches forming a bar to reinforce the ends of buttonholes, end of fly-zipper openings, and stress points on pants, jeans, overalls, and work clothes.

Baste: long stitches used to hold fabric pieces together temporarily. Basting stitches can be made by hand or machine, generally at six stitches per inch.

Hand-basting: long stitches sewn by machine. Ends are not fastened or backstitched. Before stitches are removed, threads are snipped every few inches.

Machine-basting: long stitches sewn by machine. Ends are not fastened or backstitched. Before stitches are removed, threads are snipped every few inches.

Pin-basting: pins are used to hold fabric pieces together, placed so they can be easily removed as fabric is stitched. Enough pins are used to keep layers from slipping.

Belting: a stiff narrow band made of heavy woven material, available in various widths and weights, used as interlining, backing reinforcing waistbands, and fabric-covered belts.

Betweens needle: (See Chapter 1.)

Bias: bias is a line diagonally across the grain of the fabric. True bias is at 45 degree angle. Fabric cut on the true bias has the maximum stretchability of woven fabric. (See Chapter 10.)

Bias binding/Tape: 1. single- or double-fold of strips cut on true bias in which one edge is stitched to the garment edges as a finish or trim. **2.** a bias strip of fabric used to finish and strengthen a raw edge. The bias strip is folded so that it encases the edge and shows on both the right and wrong sides. (See Chapter 10.)

Bias cut: cutting fabric on the bias.

Bias strip: a bias strip used to finish and strengthen a raw edge. The bias strip is folded so that it encases the edge and shows on both the right and wrong sides.

Blend: yarns composed of two or more different fibers mixed together before spinning into a single yarn.

Blindstitch: a small hand stitch used for hemming that is almost invisible. The thread is concealed by slipping the needle through a fold in the cloth with each stitch.

Blind tucks: a number of tucks sewn so the fold of one tuck meets the stitching line of the next tuck on the inside of the garment.

Bobbin: a small round spool of thread that locks with the top thread on the machine when sewing.

Bolt: unit in which fabric is packaged by the manufacturer and sold to fabric stores.

Bonded fabric: a fabric with a tricot backing or a lightweight underlining that is permanently sealed together by an adhesive for added body and reinforcement.

Boning: flexible narrow strips of featherboning or stiff nylon strip used to stiffen seams and edges of close-fitting garments to prevent them from slipping. For example, the bodice on a strapless dress (see Chapter 18).

Buttonhole: a finished opening for a button either by machine or hand used with a button to secure the garment. (See Chapter 21.)

Buttonholer: attachment to make worked buttonholes of various sizes on a commercial machine. Machine-made buttonholes can be made faster by hand.

Buttonhole twist: a thick natural fiber silk thread used for handworked buttonholes and for other fine tailoring.

Button loop: made of bias tubing, thread or cord and looped to serve as a buttonhole. They are usually placed to extend beyond the edge of the garment in lieu of the extension of the garment.

Button shank: an extension of thread, plastic, or metal on the underside of a button. The shank allows the button to be held up from the fabric and to rest on top of the buttonhole.

Cable cord: soft cotton yarn rope used for cording and tubing; available in several sizes from $\frac{1}{8}$ of an inch to 1 inch in thickness.

Canvas: heavy durable cotton material made from coarse, hard-twisted yarns used as utility fabric. Also used to interface the coat front and in other parts of coat construction.

Casing: a folded-over edge of a garment or an applied strip creating a tunneled section, through which elastic or a drawstring or ribbon is threaded.

Catch stitch: hand-worked, short backstitches, taken alternately from left to right, ply by ply, to form a close cross-stitch. Used especially for hemming.

Center front/Center back: the line on a pattern or garment indicating the position of the vertical center of the bodice, skirt, or pant.

Clean finish: any method (zigzag stitched, surged, or turned under) used to finish the raw edges of a garment piece, usually on hems and facings.

Clip: a small cut into the seam allowance almost to the stitch line. Used on curved seams to release strain and help the seam lie flat when turned, as in necklines, or in corners of squared seams as in collars, facings, and necklines.

Collar: a cloth band or folded over piece of fabric attached to the neckline of a shirt, blouse, or dress. (See Chapter 15.)

Collar breakline: the edge of the upper lapel, folded back to make the revers.

Collar stand: the part of the collar from the creaseline down to the neckline.

Crease: a line made by folding the fabric and pressing the fold on this specified line.

Crewel needle: a long oval-eyed needle, medium length; size ranges from 1 to 12, used for multiple strands of thread or embroidery.

Crimping: A stitching method that slightly puckers the fabric and makes excess ease fit into the seam.

Crinoline: a course, stiff, cotton fabric which is heavily sized; used to stiffen petticoats, to give body to contour belts, and to make the headings in curtains and draperies. Similar to buckram, but lighter in weight.

Crosswise grain: See *grain.*

Crotch seam: term used for place in pants where the legs meet and a curved seam is formed.

Cuff: finish detail, varying in width, for the lower edge of sleeves or pants, consisting of a separate sewn or turned-back band.

Cutting line: a heavy dark, long, unbroken line printed on a pattern; indicates where the pattern must be cut.

Custom finish: perfection in fit, detail, and construction. Usually designed and made for one specific customer.

Darts: to take up excess fabric of a determined amount from a specific width and tapered to nothing at one or both ends; used to aid in fitting the garment over the body curves. (See Chapter 8.)

Dart legs: the stitch line on both sides of the dart.

Dart point: the vanishing point and the small end of the dart.

Wide end of dart: the widest end of the dart legs.

Bust darts: the bust fitting dart helps the garment fit over the bust area. Usually begin at the shoulder or side seam and finish 2 inches from the bust point (apex).

Skirt/pant darts: these darts bring in the waist of a skirt or pants. Usually the front darts are shorter than the back darts.

Fisheye dart: the french dart is a diagonal dart originating from any point between the hipline to two inches above the waist along the side seam and tapering to the bust point (apex).

Decorative stitching: a zigzag machine stitch to create a design effect. Hand embroidery stitches are also considered decorative.

Directional stitching: stitching in the direction that is with the grain to prevent the fabric from stretching. Used as a preliminary or permanent stitch.

Double knit: (See Chapter 1.)

Ease: the even distribution of slight fullness when one section of a seam is joined to a slightly shorter section without forming gathers or tucks. Used to shape set-in sleeves, princess seams, and other areas.

Ease allowance: the amount added to pattern measurements to make garments more comfortable and allow for easier movement.

Edging: narrow decorative border treatment, usually using embroidery or lace, of raw edges, particularly on seams, hems, and necklines.

Edgestitch: to machine stitch close to a finished edge from the correct side of the fabric.

Enclosed seam: a seam allowance along a faced edge that is stitched and turned to form an enclosed seam between two layers of fabric.

Fabric: a woven, knitted, felted, bonded, or laminated material of which a garment is made. Fabrics are made of both natural and synthetic fibers. Fabric finishes vary in durability and amount of flame resistance.

Facing: a duplicate layer of fabric stitched to a raw edge on a garment for the purpose of finishing it. It is turned to the wrong side of the garment and lies flat.

Fagoting: open thread work, used as a decorative stitch between two hemmed edges.

Felt: nonwoven fabric that is made of matted fibers of wool, fur, or mohair, often mixed with cotton or rayon. Heat, moisture, and pressure are applied to the fibers to form a solid mass.

Findings: term used for sewing notions or smaller items needed to make a garment, such as interfacings, zipper, buttons, and thread.

Fingerpress: the process of using fingers, usually with some seam, to press a seam that should not be flat pressed with an iron, such as a sleeve cap.

Finishing: a process to give edges of seams, facings, hems, necklines, and other sections of a garment a professional look.

Flat-felled seam: a double-stitched seam for some shirts and pants. One piece is turned in and stitched on top of the first to give a finished effect on both sides of the garment.

Fly: a type of closure that conceals the zipper or button openings in shorts and pants.

Foundation garment: a finished interior garment made of heavier, supporting fabric and fitted to the body shape to hold a strapless garment in place.

Fray: the result of abrasion on a raw edge whereby the yarn ends work out of the fabric.

Gather: to draw up fabric fullness on a line of stitching.

Gathering stitch: a longer machine stitch (about 8 stitches per inch) used to draw up fullness on the stitch line.

Gimp: a fine cord-like thread used to outline a hand-worked buttonhole.

Give: the amount of stretch on fabric that yields to pressure without tearing or breaking.

Grade: to trim each seam allowance with an enclosed seam to varying amounts in order to reduce bulk.

Grain: sewing term that refers to the lengthwise and warpwise threads of fabric.

Crosswise grain: threads that run across the fabric and are perpendicular to the selvages.

Lengthwise grain: threads that run up and down the fabric, parallel to the selvage.

Grainline: a strong, firmly woven, ribbon with crosswise ribs. In addition to being used for a decorative ribbon, it is also used for stay-tape or backing on a waistband.

Guide sheet: See *pattern guide*.

Gusset: a small fabric piece set into a slash or seam for added width and ease. Often inserted at the underarm to give ease in a sleeve.

Hand: the "feel" of the fabric; its flexibility, smoothness, and softness.

Hand basting: See *basting*.

Hem: the finished lower edge of a garment to prevent raw edges from fraying or tearing.

Hemline: the designed line on which the hem is marked, folded, faced, and turned to the underside.

Hem allowance: the extension at the bottom of skirts, dresses, blouses, sleeves, pants which are turned under and sewn with an appropriate hemming stitch.

Hemming finishes: hems may be finished by serging, using a hand or machine stitch or by using a bonding material. Special hemming devices are sometimes used to duplicate the stitch pattern and appearance of handwork.

Hemmer: an attachment provided with most home-sewing machines to enable sewing of hems by machines.

Hemming stitch: the finished simple stitch, either by hand or machine, suitable for sewing a hem up into place. Usually with a slipstitch, blindstitch, catch stitch, or edge stitch.

Hong Kong finish: a hem or seam finish by using a narrow bias strip of fabric to conceal the raw edge of a hem or a seam.

Interfacing: a carefully selected fabric placed between the garment and the facing fabrics for added body, to give support, and maintain shape. (See Chapter 17.)

Interlining: fabric cut into the same shape of the outer fabric and used in coats and jackets for warmth. Constructed separately and placed between the lining and the outer fabric. (See Chapter 1.)

Ironing: the process of sliding a heated iron on fabric used to smooth and stabilize fabric.

Join: when term is used in pattern direction, it usually means to stitch together the pieces referred to using normal seam allowance and regular stitches.

Kimono sleeve: sleeve cut in one piece with the bodice front and bodice back, seamed from shoulder down the length of the sleeve.

Lap: to fold or extend a garment piece over another.

Lapels: the front opening from the breakpoint of the garment to the turn-back of the collar.

Lengthwise grain: See *grain*.

Lining: lightweight fabric constructed like the garment and used to finish the inside of a garment. It gives a finished appearance, helps to maintain the shape of the outer layer, and adds warmth. (See Chapter 18.)

Loop turner: a rigid thin metal tool, approximately 10 inches long, with a latch and hook at one end to turn bias tubing inside out.

Match: to bring notches or other construction markings on two pieces together.

Mercerized: cotton yarns, fabric, or thread which has been finished with caustic soda to add strength and luster to fibers and make them more receptive to dyes.

Milliners needle: a small rounded eye needle, with a long length, used to make basting stitches.

Miter: to form a diagonal seam at a square corner of a neckline, hem, or bias-angled position.

Muslin: an inexpensive, plain-woven cotton fabric made from bleached or unbleached yarns; varies in weight from fine to heavy..

Muslin shell: a basic sample garment made from muslin fabric as an aid during the styling and fitting processes.

Nap: a fibrous surface produced by brushing up fibers on the fabric during the finishing process. A one-way directional pattern layout is used with the top of all pattern pieces placed in the same direction.

Needle: a small, thin, polished steel spiked device with an eye at one end and sharp point at the other.

Nonwoven fabric: terms used when referring to fabric (usually interlining or felt) formed by matting together fibers through pressure and the use of heat or chemicals.

Notch: a small v-shape or clip, marking the edge of the pattern piece, to indicate which seams match and are not to be joined.

Notions: small supplies needed to make a garment such as thread, needles, pins, buttons, and zippers.

Overcast seam: a seam finish done by hand with an overcasting stitch or by machine with a zigzag stitch.

Pattern markings: the symbols for construction such as for darts, buttonholes, notches, dots or tucks, printed on patterns. They are transferred from the pattern to the fabric by means of tailor's tacks, notches, chalk, bastings, tracing wheel, or dressmaker's carbon paper.

Pick stitch: a small durable backstitch to hand finish a zipper application. Also called hand pick stitch.

Pile: a textured fabric extending above the surface of the cloth, produced by interlacing additional looped yarns into the base, creating closely spaced loops. The depth of loops, the variety of nap surfaces, and the weights may be controlled according to the surface finish desired.

Pin basting: See *basting*.

Pin tucks: very narrow tucks that are topstitched about 1 and $\frac{1}{16}$ of an inch and $\frac{1}{8}$ of an inch wide.

Pink: cutting a serrated edge at a seam by using pinking shears to prevent fabrics from raveling. Also decorative edge used on fabrics, such as felt.

Piping: a narrow strip of cloth folded on the bias, used for trimming garments.

Pivot: to turn a square corner by leaving the needle in the fabric, lifting the presser foot, and turning the material being stitched in another direction.

Placket: a visible overlapping strip of fabric sewn in a garment opening.

Pleat: fold of fabric, usually not stitched down but may be partially stitched, used for fitting and controlling fullness.

Ply: each layer of fabric when lying out fabric to be cut.

Pocket: garment detail sewn to the correct side of a garment or set into a garment seam or opening. Used for decoration and/or function. (See Chapter 13.)

Press: lifting and placing the iron on the garment pieces during construction with or without moisture, being careful not to push the iron back and forth.

Presser foot: the attachment on the sewing machine that holds fabric steady at the point it is advanced, while the needle is stitching. The "all purpose" foot is used for most stitching.

Pressure: refers to the amount of pressure the presser foot exerts on the fabric during the stitching process. The pressure can be adjusted to suit the fabric.

Quilted: two layers of fabric stitched together with a padding between the layers. Stitching may be done by hand or machine, usually in a diamond-shaped or scroll pattern.

Raveling: small, loose threads that fall away from a cut edge of a woven fabric. Fabrics that ravel easily should be edge-finished to prevent raveling.

Raw edge: the cut edge of the garment pieces.

Regular stitch: permanent machine stitching. Normal stitch length is usually 12 stitches per inch, but this should be adjusted according to the fabric.

Reinforce: to strengthen an area that will be subject to strain. The area may be reinforced with a stay stitch close to the stitchline or with an underlay fabric piece secured with an extra row of stitching.

Release dart: a dart partially stitched so that fullness is released at the end. Also called open end dart.

Residual shrinkage: a small amount (usually with 5 percent) of shrinkage remaining in a finished fabric or garment. Residual shrinkage occurs gradually each time the garment is washed.

Revers: shaped lapels without a collar, on coats, jackets, blouses, and dress bodices.

Reversible: a garment finished so that it may be worn with either side out.

Rip: to remove stitching.

Roll: to manipulate fabric, usually along a seamline, in order to bring the seam beyond the edge to the underside of the garment.

Scissors: a cutting tool with two opposing sharpened blades which vary from 3 to 6 inches in length. They are different from shears in blade length and in the shape of the handles. The size of the handles in scissors are equal size and smaller than shears.

Seam: two or more edges of fabric held together by sewing a variety of stitches. Seams should be well constructed and appropriate for the fabric, the type of garment, and the location on the garment. (See Chapter 7.)

Seam allowance: the amount of fabric allowed for seam in joining sections of a garment or other articles together.

Seam binding: a narrow lightweight woven tape, ribbon-like, used to cover the raw edge of a hem edge. Also used as a stay for waistline and seam reinforcement.

Seam blending: trimming all seam allowances within a seam to different widths. Blending removes bulk so that the seam will lie flat.

Seam edge: the cut edge of the seam allowance. Sometimes referred to as the raw edge.

Seam finish: the finish used on the edge of the seam allowance to prevent the fabric from raveling or fraying.

Seam guide: a device attached to the bed of the machine with clearly etched lines; used to measure seam widths.

Seamline: the line designed on patterns for stitching the seam, generally $\frac{5}{8}$ of an inch from the cut edge in home sewing and $\frac{1}{2}$ or $\frac{1}{4}$ of an inch for industrial patterns.

Seam ripper: small cutting tool used for ripping out unwanted stitches. Specially designed with cutting edge at center of blade and sharp point to slip under stitched threads.

Selvage: the narrow, firmly woven finish along both lengthwise edges of the fabric. Selvage does not ravel.

Set-in sleeve: a sleeve with a fairly high cap that resembles the shape of the arm. Set-in sleeves are cut separately from the bodice and are stitched into the armhole after the shoulder and side seams are sewn. (See Chapter 14.)

Sharps needle: an all-purpose needle with a small-rounded eye, is medium length. Sizes range from 1 to 12.

Shears: a cutting tool with a 6-inch or more cutting blade and one handle larger than the other. Larger than scissors.

Shirr: to gather up fabric on the stitchline where fullness in the garment is desired. Shirring is sometimes thought of as being multiple rows of gathers.

Shrink: to relax the fibers of the fabric through moisture or steam, usually by washing or dry cleaning before using the fabric to construct a garment, to prevent further shrinking.

Silk pins: sharp, very fine, medium-length, rustproof pins, tapering to a fine point, which are less likely to leave marks on fabric.

Single knit: fabrics knit with one set of needles and one continuous yarn used to form loops across the fabric width.

Sizing: a finish applied to fabrics to add body and stiffness.

Slash: a straight cut (longer than a clip) in the body of a garment section to make a garment opening.

Sleeve board: a small, wooden ironing board, padded with silicone-treated cotton or canvas fabric, resembling a full-sized ironing board, and standing about 5 inches high; used to press seams and sleeves.

Sleeve cap: the curved upper portion of a set-in-sleeve.

Sleeve heads: extra strips of soft fabric or cotton wadding inserted around the top portion of an armscye to create a smooth line and to support the roll at the sleeve cap.

Slipstitch: an invisible hand sewing for finishing hems or facings, or for joining edges of an opening. On hems or facings, the procedure is to take up one thread in the under fabric and then slip the needle in the fold of the other edge.

Snap: a pair of circular metal fasteners, with a ball point prong and socket, used in lieu of buttons to hold garment pieces in place.

Stay: a small piece of extra fabric or tape that is sewn to an area of the garment to reinforce and secure a position. Used at the point of a slash and at waistlines.

Staystitch: regular machine stitching applied at the stitchline before garment is assembled, used to support garment edges, and prevent distortion during construction.

Stitch in the ditch: the technique of sewing a straight stitch inconspicuously in the seam well on the correct side of a previously stitched seam. Method is used to complete waistbands, cuffs, collars, and french bias binding.

Stretch fabric: specially constructed texturized yarns woven in fabric to allow it to stretch when pulled, then bounce back into shape. Stretch qualities add comfort, shape retention, and wrinkle-resistance; often seen in firmly woven denims or gabardines.

Style lines: any seamline other than shoulder seams, armhole seams, or side seams. A style line usually runs from one point of a garment to another point. For example, a yoke from side seam to side seam or a shoulder princess seam from shoulder to waistline seam.

Tack: to sew one section of a garment to another with a few somewhat loose stitches.

Tailoring: process of cutting, fitting, and sewing a garment to conform to the body by means of darts, plackets, pockets, linings, hems, and pressing.

Tailor's chalk: a small piece of chalk, approximately $1\frac{1}{2}$ inches square with two tapered edges, used to mark lines temporarily on garment hems and other alteration points.

Tailor's hem: a firm, ham-shaped cushion used for pressing areas that require shaping. One half of a ham is covered with cotton cloth for general pressing, the other half with soft wool, which is used when pressing woolen fabric to prevent shine.

Tailor's tacks: temporary small basting stitches of double thread done by hand and then cut apart. Used to mark construction symbols.

Tape measure: a narrow firmly woven tape marked with measurements in inches and metric terms used for taking body measurements and for various other measuring uses. Metal-tipped, reversible, stretch and shrink-proof tape measures are the most practical and accurate.

Taper: to cut fabric or sew fabric thickness, so it gradually narrows to nothing at the opposite end.

Tension: the relationship of the needle and bobbin threads and how they interlock to form the sewing machine stitch, creating a looser or tighter stitch.

Thread: fairly thin twisted strands of yarn used for sewing.

Throat plate: a flat metal piece that sits at the base of the sewing machine just underneath the presser foot. A fairly small hole though which the needle passes through to the bobbin thread as it stitches. This plate also has guidelines on it to aid in sewing a straight seam.

Top collar: the top part of the collar visible on the finished garment.

Top stitching: one or more rows of machine stitching made on the outside of the garment through all layers of the garment. It may be close to a seamline, or for decorative effect, or $\frac{1}{4}$ inches from an edge.

Tracing wheel: an instrument with a needle pointed or smooth-edged circular wheel at the base, used for transferring pattern markings to the fabric or pattern paper.

Tricot knit: a knit fabric created by several loops formed in a lengthwise direction.

Trim: 1. (*cut*) to cut away excess fabric and make the seam narrower after the seam has been stitched. Also, to remove or eliminate bulk and remove excess fabric in corners at any point before turning **2.** (*decorative*) different styles of braids, lace, etc., used on the outside of the garment to help style the garment.

Tuck: a stitchfold, usually straight and parallel to the fold, whereas a dart is tapered at the end. Tucks provide relaxed but definite fullness.

Twill tape: a thin strong cotton tape with woven edges in twill weave used for inner construction, usually used to reinforce and prevent stretching.

Underlay: a strip of fabric placed on the underside of the main garment piece; used for reinforcement on buttonholes, pockets, and in decorative zigzag stitching.

Underlining: the second thickness of a carefully selected fabric that is cut using the same pattern as the garment and is stitched in place with the garment seams. Used to give added body and shape. Underlining may also be strips of muslin, cut on the bias, used to underlay hems.

Understitch: understitching is achieved by folding the entire seam allowance to the facing side or underside, and stitching on the correct side of the facing close to the seam edge. This allows the seam to lay flat and keeps the seam edge from showing on the correct side of the garment.

Unit construction: a construction procedure in which each piece is sewn and pressed and kept flat for as long as possible before inserting sleeves or collars. This results in less handling of the various pieces of a garment, keeps them fresher looking and saves time.

Velcro: a two-piece fabric strip with loops on one side and a flat woolly surface on the other side, which is usually sewn to a garment area and pressed together in lieu of a closure.

Vent: a lapped opening or finished slit used in hems of tailored jackets, skirts, and sleeves. (See Chapter 18.)

Waistband: a waistline finish, encircling the waist area. Waistbands are made with a folded over band, or a seamed, contoured piece. (See Chapter 19.)

Warp: the threads or yarns that run lengthwise during the weaving process.

Wash-and-wear: term used to describe various finishes applied to fabrics. Garments made of these fabrics require little or no ironing after laundering.

Welt seam: a plain seam with both seam allowances pressed to one side and then held in place with one row of topstitching. (See Chapter 7, Seams.)

Whipstitch: a small hand-stitched vertical seam finish, only $\frac{1}{8}$ of an inch apart, stitched over the edge of a seam.

With nap: a pattern layout directive where all pattern pieces are to be placed facing the same direction, to be used with napped fabrics.

Without nap: pattern layout direction where the pattern pieces may be placed in both directions, to be used for fabrics without a nap.

Yardstick: a wooden or metal ruler one yard in length (36 inches) marked in inches or metric terms used in measuring. An aid when laying pattern pieces on straight of grain of the fabric or measuring hemlines.

Yoke: the fitted upper portion of a blouse, pants, or skirt.

Zigzag stitch: a regular stitch where all stitches are of the same width and in a straight line. The stitch length and stitch width may be set and selected for various lengths and widths, depending upon the desired use.

Zipper: a fastening device made with metal teeth or synthetic coils that make a complete closure by means of interlocking. (See Chapter 12.)

Zipper foot: a single-toed presser foot notched on both sides to accommodate the needle and facilitate stitching close to raised edges, such as zippers and cording for left or right construction.

Appendix A

FABRIC YARDAGE CONVERSION TABLE

How To Use This Table:

If the pattern calls for $1\frac{1}{2}$ yards (1.40 m) of 44″–45″ (115cm) fabric and the fabric you choose is 60″ (150cm) wide, read across the table to find that you need only $1\frac{1}{8}$ yard (1.0m) of 60″ wide fabric.

44″–45″	115cm	50″	127cm	52″–54″	140cm	58″–60″	150cm
YARD	METER	YARD	METER	YARD	METER	YARD	METER
$1\frac{3}{8}$	1.30m	$1\frac{1}{4}$	1.10m	$1\frac{1}{8}$	1.00m	1	0.90m
$1\frac{1}{2}$	1.40m	$1\frac{3}{8}$	1.30m	$1\frac{1}{4}$	1.10m	$1\frac{1}{8}$	1.00m
$1\frac{5}{8}$	1.50m	$1\frac{1}{2}$	1.40m	$1\frac{3}{8}$	1.30m	$1\frac{1}{4}$	1.10m
$1\frac{3}{4}$	1.60m	$1\frac{5}{8}$	1.50m	$1\frac{1}{2}$	1.40m	$1\frac{3}{8}$	1.30m
$1\frac{7}{8}$	1.70m	$1\frac{5}{8}$	1.50m	$1\frac{1}{2}$	1.40m	$1\frac{3}{8}$	1.30m
2	1.80m	$1\frac{3}{4}$	1.60m	$1\frac{3}{4}$	1.60m	$1\frac{5}{8}$	1.50m
$2\frac{1}{8}$	1.90m	$1\frac{3}{4}$	1.60m	$1\frac{3}{4}$	1.60m	$1\frac{3}{4}$	1.60m
$2\frac{1}{4}$	2.10m	2	1.80m	$1\frac{7}{8}$	1.70m	$1\frac{3}{4}$	1.60m
$2\frac{3}{8}$	2.20m	$2\frac{1}{8}$	1.90m	2	1.80m	$1\frac{7}{8}$	1.70m
$2\frac{1}{2}$	2.30m	$2\frac{1}{4}$	2.10m	2	1.80m	$1\frac{7}{8}$	1.70m
$2\frac{5}{8}$	2.40m	$2\frac{3}{8}$	2.20m	$2\frac{1}{4}$	2.10m	2	1.80m
$2\frac{3}{4}$	2.50m	$2\frac{3}{8}$	2.20m	$2\frac{1}{4}$	2.10m	2	1.80m
$2\frac{7}{8}$	2.60m	$2\frac{5}{8}$	2.40m	$2\frac{3}{8}$	2.20m	$2\frac{1}{4}$	2.10m
3	2.70m	$2\frac{3}{4}$	2.50m	$2\frac{5}{8}$	2.40m	$2\frac{3}{8}$	2.20m
$3\frac{1}{4}$	3.00m	3	2.70m	$2\frac{3}{4}$	2.50m	$2\frac{5}{8}$	2.40m
$3\frac{1}{2}$	3.20m	$3\frac{1}{4}$	3.00m	$2\frac{7}{8}$	2.60m	$2\frac{3}{4}$	2.50m
$3\frac{3}{4}$	3.40m	$3\frac{3}{8}$	3.10m	$3\frac{1}{8}$	2.90m	$2\frac{7}{8}$	2.60m
4	3.70m	$3\frac{3}{4}$	3.40m	$3\frac{1}{2}$	3.20m	3	2.70m

INCHES–YARD EQUIVALENTS

INCHES	YARDS	INCHES	YARDS
1″	0.03yds	19″	0.53yds
2″	0.05yds	20″	0.56yds
3″	0.08yds	21″	0.58yds
4″	0.11yds	22″	0.61yds
5″	0.14yds	23″	0.64yds
6″	0.17yds	24″	0.67yds
7″	0.19yds	25″	0.69yds
8″	0.22yds	26″	0.72yds
9″	0.25yds	27″	0.75yds
10″	0.28yds	28″	0.78yds
11″	0.31yds	29″	0.81yds
12″	0.33yds	30″	0.83yds
13″	0.36yds	31″	0.86yds
14″	0.39yds	32″	0.89yds
15″	0.42yds	33″	0.92yds
16″	0.44yds	34″	0.94yds
17″	0.47yds	35″	0.97yds
18″	0.50yds	36″	1.00yd

EQUIVALENTS
FRACTION – DECIMAL – METRIC

INCHES (FRACTION)	INCHES (DECIMAL)	CENTIMETERS
$\frac{1}{16}$	0.0625	0.1588
$\frac{1}{8}$	0.125	0.3175
$\frac{3}{16}$	0.1875	0.4763
$\frac{1}{4}$	0.25	0.635
$\frac{5}{16}$	0.3125	0.7938
$\frac{1}{3}$	0.3333	0.8466
$\frac{3}{8}$	0.375	0.9525
$\frac{1}{2}$	0.5	1.27
$\frac{9}{16}$	0.5625	1.4279
$\frac{5}{8}$	0.625	1.5875
$\frac{2}{3}$	0.6666	1.693
$\frac{3}{4}$	0.75	1.9
$\frac{13}{16}$	0.8125	2.06
$\frac{7}{8}$	0.875	2.223
1	1.0	2.54

Appendix B

Sewing References:

Threads Magazine
1-800-477-8727
www.tauton.com

Sew News Magazine
741 Corporate Circle, Suite A
Golden, CO 80401
www.sewnews.com

Clotilde's Sewing Savvy
www.clotildessewingsavvy.com

Pattern Websites:

Pattern Review
www.patternreview.com

Vogue Patterns
www.voguepatterns.com

McCall Patterns
www.mccall.com

Butterick Patterns
www.butterickpatterns.com

Simplicity Patterns
www.simplicity.com

FASHION PATTERNS by Coni
www.fashionpatterns.com

Fabric Information Resources:

Profiling Fabrics: Properties, Performance &
Construction Techniques
(Debbie Ann Gioello, Fairchild Books)

Sewing Associations:

American Sewing Guild
9660 Hillcroft, Suite 510
Houston, TX 77096
713-729-3000
www.asg.org

Home Sewing Association
P.O. Box 1312
Monroeville, PA 15146
412-372-5950
www.sewing.org

The Professional Association of Custom Clothiers
www.paccprofessionals.com

Sewing Educator's Alliance
2724 2nd Avenue
Des Moines, IA 50313
1-800-4SEWING

Index